MPI—The Complete Reference

Volume 2, The MPI-2 Extensions

MPI—The Complete Reference

Volume 2, The MPI-2 Extensions

William Gropp
Steven Huss-Lederman
Andrew Lumsdaine
Ewing Lusk
Bill Nitzberg
William Saphir
Marc Snir

The MIT Press
Cambridge, Massachusetts
London, England

Second printing, 1999

Parts of this book come from "MPI-2: Extensions to the Message-Passing Interface" by the Message Passing Interface Forum, © the University of Tennessee. These sections were reprinted by permission of the University of Tennessee.

This book was set in LATEX by the authors and was printed and bound in the United States of America.

Library of Congress Cataloging-in-Publication Data

MPI—the complete reference/Marc Snir . . . [et. al.]. William Gropp . . . [et al.].
    p.   cm.—(Scientific and engineering computation)
Includes bibliographical references (p.) and index.
Contents: Vol. 1. The MPI core—Vol. 2. The MPI-2 extensions.
ISBN 0-262-69215-5 (v. 1: pbk. : alk. paper).—ISBN 0-262-69216-3 (v. 2: pbk. : alk. paper).
1. Parallel programming (Electronic computers) 2. Subroutines (Computer programs) I. Snir, Marc. II. Gropp, William. III. Series.
QA76.642.M65   1998
004'.35—dc21   98-25604
                                                                                        CIP

Contents

Series Foreword

The world of modern computing potentially offers many helpful methods and tools to scientists and engineers, but the fast pace of change in computer hardware, software, and algorithms often makes practical use of the newest computing technology difficult. The Scientific and Engineering Computation series focuses on rapid advances in computing technologies, with the aim of facilitating transfer of these technologies to applications in science and engineering. It will include books on theories, methods, and original applications in such areas as parallelism, large-scale simulations, time-critical computing, computer-aided design and engineering, use of computers in manufacturing, visualization of scientific data, and human-machine interface technology.

The series is intended to help scientists and engineers understand the current world of advanced computation and to anticipate future developments that will affect their computing environments and open up new capabilities and modes of computation.

This book is about MPI-2, a set of significant extensions to the Message Passing Interface (MPI) specification. Together with the second edition of *MPI—The Complete Reference: Volume 1, The MPI Core*, by Marc Snir, Steve Otto, Steven Huss-Lederman, David W. Walker, and Jack Dongarra (also in this series), it provides an annotated reference manual for all of MPI. The reader can consult a third book in the series, *Using MPI: Portable Parallel Programming with the Message Passing Interface*, by William Gropp, Ewing Lusk, and Anthony Skjellum, for a tutorial introduction to MPI.

Janusz S. Kowalik

Preface

About This Book

This book describes the new features of MPI that represent the most significant extensions to MPI-1. We repeat the material already published in the MPI-2 specification document [7], though an attempt to clarify has been made. In Chapter 1 we cover basic concepts and terms used in this book. Chapter 2 covers miscellaneous matters, such as the use of MPI with threads and mixed-language programming with MPI functions and objects. In Chapter 3 we discuss MPI's approach to dynamic process creation and the connection of two independently started MPI programs to form a single program. Chapter 4 describes MPI's one-sided operations, which extend the MPI programming model in the direction of shared memory. New extensions to MPI's collective operations are described in Chapter 5. Chapter 6 contains new MPI features that promote the interaction of MPI programs with other systems. In Chapter 7 we discuss MPI's operations for specifying parallel I/O. Such operations are increasingly important for handling I/O bottlenecks. Chapter 8 describes language binding issues that arise when MPI is used in C++ or Fortran-90 programs. Chapter 9 provides a summary and description of the current (as of April 1998) status of MPI-2 implementation and adoption.

The companion volume to this book, the second edition of *MPI—The Complete Reference: Volume 1, The MPI Core* [23] includes those parts of the MPI-2 standard that are clarifications of MPI-1 definitions or minor extensions to MPI-1 functionality. This structure enables one to find all the relevant definitions and commentary on a particular MPI function in a single place.

Neither *MPI—The Complete Reference: Volume 1, The MPI Core* nor this book are official versions of the MPI standard; the standards are available from http://www.mpi-forum.org. In the case of any differences between these books and the standards, the standards take precedence.

MIT Press is maintaining a Web page for this book, by which one can gain access to errata and corrections, should they be necessary. The URL for this page is http://mitpress.mit.edu/book-home.tcl?isbn=0262571234.

Acknowledgments

Our primary acknowledgment is to the MPI Forum itself, whose hard work at and between meetings led to the definition of the MPI standard. Those (besides ourselves) who attended at least one meeting are Greg Astfalk, Robert Babb, Ed

Benson, Rajesh Bordawekar, Pete Bradley, Peter Brennan, Ron Brightwell, Maciej Brodowicz, Eric Brunner, Greg Burns, Margaret Cahir, Pang Chen, Ying Chen, Albert Cheng, Yong Cho, Joel Clark, Lyndon Clarke, Laurie Costello, Dennis Cottel, Jim Cownie, Zhenqian Cui, Suresh Damodaran-Kamal, Raja Daoud, Judith Devaney, David DiNucci, Doug Doefler, Jack Dongarra, Terry Dontje, Nathan Doss, Anne Elster, Mark Fallon, Karl Feind, Sam Fineberg, Craig Fischberg, Stephen Fleischman, Ian Foster, Hubertus Franke, Richard Frost, Al Geist, Robert George, David Greenberg, John Hagedorn, Kei Harada, Leslie Hart, Shane Hebert, Rolf Hempel, Tom Henderson, Alex Ho, Hans-Christian Hoppe, Joefon Jann, Terry Jones, Carl Kesselman, Koichi Konishi, Susan Kraus, Steve Kubica, Steve Landherr, Mario Lauria, Mark Law, Juan Leon, Lloyd Lewins, Ziyang Lu, Bob Madahar, Peter Madams, John May, Oliver McBryan, Brian McCandless, Tyce McLarty, Thom McMahon, Harish Nag, Nick Nevin, Jarek Nieplocha, Ron Oldfield, Peter Ossadnik, Steve Otto, Peter Pacheco, Yoonho Park, Perry Partow, Pratap Pattnaik, Elsie Pierce, Paul Pierce, Heidi Poxon, Jean-Pierre Prost, Boris Protopopov, James Pruyve, Rolf Rabenseifner, Joe Rieken, Peter Rigsbee, Tom Robey, Anna Rounbehler, Nobutoshi Sagawa, Arindam Saha, Eric Salo, Darren Sanders, Eric Sharakan, Andrew Sherman, Fred Shirley, Lance Shuler, A. Gordon Smith, Ian Stockdale, David Taylor, Stephen Taylor, Greg Tensa, Rajeev Thakur, Marydell Tholburn, Dick Treumann, Simon Tsang, Manuel Ujaldon, David Walker, Jerrell Watts, Klaus Wolf, Parkson Wong, and Dave Wright.

We also acknowledge the valuable input from many persons around the world who participated in MPI Forum discussions via e-mail.

The following institutions supported the MPI-2 project through time and travel support for the people listed above: Argonne National Laboratory; Bolt, Beranek, and Newman; California Institute of Technology; Center for Computing Sciences; Convex Computer Corporation; Cray Research; Digital Equipment Corporation; Dolphin Interconnect Solutions, Inc.; Edinburgh Parallel Computing Centre; General Electric Company; German National Research Center for Information Technology; Hewlett-Packard; Hitachi; Hughes Aircraft Company; Intel Corporation; International Business Machines; Khoral Research; Lawrence Livermore National Laboratory; Los Alamos National Laboratory; MPI Software Techology, Inc.; Mississippi State University; NEC Corporation; National Aeronautics and Space Administration; National Energy Research Scientific Computing Center; National Institute of Standards and Technology; National Oceanic and Atmospheric Adminstration; Oak Ridge National Laboratory; Ohio State University; PALLAS GmbH; Pacific

Northwest National Laboratory; Pratt & Whitney; San Diego Supercomputer Center; Sanders, A Lockheed-Martin Company; Sandia National Laboratories; Schlumberger; Scientific Computing Associates, Inc.; Silicon Graphics Incorporated; Sky Computers; Sun Microsystems Computer Corporation; Syracuse University; The MITRE Corporation; Thinking Machines Corporation; the United States Navy; the University of Colorado; the University of Denver; the University of Houston; the University of Illinois; the University of Maryland; the University of Notre Dame; the University of San Fransisco; the University of Stuttgart Computing Center; and the University of Wisconsin.

MPI-2 operated on a very tight budget (in reality, it had no budget when the first meeting was announced). The institutions listed above helped the MPI-2 effort by supporting the efforts and travel of the members of the MPI Forum. Direct support was given by NSF and DARPA under NSF contract CDA-9115428 for travel by U.S. academic participants and Esprit under project HPC Standards (21111) for European participants.

MPI—The Complete Reference

Volume 2, The MPI-2 Extensions

1 Introduction

In this chapter we summarize the process that led to MPI-2. We also describe notations used in this book and some MPI conventions and design characteristics that make the rest of the book easier to understand. We address language binding issues here that are common to all chapters. We conclude with comments on implementation and runtime issues. Most of the material in this chapter recapitulates terms and definitions contained in the companion book *MPI—The Complete Reference: Volume 1, The MPI Core*. It is repeated here for completeness.

1.1 MPI-1

The original MPI standard of 1994, which we call MPI-1, arose from the desire of the parallel computing community to have a single library interface for the widely used message-passing model of parallel computation. The intention was that such a specification would be implemented efficiently on a wide variety of platforms.

As an effort to establish a community-based standard, MPI was successful. MPI-1 both standardized existing practice and incorporated a number of research ideas that had not been part of existing high-performance message-passing systems. Implementations appeared rapidly, and now MPI is a standard component of the system software on all parallel computers. A number of freely available implementations exist for heterogeneous workstation networks as well as for single parallel machines. Many large application codes have been converted to MPI from older, vendor-specific message-passing interfaces, and the process is accelerating. MPI is now ubiquitous.

The original MPI Forum limited the scope of MPI in order to be able to address a manageable set of topics in the time it had allocated itself. Important topics that were deliberately omitted included the following:

dynamic processes: MPI programs were assumed to consist of a fixed number of processes, all started simultaneously by some mechanism external to the MPI program.

input/output: The issue of I/O to files was considered an active area of research, not yet ready for standardization.

one-sided operations: MPI-1 adhered to the strict message-passing programming model, in which data is copied from the address space of one process to that of another only by a cooperative pair of function calls, one in each process (send/receive).

1.2   MPI-2

As users began to convert their applications to MPI, they found that although MPI was a large and comprehensive library, they wanted still more functionality:

• PVM (Parallel Virtual Machine) users had come to expect dynamic process management, and a number of applications relied on it. This capability is relatively easy to provide on workstation networks and symmetric multiprocessors, but difficult on massively parallel processors (MPPs), where both hardware and software resources may have to be rescheduled. Furthermore, the rise of distributed applications required a standard mechanism for separately started MPI programs to establish contact and communicate.

• The Cray T3D *shmem* interface promoted the use of one-sided communication.

• Parallel file systems from IBM and Intel, as well as experimental I/O interfaces from various research groups, demonstrated the feasibility and advantages of a portable, high-performance interface that could be used in multiple I/O environments.

• Experience with MPI led users to request a number of convenience features, particularly for mixed language programming.

• Increasing use of C++ and Fortran-90 led to requests for standard C++ bindings for all MPI functions and recommendations on how to use MPI in Fortran-90 programs.

• Implementation of and experience with the use of MPI uncovered several ambiguities in the standard. It was desirable to clear these up as quickly as possible.

To promote the continued use of MPI and benefit a wide class of parallel programmers, the MPI Forum began meeting again in March of 1995. The "MPI-2" Forum comprised both veterans of the MPI-1 process and many new participants, representing both vendors that had not been particularly active in MPI-1 and new library and application writers. The Forum continued operation in the same way as before, encouraging anyone who wished to attend meetings and posting its e-mail discussions and intermediate documents on the Internet for public discussion. The result was the document MPI-2: *Extensions to the Message-Passing Interface* [5], which together with [4] now constitutes the official MPI standard.

The majority of the Forum's work was in new areas, such as one-sided operations, dynamic process management, and parallel I/O. Considerable effort was also expended on "MPI-1-like" features such as improved datatype handling, C++ bindings for the MPI-1 functions, and the clarification of ambiguities in the MPI-1 standard. In this book we focus on that part of MPI-2 that breaks new ground. We leave the other material to *MPI—The Complete Reference: Volume 1, The MPI Core*, published simultaneously with this book. We shall henceforward refer to that book as Book I. Some material in this book references material in *MPI—The Complete Reference: Volume 1, The MPI Core*. This material is indicated by a section number or page number prefaced with a Roman numeral one. For example, Chapter 2 of *MPI—The Complete Reference: Volume 1, the MPI Core* is written as Chapter I-2.

The official documents of the Forum, including the the standard, are available from the MPI Forum Web page at `http://www.mpi-forum.org`. Both Postscript and HTML versions are available. Neither *MPI—The Complete Reference: Volume 1, The MPI Core* nor this book are official versions of the MPI standard; in the case of any difference between these books and the standards, the standards take precedence.

1.3   MPI **Conventions and Design Choices**

In this section we explain notation used throughout the book to help the reader navigate the various parts of the MPI standard.

1.3.1   Document Notation

As in the standard itself, we set off with specific notation certain classes of remarks that are not part of the description of the MPI standard.

Rationale.   The rationale for the design choices made in the interface specification is set off in this format. Some readers may wish to skip these sections, while readers interested in interface design may want to read them carefully. ☐

Advice to users.   Material aimed at users and that illustrates usage is set off in this format. Some readers may wish to skip these sections, while readers interested in programming in MPI may want to read them carefully. ☐

Advice to implementors.   Material that is primarily commentary to implementors is set off in this format. Some readers may wish to skip these sections, while readers interested in MPI implementations may want to read them carefully. ☐

1.3.2   Naming Conventions

MPI-1 used informal naming conventions. In many cases, MPI-1 names for C functions are of the form Class_action_subset and in Fortran of the form CLASS_ACTION_-SUBSET, but this rule is not uniformly applied. In MPI-2, an attempt has been made to standardize names of new functions according to the following rules. In addition, the C++ bindings for MPI-1 functions also follow these rules (see Section 1.6.4). C and Fortran names for MPI-1 functions have not been changed.

- In C, all routines associated with a particular type of MPI object should be of the form Class_action_subset or, if no subset exists, of the form Class_action. In Fortran, all routines associated with a particular type of MPI object should be of the form CLASS_ACTION_SUBSET or, if no subset exists, of the form CLASS_ACTION. In C++, all entities are defined within the **MPI** namespace and a routine associated with a particular type of MPI object is a method on **Class**. Thus, the entire C++ function name is **MPI::Class::Action_subset**. If the routine is associated with a certain class, but does not make sense as an object method, it is a static member function of the class.
- If the routine is not associated with a class, the name should be of the form Action_subset in C and ACTION_SUBSET in Fortran, and in C++ should be scoped in the **MPI** namespace, **MPI::Action_subset**.
- The names of certain actions have been standardized. In particular, **Create** creates a new object, **Get** retrieves information about an object, **Set** sets this information, **Delete** deletes information, **Is** asks whether or not an object has a certain property.

These rules are strictly followed by the C++ binding, but are sometimes violated by the C and Fortran bindings, especially in MPI-1. The most common exceptions are the omission of the **Class** name from the routine and the omission of the **Action** where one can be inferred. In such cases, the language neutral name is the same as for C and Fortran, but differs from the C++ name. An example of this is the language neutral name of MPI_FINALIZED, with C name MPI_Finalized and Fortran name MPI_FINALIZED, but a C++ name of MPI::Is_finalized.

Rationale.   The naming conventions are often violated so as to have shorter names for common operations. Thus, MPI_SEND, rather than MPI_COMM_SEND, as would be required by a strict application of the naming conventions. Also, the MPI-1 Forum did not follow an explicit set of rules so that exceptions are more frequent in MPI-1 than in MPI-2. □

MPI identifiers are limited to 30 characters (31 with the profiling interface). This is done to avoid exceeding the limit on some compilation systems.

1.3.3   Procedure Specification

MPI procedures are specified using a language-independent notation. The arguments of procedure calls are marked as IN, OUT or INOUT. The meanings of these are:

- if the call may use the input value but does not update an argument, it is marked IN,
- if the call may update an argument but does not use its input value, it is marked OUT, and
- if the call may both use and update an argument, it is marked INOUT.

There is one special case—if an argument is a handle to an opaque object (these terms are defined in Section 1.5.1), and the object is updated by the procedure call, then the argument is marked OUT. It is marked this way even though the handle itself is not modified—we use the OUT attribute to denote that what the handle *references* is updated. Thus, in C++, IN arguments are either references or pointers to `const` objects. Similarly, a send buffer is marked as an IN argument and a receive buffer is marked as an OUT argument.

Rationale.   The definition of MPI tries to avoid, to the largest extent possible, the use of INOUT arguments, because such use is error-prone, especially for scalar arguments. ▯

MPI's use of IN, OUT and INOUT does not always translate into the corresponding language concept in bindings (e.g., `INTENT` in Fortran 90 bindings or `const` in C++ bindings). For instance, MPI marks the buffer argument of a receive call as OUT, but the "constant" MPI_BOTTOM can be passed to OUT buffer arguments, in which case the address of the updated variables is carried by the `datatype` argument (see Section I-3.8). Also, MPI_STATUS_IGNORE can be passed as the OUT status argument of a receive call, to indicate that no `status` need be computed and returned by the call. In C++, IN arguments are either references or pointers to `const` objects.

In several cases an argument is used as IN by some processes and OUT by other processes. Such an argument is, syntactically, an INOUT argument and is marked as such, although semantically it is not used in one call both for input and for output on a single process.

Another frequent situation arises when an argument value is needed only by a subset of the processes. When an argument is not significant at a process then an arbitrary value can be passed as an argument.

Unless specified otherwise, an argument of type OUT or type INOUT cannot be aliased with any other argument passed to an MPI procedure. Two arguments are aliased if they refer to the same or overlapping storage locations. An example of argument aliasing in C appears below. If we define a C procedure like this,

```
void copyIntBuffer( int *pin, int *pout, int len )
{
    int i;
    for (i=0; i<len; ++i) *pout++ = *pin++;
}
```

then a call to it in the following code fragment has aliased arguments.

```
int a[10];
copyIntBuffer( a, a+3, 7 );
```

Although the C language allows this, such usage of MPI procedures is forbidden unless otherwise specified. Note that Fortran prohibits aliasing of arguments.

All MPI functions are first specified in the language-independent notation. Immediately below this, the ISO C version of the function is shown followed by a version of the same function in Fortran and then in C++. Fortran in this book refers to Fortran 90; see Section 1.6.

1.4 Semantic Terms

When discussing MPI procedures the following semantic terms are used.

blocking: A procedure is blocking if return from the procedure indicates the user is allowed to reuse resources specified in the call.

nonblocking: A procedure is nonblocking if the procedure may return before the operation affected by the procedure call completes, and before the user is allowed to reuse resources (such as buffers) specified in the call. A call to a nonblocking procedure **starts** an operation. The call **completes** when the procedure returns, but the operation started may not be completed yet, if the call is nonblocking. The operation **completes** when all changes in the calling process state effected by the call have taken place, and the user is allowed to reuse all resources specified in the call. Thus, a send operation completes when data have been copied out of the sender memory, and the send buffer can be reused. This completion is an asynchronous event that may occur after the send call returned, while the sending process executes unrelated code. It may also occur before the communication initiated by the send operation completes (the data may not have been received yet).

Typically, a **request** object is associated with an operation when the operation is started by a nonblocking procedure. The user can use this object to test or wait for the completion of the operation. When the test succeeds or the wait completes, then the request is **completed** and the operation completion becomes visible to the calling process. Note that the word "complete" is used with respect to operations, requests, and communications, and refers to a possibly distinct event in each case.

local: A procedure is local if completion of the procedure does not depend on the execution of MPI calls by other processes.

non-local: A procedure is non-local if completion of the operation may require the execution of some MPI procedure on another process.

collective: A procedure is collective if all processes in a process group need to invoke the procedure. A collective call may or may not be **synchronizing**. If it is, then the completion of the call on any process in the group will require that all other processes in the group start their matching call. Collective calls over the same communicator must be executed in the same order by all members of the process group.

predefined: A predefined datatype is a datatype with a predefined (constant) name (such as MPI_INT, MPI_FLOAT_INT, or MPI_UB) or a datatype constructed with MPI_TYPE_CREATE_F90_INTEGER, MPI_TYPE_CREATE_F90_REAL, or MPI_TYPE_CREATE_F90_COMPLEX. The former are **named** whereas the latter are **unnamed**.

derived: A derived datatype is any datatype that is not predefined.

portable: A datatype is portable if it is a predefined datatype or is derived from a portable datatype using only the type constructors MPI_TYPE_CONTIGUOUS, MPI_TYPE_VECTOR, MPI_TYPE_INDEXED, MPI_TYPE_INDEXED_BLOCK, MPI_TYPE_CREATE_SUBARRAY, MPI_TYPE_DUP, or MPI_TYPE_CREATE_DARRAY. Such a datatype is portable because all displacements in the datatype are in terms of extents of one predefined datatype. Therefore, if such a datatype fits a data layout in one memory, it will fit the corresponding data layout in another memory if the same declarations were used, even if the two systems have different architectures. On the other hand, if a datatype was constructed using MPI_TYPE_CREATE_HINDEXED, MPI_TYPE_CREATE_HVECTOR or MPI_TYPE_CREATE_STRUCT, then the datatype contains explicit byte displacements (e.g., providing padding to meet alignment restrictions). These displacements are unlikely to be chosen correctly if they fit data layout on one memory but are used for data layouts on another process running on a processor with a different architecture.

equivalent: Two datatypes are equivalent if they appear to have been created with the same sequence of calls (and arguments) and thus have the same typemap. Two equivalent datatypes do not necessarily have the same cached attributes or the same names.

1.5 Function Argument Data Types

Here we discuss the host language datatypes used in calling MPI functions.

1.5.1 Opaque Objects

MPI manages **system memory** that is used for buffering messages and for storing internal representations of various MPI objects such as groups, communicators, datatypes, etc. This memory is not directly accessible to the user, and objects stored there are **opaque**: their size and structure are not visible to the user. Opaque objects are accessed via **handles** that exist in user space. MPI procedures that operate on opaque objects are passed handle arguments to access these objects. In addition to their use by MPI calls for object access, handles can participate in assignments and comparisons.

In Fortran, all handles have type `INTEGER`. In C and C++, a different handle type is defined for each category of objects. In addition, handles themselves are distinct objects in C++. The C and C++ types must support the use of the assignment and equality operators.

Advice to implementors. In Fortran, the handle can be an index into a table of opaque objects in a system table; in C it can be such an index or a pointer to the object. C++ handles can simply "wrap up" a table index or pointer. ▯

Opaque objects are allocated and deallocated by calls that are specific to each object type. These are listed in the sections where the objects are described. The calls accept a handle argument of matching type. In an allocate call this is an OUT argument that returns a valid reference to the object. In a call to deallocate, this is an INOUT argument that returns with an "invalid handle" value. MPI provides an "invalid handle" constant for each object type. Comparisons to this constant are used to test for validity of the handle.

A call to a deallocate routine invalidates the handle and marks the object for deallocation. The object is not accessible to the user after the call. However, MPI need not deallocate the object immediately. Any operation pending (at the time of the deallocate) that involves this object will complete normally; the object will be deallocated afterwards.

An opaque object and its handle are significant only at the process where the object was created and cannot be transferred to another process.

MPI provides certain predefined opaque objects and predefined, static handles to these objects. The user must not free such objects. In C++, this is enforced by declaring the handles to these predefined objects to be `static const`.

Rationale. This design hides the internal representation used for MPI data structures, thus allowing similar calls in C, C++, and Fortran. It also avoids conflicts with the typing rules in these languages, and easily allows future extensions of functionality. The mechanism for opaque objects used here loosely follows the POSIX Fortran binding standard [12].

The explicit separation of handles in user space and objects in system space allows space-reclaiming and deallocation calls to be made at appropriate points in the user program. If the opaque objects were in user space, one would have to be very careful not to go out of scope before any pending operation requiring that object completed. The specified design allows an object to be marked for deallocation, the user program can then go out of scope, and the object itself still persists until any pending operations are complete.

The requirement that handles support assignment/comparison is made since such operations are common. This restricts the domain of possible implementations. The alternative would have been to allow handles to have been an arbitrary, opaque type. This would force the introduction of routines to do assignment and comparison, adding complexity, and was therefore ruled out. □

Advice to users. A user may accidently create a dangling reference by assigning to a handle the value of another handle, and then deallocating the object associated with these handles. Conversely, if a handle variable is deallocated before the associated object is freed, then the object becomes inaccessible (this may occur, for example, if the handle is a local variable within a subroutine, and the subroutine is exited before the associated object is deallocated). It is the user's responsibility to avoid adding or deleting references to opaque objects, except as a result of MPI calls that allocate or deallocate such objects. ▯

Advice to implementors.   The intended semantics of opaque objects is that opaque objects are separate from one another; each call to allocate such an object copies all the information required for the object. Implementations may avoid excessive copying by substituting referencing for copying. For example, a derived datatype may contain references to its components, rather then copies of its components; a call to MPI_COMM_GROUP may return a reference to the group associated with the communicator, rather than a copy of this group. In such cases, the implementation must maintain reference counts, and allocate and deallocate objects in such a way that the visible effect is as if the objects were copied. ▯

1.5.2   Array Arguments

An MPI call may need an argument that is an array of opaque objects. Such an array is accessed via an array of handles. The array-of-handles is an array with entries that are handles to objects of the same type in consecutive locations in the array. Whenever such an array is used, an additional len argument is required to indicate the number of valid entries (unless this number can be derived otherwise). The valid entries are at the beginning of the array; len indicates how many of them there are, and need not be the size of the entire array. The same approach is followed for other array arguments. In some cases NULL handles are considered valid entries.

1.5.3   State

MPI procedures use at various places arguments with *state* types. The values of such a data type are all identified by names, and no operation is defined on them. For example, the MPI_TYPE_CREATE_SUBARRAY routine has a state argument order with values MPI_ORDER_C and MPI_ORDER_FORTRAN.

1.5.4   Named Constants

MPI procedures sometimes assign a special meaning to a special value of a basic type argument; for example, tag is an integer-valued argument of point-to-point communication operations, with a special wild-card value, MPI_ANY_TAG. Such arguments will have a range of regular values that is a proper subrange of the range of values of the corresponding basic type; special values (such as MPI_ANY_TAG) will be outside the regular range. The range of regular values, such as tag, can be queried using the MPI environmental inquiry functions. The range of other values, such as source, depends on values given by other MPI routines (in the case of source it is the communicator size).

MPI also provides predefined named constant handles, such as MPI_COMM-WORLD.

All named constants, with the exceptions noted below for Fortran, can be used in initialization expressions or assignments.[1] These constants do not change values during execution. Opaque objects accessed by constant handles are defined and do not change value between MPI initialization (MPI_INIT) and MPI completion (MPI_FINALIZE).

The constants that cannot be used in initialization expressions or assignments in Fortran are:

```
MPI_BOTTOM
MPI_STATUS_IGNORE
MPI_STATUSES_IGNORE
MPI_ERRCODES_IGNORE
MPI_IN_PLACE
MPI_ARGV_NULL
MPI_ARGVS_NULL
```

Advice to implementors. In Fortran the implementation of these special constants may require the use of language constructs that are outside the Fortran standard. Using special values for the constants (e.g., by defining them through parameter statements) is not possible because an implementation cannot distinguish these values from legal data. Typically, these constants are implemented as predefined static variables (e.g., a variable in an MPI-declared COMMON block), relying on the fact that the target compiler passes data by address. Inside the subroutine, this address can be extracted by some mechanism outside the Fortran standard (e.g., by Fortran extensions or by implementing the function in C). □

1.5.5 Choice

MPI functions sometimes use arguments with a *choice* (or union) data type. Distinct calls to the same routine may pass by reference actual arguments of different types. The mechanism for providing such arguments will differ from language to language. For Fortran, the book uses <type> to represent a choice variable; for C and C++, we use void *.

---

[1]They still are not quite the same as language constants. For example, they cannot be used as case labels in a C switch statement.

1.5.6 Addresses

Some MPI procedures use *address* arguments that represent an absolute address in
the calling program. The datatype of such an argument is MPI_Aint in C, MPI::Aint
in C++ and INTEGER (KIND=MPI_ADDRESS_KIND) in Fortran. The MPI constant
MPI_BOTTOM indicates the start of the address range.

1.5.7 File Offsets

For I/O (defined in MPI-2) there is a need to give the size, displacement, and offset
into a file. These quantities can easily be larger than 32 bits which can be the
default size of a Fortran integer. To overcome this, these quantities are declared to
be INTEGER (KIND=MPI_OFFSET_KIND) in Fortran. In C one uses MPI_Offset whereas
in C++ one uses MPI::Offset.

1.6 Language Binding

This section defines the rules for MPI language binding in general and for Fortran,
ISO C, and C++, in particular. (Note that ANSI C has been replaced by ISO
C.) Defined here are various object representations, as well as the naming conventions used for expressing this standard. The actual calling sequences are defined
elsewhere.

MPI bindings are for Fortran 90, though they are designed to be usable in Fortran
77 environments as much as possible.

Since the word PARAMETER is a keyword in the Fortran language, we use the word
"argument" to denote the arguments to a subroutine. These are normally referred
to as parameters in C and C++, however, we expect that C and C++ programmers
will understand the word "argument" (which has no specific meaning in C/C++),
thus allowing us to avoid unnecessary confusion for Fortran programmers.

Since Fortran is case insensitive, linkers may use either lowercase or uppercase
when resolving Fortran names. Users of case-sensitive languages should avoid the
"mpi_" and "pmpi_" prefixes.

1.6.1 Deprecated Names and Functions

A number of chapters refer to deprecated or replaced MPI-1 constructs. These are
constructs that continue to be part of the MPI standard, but that users are recommended to discontinue using, since MPI-2 provides better solutions. For example,
the Fortran binding for MPI-1 functions that have address arguments uses INTEGER.
This is not consistent with the C binding, and causes problems on machines with

32-bit INTEGERs and 64-bit addresses. In MPI-2, these functions have new names and new bindings for the address arguments. The use of the old functions is deprecated. For consistency, here and in a few other cases, new C functions are also provided, even though the new functions are equivalent to the old functions. The old names are deprecated. Another example is provided by the MPI-1 predefined datatypes MPI_UB and MPI_LB. They are deprecated, since their use is awkward and error-prone, while the MPI-2 function MPI_TYPE_CREATE_RESIZED provides a more convenient mechanism for resizing a datatype.

Table 1.1 provides a list of all of the deprecated constructs. Note that the constants MPI_LB and MPI_UB are replaced by the function MPI_TYPE_CREATE_RESIZED; this is because their principal use was as input datatypes to MPI_TYPE_STRUCT to create resized datatypes. Also note that some C typedefs and Fortran subroutine names are included in this list; they are the types of callback functions.

1.6.2 Fortran Binding Issues

MPI-1 provided bindings for Fortran 77. MPI-2 retains these bindings but they are now interpreted in the context of the Fortran 90 standard. MPI can still be used with most Fortran 77 compilers, as noted below. When the term Fortran is used it means Fortran 90.

All MPI names have an MPI_ prefix, and all characters are capitals. Programs must not declare variables, parameters, or functions with names beginning with the prefix MPI_. To avoid conflicting with the profiling interface, programs should also avoid functions with the prefix PMPI_. This is mandated to avoid possible name collisions.

All MPI Fortran subroutines have a return code in the last argument. A few MPI operations that are functions do not have the return code argument. The return code value for successful completion is MPI_SUCCESS. Other error codes are implementation dependent. Error codes are discussed in Section I-7.5.

Constants representing the maximum length of a string are one smaller in Fortran than in C and C++ as discussed in Section 2.2.8.

Handles are represented in Fortran as INTEGERs. Binary-valued variables are of type LOGICAL.

Array arguments are indexed from one. Address arguments are INTEGERs of kind MPI_ADDRESS_KIND. File displacements are INTEGERs of kind MPI_OFFSET_KIND.

The MPI Fortran binding is inconsistent with the Fortran 90 standard in several respects. These inconsistencies, such as register optimization problems, have implications for user codes that are discussed in detail in Section 8.2.2. They are also inconsistent with Fortran 77.

Table 1.1
Deprecated functions, constants, and typedefs in MPI.

Deprecated	MPI-2 Replacement
MPI_ADDRESS	MPI_GET_ADDRESS
MPI_TYPE_HINDEXED	MPI_TYPE_CREATE_HINDEXED
MPI_TYPE_HVECTOR	MPI_TYPE_CREATE_HVECTOR
MPI_TYPE_STRUCT	MPI_TYPE_CREATE_STRUCT
MPI_TYPE_EXTENT	MPI_TYPE_GET_EXTENT
MPI_TYPE_UB	MPI_TYPE_GET_EXTENT
MPI_TYPE_LB	MPI_TYPE_GET_EXTENT
MPI_LB	MPI_TYPE_CREATE_RESIZED
MPI_UB	MPI_TYPE_CREATE_RESIZED
MPI_ERRHANDLER_CREATE	MPI_COMM_CREATE_ERRHANDLER
MPI_ERRHANDLER_GET	MPI_COMM_GET_ERRHANDLER
MPI_ERRHANDLER_SET	MPI_COMM_SET_ERRHANDLER
MPI_Handler_function	MPI_Comm_errhandler_fn
MPI_KEYVAL_CREATE	MPI_COMM_CREATE_KEYVAL
MPI_KEYVAL_FREE	MPI_COMM_FREE_KEYVAL
MPI_DUP_FN	MPI_COMM_DUP_FN
MPI_NULL_COPY_FN	MPI_COMM_NULL_COPY_FN
MPI_NULL_DELETE_FN	MPI_COMM_NULL_DELETE_FN
MPI_Copy_function	MPI_Comm_copy_attr_function
COPY_FUNCTION	COMM_COPY_ATTR_FN
MPI_Delete_function	MPI_Comm_delete_attr_function
DELETE_FUNCTION	COMM_DELETE_ATTR_FN
MPI_ATTR_DELETE	MPI_COMM_DELETE_ATTR
MPI_ATTR_GET	MPI_COMM_GET_ATTR
MPI_ATTR_PUT	MPI_COMM_SET_ATTR

- An MPI subroutine with a choice argument may be called with different argument types.
- An MPI subroutine with an assumed-size dummy argument may be passed an actual scalar argument.
- Many MPI routines assume that actual arguments are passed by address and that arguments are not copied on entrance to or exit from the subroutine.

- An MPI implementation may read or modify user data (e.g., communication buffers used by nonblocking communications) concurrently with a user program executing outside MPI calls.
- Several named "constants," such as MPI_BOTTOM, MPI_STATUS_IGNORE, and MPI_ERRCODES_IGNORE, are not ordinary Fortran constants and require a special implementation. See Section 1.5.4 for more information.

Additionally, MPI is inconsistent with Fortran 77 in a number of ways, as noted below.

- MPI identifiers exceed 6 characters.
- MPI identifiers may contain underscores after the first character.
- MPI requires an include file, mpif.h. On systems that do not support include files, the implementation should specify the values of named constants.
- Many routines in MPI-2 have KIND-parameterized integers (e.g., MPI_ADDRESS_KIND and MPI_OFFSET_KIND) that hold address information. On systems that do not support Fortran 90-style parameterized types, INTEGER*8 or INTEGER should be used instead.
- The memory allocation routine MPI_ALLOC_MEM can't be usefully used in Fortran without a language extension that allows the allocated memory to be associated with a Fortran variable.

1.6.3 C Binding Issues

We use the ISO C declaration format. All MPI names have an MPI_ prefix, defined constants are in all capital letters, and defined types and functions have exactly one capital letter immediately following the prefix. Programs must not declare variables or functions with names beginning with the prefix MPI_. To support the profiling interface, programs should not declare functions with names beginning with the prefix PMPI_.

The definition of named constants, function prototypes, and type definitions must be supplied in an include file mpi.h.

Almost all C functions return an error code. The successful return code will be MPI_SUCCESS, but failure return codes are implementation dependent (See Section I-7.5).

Type declarations are provided for handles to each category of opaque objects.

Array arguments are indexed from zero.

Logical flags are integers with value 0 meaning "false" and a non-zero value meaning "true."

Choice arguments are pointers of type `void *`.

Address arguments are of MPI-defined type MPI_Aint. File displacements are of type MPI_Offset. MPI_Aint is defined to be an integer of the size needed to hold any valid address on the target architecture. MPI_Offset is defined to be an integer of the size needed to hold any valid file size on the target architecture.

1.6.4   C++ Binding Issues

There are places in the standard that give rules for C and not for C++. In these cases, the C rule should be applied to the C++ case, as appropriate. In particular, the values of constants given in the text are the ones for C and Fortran. In general, it is easy to determine the C++ constant from the C constant. To help C++ users, the first reference to a constant listed in the index under the C name also has the C++ name in the text. There are also several C++ types that do not exist in C, including MPI::BOOL, MPI::COMPLEX, MPI::DOUBLE_COMPLEX, and MPI::LONG_DOUBLE_COMPLEX. Several C++ types have names that are not easily derivable from the C name, including MPI::F_COMPLEX, MPI::F_DOUBLE_COMPLEX, MPI::TWOINT, MPI::TWOREAL, MPI::TWODOUBLE_PRECISION, and MPI::TWOINTEGER. There is also the C++ only error handler MPI::ERRORS_THROW_EXCEPTIONS. Finally, there is no constant comparable to MPI_STATUS_IGNORE.

We use the ANSI C++ declaration format. All MPI names are declared within the scope of a namespace called `MPI` and therefore are referenced with an `MPI::` prefix. Defined constants are in all capital letters, and class names, defined types, and functions have only their first letter capitalized. Programs must not declare variables or functions in the `MPI` namespace. This is mandated to avoid possible name collisions.

The members of the `MPI` namespace are those classes corresponding to objects implicitly used by MPI. An abbreviated definition of the `MPI` namespace for MPI-1 and its member classes is as follows:

```
namespace MPI {
  class Comm                          {...};
  class Intracomm : public Comm       {...};
  class Graphcomm : public Intracomm  {...};
  class Cartcomm  : public Intracomm  {...};
  class Intercomm : public Comm       {...};
  class Datatype                      {...};
  class Errhandler                    {...};
```

```
  class Exception                        {...};
  class Group                            {...};
  class Op                               {...};
  class Request                          {...};
  class Prequest   : public Request      {...};
  class Status                           {...};
};
```

Additionally, the following classes are defined for MPI-2:

```
namespace MPI {
  class File                             {...};
  class Grequest   : public Request      {...};
  class Info                             {...};
  class Win                              {...};
};
```

Note that there are a small number of derived classes and that virtual inheritance is *not* used. To the greatest extent possible, the C++ bindings for MPI functions are member functions of these classes.

The definition of named constants, function prototypes, and type definitions must be supplied in an include file mpi.h.

Advice to implementors.   The file mpi.h may contain both the C and C++ definitions. Usually one can simply use the pre-defined preprocessor symbol (generally __cplusplus, but not required) to see if one is using C++ to protect the C++ definitions. It is possible that a C compiler will require that the source protected this way be legal C code. In this case, all the C++ definitions can be placed in a different include file and the "#include" directive can be used to include the necessary C++ definitions in the mpi.h file. ☐

C++ functions that create objects or return information usually place the object or information in the return value. Since the language neutral prototypes of MPI functions include the C++ return value as an OUT parameter, semantic descriptions of MPI functions refer to the C++ return value by that parameter name (see Section 8.1.11). The remaining C++ functions return void.

In some circumstances, MPI permits users to indicate that they do not want a return value. For example, the user may indicate that the status is not to be filled in. Unlike C and Fortran where this is achieved through a special input value, in

C++ this is done by having two bindings where one has the optional argument and one does not.

C++ functions do not return error codes. If the default error handler has been set to MPI::ERRORS_THROW_EXCEPTIONS, the C++ exception mechanism is used to signal an error by throwing an `MPI::Exception` object.

It should be noted that the default error handler (i.e., MPI::ERRORS_ARE_-FATAL) on a given type has not changed. User error handlers are also permitted. MPI::ERRORS_RETURN simply returns control to the calling function; there is no provision for the user to retrieve the error code.

User callback functions that return integer error codes should not throw exceptions; the returned error will be handled by the MPI implementation by invoking the appropriate error handler.

Advice to users.   C++ programmers that want to handle MPI errors on their own should use the MPI::ERRORS_THROW_EXCEPTIONS error handler, rather than MPI::ERRORS_RETURN, which is used for that purpose in C. Care should be taken using exceptions in mixed language situations. ☐

Opaque object handles must be objects in themselves, and have the assignment and equality operators overridden to perform semantically like their C and Fortran counterparts.

Array arguments are indexed from zero.

Logical flags are of type `bool`.

Choice arguments are pointers of type `void *`.

Address arguments are of MPI-defined integer type MPI::Aint, defined to be an integer of the size needed to hold any valid address on the target architecture. Analogously, MPI::Offset is an integer to hold file offsets.

Most MPI functions are methods of MPI C++ classes. MPI class names are generated from the language neutral MPI types by dropping the MPI_ prefix and scoping the type within the MPI namespace. For example, MPI_DATATYPE becomes `MPI::Datatype`.

The names of MPI-2 functions generally follow the naming rules given. In some circumstances, the new MPI-2 function is related to an MPI-1 function with a name that does not follow the naming conventions. In this circumstance, the language-neutral name is analogous to the MPI-1 name even though this gives an MPI-2 name that violates the naming conventions. The C and Fortran names are the same as the language-neutral name in this case. However, the C++ names for MPI-1 do reflect the naming rules and can differ from the C and Fortran names. Thus, the analogous name in C++ to the MPI-1 name is different from the language-neutral name. This results in the C++ name differing from the language-neutral name. An example of this is the language-neutral name of MPI_FINALIZED and a C++ name of MPI::Is_finalized.

In C++, function **typedef**s are made publicly within appropriate classes. However, these declarations then become somewhat cumbersome, as in the following case. The complete typedef for the generalized request query callback function would look like

```
namespace MPI {
  class Request {
   // ...
  };

  class Grequest : public MPI::Request {
   // ...
    typedef int Query_function(void* extra_state,
                               MPI::Status& status);
  };
};
```

Rather than including this scaffolding when declaring C++ **typedef**s, we use an abbreviated form. In particular, we explicitly indicate the class and namespace scope for the **typedef** of the function. Thus, the example above is shown in the text as follows:

```
typedef int MPI::Grequest::Query_function(void* extra_state,
                                           MPI::Status& status);
```

Besides the member functions which constitute the C++ language bindings for MPI, the C++ language interface has additional functions (as required by the C++ language). In particular, the C++ language interface defines methods for construction, destruction, copying, assignment, comparison, and mixed-language operability for all MPI member classes.

The default constructor and destructor are prototyped as follows:

```
MPI::<CLASS>()
```

```
~MPI::<CLASS>()
```

In terms of construction and destruction, opaque MPI user-level objects behave like handles. Default constructors for all MPI objects except MPI::**Status** create corresponding MPI::*_NULL handles. That is, when an MPI object is instantiated, comparing it with its corresponding MPI::*_NULL object will return true. The default constructors do not create new MPI opaque objects. Some classes have a member function Create() for this purpose.

The destructor for each MPI user-level object does *not* invoke the corresponding MPI_*_FREE function (if it exists).

The copy constructor and assignment operator are prototyped as follows:

```
MPI::<CLASS>(const MPI::<CLASS>& data)
```

```
MPI::<CLASS>& MPI::<CLASS>::operator=(const MPI::<CLASS>& data)
```

In terms of copying and assignment, opaque MPI user-level objects behave like handles. Copy constructors perform handle-based (shallow) copies. MPI::Status objects are exceptions to this rule. These objects perform deep copies for assignment and copy construction.

The comparison operators are prototyped as follows:

```
bool MPI::<CLASS>::operator==(const MPI::<CLASS>& data) const
```

```
bool MPI::<CLASS>::operator!=(const MPI::<CLASS>& data) const
```

The member function operator==() returns true only when the handles reference the same internal MPI object, false otherwise. operator!=() returns the boolean complement of operator==(). However, since the Status class is not a handle to an underlying MPI object, it does not make sense to compare Status instances. Therefore, the operator==() and operator!=() functions are not defined on the Status class.

Constants are singleton objects and are declared const. Note that not all globally defined MPI objects are constant. For example, MPI::COMM_WORLD and MPI::COMM_SELF are not const.

1.7 Processes

An MPI program consists of autonomous processes, each executing its own code, in an MIMD style. The codes executed by each process need not be identical. The processes communicate via calls to MPI communication primitives. Typically, each process executes in its own address space, although shared-memory implementations of MPI are possible.

MPI specifies the behavior of a parallel program assuming that only MPI calls are used. The interaction of an MPI program with other possible means of communication, I/O, and process management is not specified. Unless otherwise stated in the specification of the standard, MPI places no requirements on the result of its interaction with external mechanisms that provide similar or equivalent functionality. This includes, but is not limited to, interactions with external mechanisms for process control, shared and remote memory access, file system access and control, interprocess communication, process signaling, and terminal I/O. High-quality implementations should strive to make the results of such interactions intuitive to users, and attempt to document restrictions where deemed necessary.

Advice to users.   There is no requirement that MPI processes be the same as POSIX processes. □

Advice to implementors.   Implementations that support such additional mechanisms for functionality supported within MPI are expected to document how these interact with MPI. □

The interaction of MPI and threads is defined in Section 2.1.

1.8   Error Handling

MPI provides the user with reliable message transmission. A message sent is always received correctly, and the user does not need to check for transmission errors, time-outs, or other error conditions. In other words, MPI does not provide mechanisms for dealing with failures in the communication system. If the MPI implementation is built on an unreliable underlying mechanism, then it is the job of the implementor of the MPI subsystem to insulate the user from this unreliability, or to reflect unrecoverable errors as failures. Whenever possible, such failures will be reflected as errors in the relevant communication call. Similarly, MPI itself provides no mechanisms for handling processor failures.

Of course, MPI programs may still be erroneous. A **program error** can occur when an MPI call is made with an incorrect argument (e.g., non-existent destination in a send operation, buffer too small in a receive operation, etc.). This type of error would occur in any implementation. In addition, a **resource error** may occur when a program exceeds the amount of available system resources (number of pending messages, system buffers, etc.). The occurrence of this type of error depends on the amount of available resources in the system and the resource allocation mechanism used; this may differ from system to system. A high-quality implementation will provide generous limits on the important resources so as to alleviate the portability problem this represents.

In C and Fortran, almost all MPI calls return a code that indicates successful completion of the operation. Whenever possible, MPI calls return an error code if an error occurred during the call. By default, an error detected during the execution of the MPI library causes the parallel computation to abort, except for file operations. However, MPI provides mechanisms for users to change this default and to handle recoverable errors. The user may specify that no error is fatal, and handle error codes returned by MPI calls by himself or herself. Also, the user may provide his or her own error-handling routines, which will be invoked whenever an MPI call returns abnormally. The MPI error handling facilities are described in I-7.5.1 (recall that I-7.5.1 refers to the companion book, *MPI: The Complete Reference, Volume 1*). The return values of C++ functions are not error codes. If the default error handler has been set to MPI::ERRORS_THROW_EXCEPTIONS, the C++ exception mechanism is used to signal an error by throwing an `MPI::Exception` object.

Several factors limit the ability of MPI calls to return with meaningful error codes when an error occurs. MPI may not be able to detect some errors; other errors may be too expensive to detect in normal execution mode; finally, some errors may be "catastrophic" and may prevent MPI from returning control to the caller in a consistent state.

Another subtle issue arises because of the nature of asynchronous communications: MPI calls may initiate operations that continue asynchronously after the call returns. Thus, the operation may return with a code indicating successful completion, yet later cause an error exception to be raised. If there is a subsequent call that relates to the same operation (e.g., a call that verifies that an asynchronous operation has completed) then the error argument associated with this call will be used to indicate the nature of the error. In a few cases, the error may occur after all calls that relate to the operation have completed, so that no error value can be used to indicate the nature of the error (e.g., an error on the receiver in a send with the ready mode). Such an error must be treated as fatal, since information cannot be returned for the user to recover from it.

MPI does not specify the state of a computation after an erroneous MPI call has occurred. The desired behavior is that a relevant error code be returned, and the effect of the error be localized to the greatest possible extent. For example, it is highly desirable that an erroneous receive call will not cause any part of the receiver's memory to be overwritten beyond the area specified for receiving the message.

Implementations may go beyond the MPI standard in supporting in a meaningful manner MPI calls that are defined by the standard to be erroneous. For example, MPI specifies strict type-matching rules between matching send and receive operations: it is erroneous to send a floating-point variable and receive an integer. Implementations may go beyond these type matching rules, and provide automatic type conversion in such situations. It will be helpful to generate warnings for such non-conforming behavior.

MPI-2 defines a way for users to create new error codes as defined in Section 6.5.

1.9   Implementation Issues

There are a number of areas where an MPI implementation may interact with the operating environment and system. While MPI does not mandate that any services (such as signal handling) be provided, it does strongly suggest the behavior to be provided if those services are available. This is an important point in achieving portability across platforms that provide the same set of services.

1.9.1   Independence of Basic Runtime Routines

MPI programs require that library routines that are part of the basic language environment (such as WRITE in Fortran and printf() and malloc() in ISO C) and are executed after MPI_INIT and before MPI_FINALIZE operate independently and that their *completion* is independent of the action of other processes in an MPI program.

Note that this in no way prevents the creation of library routines that provide parallel services whose operation is collective. However, the following program is expected to complete in an ISO C environment regardless of the size of MPI_COMM_WORLD (assuming that printf() is available at the executing nodes).

```
int rank;
MPI_Init((void *)0, (void *)0);
MPI_Comm_rank(MPI_COMM_WORLD, &rank);
if (rank == 0) printf("Starting program\n");
MPI_Finalize();
```

The corresponding Fortran and C++ programs are also expected to complete.

An example of what is *not* required is any particular ordering of the action of these routines when called by several tasks. For example, MPI makes neither requirements nor recommendations for the output from the following program (again assuming that I/O is available at the executing nodes).

```
MPI_Comm_rank(MPI_COMM_WORLD, &rank);
printf("Output from task rank %d\n", rank);
```

In addition, calls that fail because of resource exhaustion or other error are not considered a violation of the requirements here (however, they are required to complete, just not to complete successfully).

1.9.2 Interaction with Signals

MPI does not specify the interaction of processes with signals and does not require that MPI be signal safe. The implementation may reserve some signals for its own use. It is required that the implementation document which signals it uses, and it is strongly recommended that it not use SIGALRM, SIGFPE, or SIGIO. Implementations may also prohibit the use of MPI calls from within signal handlers.

In multithreaded environments, users can avoid conflicts between signals and the MPI library by catching signals only on threads that do not execute MPI calls. High quality single-threaded implementations will be signal safe: an MPI call suspended by a signal will resume and complete normally after the signal is handled.

2 Miscellany

This chapter contains topics that do not fit conveniently into other chapters. The first section deals with the interaction of threads with MPI. The MPI standard does not mandate thread support, but specifies the behavior of **thread-compliant** MPI implementations. New calls are provided for querying and controlling the level of thread support provided by the MPI library. Regardless of the level of thread support, all implementations must provide the new thread calls for portability.

The second section deals with interoperability of C, C++ and Fortran language, that is, support for mixed language parallel programs.

The third section presents the MPI functions that create and manipulate info objects. These objects are used by many MPI functions to pass optional information.

Finally, the last section deals with the MPI functions for the allocation and deallocation of "special" memory.

2.1 MPI and Threads

This section specifies the interaction between MPI calls and threads. The section lists minimal requirements for **thread-compliant** MPI implementations. MPI may be implemented in environments where threads are not supported or perform poorly. Therefore, it is not required that all MPI implementations be thread-compliant. This section also describes functions that can be used for initializing and querying the thread environment. These functions are supported by all MPI implementations, even if they are not thread-compliant.

This section generally assumes a thread package similar to POSIX threads [15], but the syntax and semantics of thread calls are not specified here—these are beyond the scope of this document.

2.1.1 General

In a thread-compliant implementation, an MPI process is a process that may be multithreaded. Each thread can issue MPI calls; however, threads are not separately addressable: a rank in a send or receive call identifies a process, not a thread. A message sent to a process can be received by any thread in this process.

Rationale. This model corresponds to the POSIX model of interprocess communication: the fact that a process is multithreaded, rather than single-threaded, does not affect the external interface of this process. MPI implementations where MPI "processes" are POSIX threads inside a single POSIX process are not thread-compliant by this definition (indeed, their "processes" are single-threaded). ☐

Advice to users.   It is the user's responsibility to prevent races when threads within the same application post conflicting communication calls. The user can make sure that two threads in the same process will not issue conflicting communication calls by using distinct communicators at each thread. □

The two main requirements for a thread-compliant implementation are listed below.

1.   All MPI calls are *thread-safe*. That is, two concurrently running threads may make MPI calls and the outcome will be as if the calls executed in some order, even if their execution is interleaved.

2.   Blocking MPI calls will block the calling thread only, allowing another thread to execute, if available. The calling thread will be blocked until the event on which it is waiting occurs. Once the blocked communication is enabled and can proceed, then the call will complete and the thread will be marked runnable, within a finite time. A blocked thread will not prevent progress of other runnable threads in the same process, and will not prevent them from executing MPI calls.

Example 2.1   Process 0 consists of two threads. The first thread executes a blocking send call MPI_Send(buff1, count, type, 0, 0, comm), whereas the second thread executes a blocking receive call MPI_Recv(buff2, count, type, 0, 0, comm, &status). That is, the first thread sends a message that is received by the second thread. This communication should always succeed. According to the first requirement, the execution will correspond to some interleaving of the two calls. According to the second requirement, an MPI call can only block the calling thread and must not prevent progress of the other thread. If the send call went ahead of the receive call, then the sending thread may block, but this will not prevent the receiving thread from executing. Thus, the receive call will occur. Once both calls occur, the communication is enabled and both calls will complete. On the other hand, a single-threaded process that posts a send, followed by a matching receive, may deadlock. (However, using an isend will not cause deadlock.) The progress requirement for multithreaded implementations is stronger, as a blocked call cannot prevent progress in other threads.

Advice to implementors.   MPI calls can be made thread-safe by executing only one at a time, for example, by protecting MPI code with one process-global lock. However, blocked operations cannot hold the lock, as this would prevent progress of other threads in the process. The lock is held only for the duration of an atomic, locally-completing suboperation such as posting a send or completing a send, and is released in between. Finer locks can provide more concurrency, at the expense of higher locking overheads. Concurrency can also be achieved by having some of the MPI protocol executed by separate server threads. ☐

2.1.2 Clarifications

Initialization and completion. Exactly one thread per process calls MPI-FINALIZE and this should occur on the same thread that initialized MPI. We call this thread the **main thread**. The call should occur only after all the process threads have reached the state where it is legitimate to call MPI_FINALIZE (see Section I-7.2).

Rationale. This constraint may simplify implementation. ☐

Multiple threads completing the same request. A program in which two threads block, waiting on the same request, is erroneous. Similarly, the same request cannot appear in the array of requests of two concurrent MPI-WAIT{ANY|SOME|ALL} calls. In MPI, a request can only be completed once. Any combination of wait or test which violates this rule is erroneous.

Rationale. This is consistent with the view that a multithreaded execution corresponds to an interleaving of the MPI calls. In a single-threaded implementation, once a wait is posted on a request the request handle will be nullified before it is possible to post a second wait on the same handle. With threads, an MPI-WAIT{ANY|SOME|ALL} may be blocked without having nullified its request(s) so it becomes the user's responsibility to avoid using the same request in an MPI-WAIT on another thread. This constraint also simplifies implementation, as only one thread will be blocked on any communication or I/O event. ☐

Probe. A receive call that uses source and tag values returned by a preceding call to MPI_PROBE or MPI_IPROBE will receive the message matched by the probe call only if there was no other matching receive after the probe and before that receive. In a multithreaded environment, it is up to the user to enforce this condition using suitable mutual exclusion logic. This can be enforced by making sure that each communicator is used by only one thread on each process.

Collective calls. Matching of collective calls on a communicator, window, or file handle is done according to the order in which the calls are issued at each process. If concurrent threads issue such calls on the same communicator, window or file handle, it is up to the user to make sure the calls are correctly ordered, using interthread synchronization.

Exception handlers.   An exception handler does not necessarily execute in the context of the thread that made the exception-raising MPI call; the exception handler may be executed by a thread that is distinct from the thread that will return the error code.

Rationale.   The MPI implementation may be multithreaded, so that part of the communication protocol may execute on a thread that is distinct from the thread that made the MPI call. The design allows the exception handler to be executed by the thread where the exception occurred. □

Interaction with signals and cancellations.   The outcome is undefined if a thread that executes an MPI call is cancelled (by another thread), or if a thread catches a signal while executing an MPI call. However, a thread of an MPI process may terminate, and may catch signals or be cancelled by another thread when not executing MPI calls.

Rationale.   Few C library functions are signal-safe, and many have cancellation points—points where the thread executing them may be cancelled. The above restriction simplifies implementation (no need for the MPI library to be "async-cancel-safe" or "async-signal-safe"). □

Advice to users.   Users can catch signals in separate, non-MPI threads (e.g., by masking signals on MPI calling threads, and unmasking them in one or more non-MPI threads). A good programming practice is to have a distinct thread blocked in a call to `sigwait` for each expected user signal. Users must not catch signals used by the MPI implementation; as each MPI implementation is required to document the signals used internally, users can avoid these signals. □

Advice to implementors.   The MPI library should not invoke library calls that are not thread-safe, if multiple threads execute. □

2.1.3   Initialization

The following function may be used to initialize MPI, and initialize the MPI thread environment, instead of MPI_INIT.

MPI_INIT_THREAD(required, provided)

| IN | required | desired level of thread support (integer) |
| OUT | provided | provided level of thread support (integer) |

```
int MPI_Init_thread(int *argc, char ***argv, int required,
    int *provided)
```

```
MPI_INIT_THREAD(REQUIRED, PROVIDED, IERROR)
    INTEGER REQUIRED, PROVIDED, IERROR
```

```
int MPI::Init_thread(int& argc, char**& argv, int required)
```

```
int MPI::Init_thread(int required)
```

Passing argc and argv is optional in C and C++ (these arguments are not passed in Fortran). In C, this is accomplished by passing NULL as argument value. In C++, this is accomplished with two separate bindings to cover these two cases. When argc and argv are supplied, these should be the values passed to main. This is the same as for MPI_INIT (Chapter I-7).

This call initializes MPI in the same way that a call to MPI_INIT would. In addition, it initializes the thread environment. The argument required is used to specify the desired level of thread support. The possible values are listed in increasing order of thread support.

MPI_THREAD_SINGLE: Only one thread will execute.

MPI_THREAD_FUNNELED: The process may be multithreaded, but only the main thread will make MPI calls (all MPI calls are "funneled" to the main thread). The main thread is the one that initializes and finalizes MPI.

MPI_THREAD_SERIALIZED: The process may be multithreaded, and multiple threads may make MPI calls, but only one at a time: MPI calls are not made concurrently from two distinct threads of the same process (all MPI calls are "serialized").

MPI_THREAD_MULTIPLE: Multiple threads may call MPI, with no restrictions.

These values are monotonic; that is, MPI_THREAD_SINGLE < MPI_THREAD_-FUNNELED < MPI_THREAD_SERIALIZED < MPI_THREAD_MULTIPLE.
Note that the C++ names begin with MPI::THREAD rather than MPI_THREAD.

Different processes in MPI_COMM_WORLD may require different levels of thread support.

The call returns in provided information about the actual level of thread support that will be provided by MPI. It can be one of the four values listed above.

The levels of thread support that can be provided by MPI_INIT_THREAD will depend on the implementation, and may depend on information provided by the user before the program started to execute (e.g., with arguments to mpiexec). If possible, the call will return provided = required. Failing this, the call will return the least supported level such that provided > required (thus providing a stronger level of support than required by the user). Finally, if the user requirement cannot be satisfied, then the call will return in provided the highest supported level.

A **thread-compliant** MPI implementation will be able to return provided = MPI_THREAD_MULTIPLE. Such an implementation may always return provided = MPI_THREAD_MULTIPLE, irrespective of the value of required. At the other extreme, an MPI library that is not thread-compliant may always return provided = MPI_THREAD_SINGLE, irrespective of the value of required.

A call to MPI_INIT has the same effect as a call to MPI_INIT_THREAD with required = MPI_THREAD_SINGLE.

Vendors may provide (implementation dependent) means to specify the levels of thread support available when the MPI program is started. This will affect the outcome of calls to MPI_INIT and MPI_INIT_THREAD. Suppose, for example, that an MPI program has been started so that only MPI_THREAD_MULTIPLE is available. Then MPI_INIT_THREAD will return provided = MPI_THREAD_MULTIPLE, irrespective of the value of required; a call to MPI_INIT will also initialize the MPI thread support level to MPI_THREAD_MULTIPLE. Suppose, on the other hand, that an MPI program has been started so that all four levels of thread support are available. Then, a call to MPI_INIT_THREAD will return provided = required; on the other hand, a call to MPI_INIT will initialize the MPI thread support level to MPI_THREAD_SINGLE.

Advice to users.   Users should require the lowest level of thread support that is compatible with their code. This leaves the most freedom for optimizations by the MPI implementation. □

Rationale.   Various optimizations are possible when MPI code is executed single-threaded, or is executed on multiple threads, but not concurrently: mutual exclusion code may be omitted. Furthermore, if only one thread executes, then the MPI library can use library functions that are not thread-safe, without risking conflicts with user threads. Thus, a lower level of thread support may be associated with a lower overhead for MPI calls. Therefore, the current design provides the user with a mechanism for requiring the lowest level of thread support that is required by its program.

The model of one communication thread, multiple computation threads fits many applications well. For example, if the process code is a sequential Fortran/C/C++ program with MPI calls that has been parallelized by a compiler for execution on an SMP node, in a cluster of SMPs, then the process computation is multithreaded, but MPI calls will likely execute on a single thread.

The design accommodates a static specification of the thread support level (e.g., with arguments to mpiexec), for environments that require static binding of libraries, and for compatibility for current multithreaded MPI codes. □

Advice to implementors.   If provided is not MPI_THREAD_SINGLE then the MPI library should not invoke C/C++/Fortran library calls that are not thread-safe. For example, in an environment where `malloc` is not thread-safe, `malloc` should not be used by the MPI library.

Some implementors may want to use different MPI libraries for different levels of thread support. They can do so using dynamic linking and selecting which library will be linked when MPI_INIT_THREAD is invoked. If this is not possible, then optimizations for lower levels of thread support will occur only when the level of thread support required is specified at link time. □

The following function can be used to query the current level of thread support.

MPI_QUERY_THREAD(provided)

| OUT | provided | provided level of thread support (integer) |

```
int MPI_Query_thread(int *provided)
```

```
MPI_QUERY_THREAD(PROVIDED, IERROR)
    INTEGER PROVIDED, IERROR
```

```
int MPI::Query_thread()
```

The call returns in provided the current level of thread support. This will be the value returned in provided by MPI_INIT_THREAD, if MPI was initialized by a call to MPI_INIT_THREAD(). If MPI was initialized with MPI_INIT, then it is as if required was MPI_THREAD_SINGLE in MPI_INIT_THREAD. The value of provided can be different from this value.

MPI_IS_THREAD_MAIN(flag)

   OUT   flag   true if calling thread is main thread, false otherwise
                                        (logical)

```
int MPI_Is_thread_main(int *flag)
```

```
MPI_IS_THREAD_MAIN(FLAG, IERROR)
    LOGICAL FLAG
    INTEGER IERROR
```

```
bool MPI::Is_thread_main()
```

This function can be called by a thread to find out whether it is the main thread (the thread that called MPI_INIT or MPI_INIT_THREAD).

All routines listed in this section must be supported by all MPI implementations.

Rationale. MPI libraries are required to provide these calls even if they do not support threads, so that portable code that contains invocations to these functions be able to link correctly. MPI_INIT continues to be supported so as to provide compatibility with current MPI codes. □

Advice to users. It is possible to spawn threads before MPI is initialized, but no MPI call other than MPI_INITIALIZED should be executed by these threads, until MPI_INIT_THREAD is invoked by one thread (which, thereby, becomes the main thread). In particular, it is possible to enter the MPI execution with a multithreaded process.

The level of thread support provided is a global property of the MPI process that can be specified only once, when MPI is initialized on that process (or before). Portable third-party libraries should be written so as to accommodate any provided level of thread support. Otherwise, their usage will be restricted to specific level(s) of thread support. If such a library can run only with specific level(s) of thread support, for example, only with MPI_THREAD_MULTIPLE, then MPI_QUERY_THREAD can be used to check whether the user initialized MPI to the correct level of thread support and, if not, raise an exception. □

Example 2.2 Using a thread to process asynchronous messages.

This program shows how a thread can be created that waits in a receive loop, processing messages as they arrive. In this example, a message with a tag of zero causes the thread to exit.

```
void receive_thread(void *ptr);
int main( int argc, char **argv )
{
    int provided, rank, data;
    MPI_Comm thread_comm;
    pthread_t thread;

    MPI_Init_thread( 0, 0, MPI_THREAD_MULTIPLE, &provided );
    if (provided < MPI_THREAD_MULTIPLE)
        MPI_Abort( MPI_COMM_WORLD, 0 );

    /* Create a communicator just for communication
       with the thread */
    MPI_Comm_dup( MPI_COMM_WORLD, &thread_comm );
    MPI_Comm_rank( thread_comm, &rank );
    if (rank == 0) {
        pthread_create(&thread, NULL, receive_thread, &thread_comm);
    }
    ...
    /* perform work.  Processes with any rank can execute */
        MPI_Send( &data, 1, MPI_INT, 0, 1, thread_comm );
    /* to have process 0 print the value of data */
    ...
    /* Tell the receive thread to exit */
    MPI_Send( MPI_BOTTOM, 0, MPI_INT, 0, 0, thread_comm );
    MPI_Finalize();
    return 0;
}
/* thread code */
void receive_thread(void *ptr)
{
    int      buf;
    MPI_Comm thread_comm = *(MPI_Comm *)ptr;
    MPI_Status status;

    while (1) {
        MPI_Recv( &buf, 1, MPI_INT, MPI_ANY_SOURCE, MPI_ANY_TAG,
                  thread_comm, &status );
```

```
        if (status.MPI_TAG == 0) return;
        printf( "Received %d from %d\n", buf, status.MPI_SOURCE );
    }
}
```

2.2 Language Interoperability

2.2.1 Introduction

It is not uncommon for library developers to use one language to develop an applications library that may be called by an application program written in a different language. MPI currently supports ISO (previously ANSI) C, C++, and Fortran bindings. It should be possible to mix these three languages in a program that uses MPI, and pass MPI-related information across language boundaries.

Moreover, MPI allows the development of client-server code, with MPI communication used between a parallel client and a parallel server. It should be possible to code the server in one language and the clients in another language. To do so, communications should be possible between applications written in different languages.

There are several issues that need to be addressed in order to achieve such interoperability.

Initialization: We need to specify how the MPI environment is initialized for all languages.

Interlanguage passing of MPI opaque objects: We need to specify how MPI object handles are passed between languages. We also need to specify what happens when an MPI object is accessed in one language, to retrieve information (e.g., attributes) set in another language.

Interlanguage communication: We need to specify how messages sent in one language can be received in another language.

It is highly desirable that the solution for interlanguage interoperability be extendable to new languages, should MPI bindings be defined for such languages.

2.2.2 Assumptions

We assume that conventions exist for programs written in one language to call functions in written in another language. These conventions specify how to link routines in different languages into one program, how to call functions in a different language, how to pass arguments between languages, and the correspondence between basic data types in different languages. In general, these conventions will be implementation-dependent. Furthermore, not every basic datatype may have a matching type in other languages. For example, C/C++ character strings may not be compatible with Fortran **CHARACTER** variables. However, we assume that a Fortran **INTEGER**, as well as a (sequence associated) Fortran array of **INTEGER**s, can be passed to a C or C++ program. We also assume that Fortran, C, and C++ have address-sized integers. This does not mean that the default-sized integers are the same size as default-sized pointers, but only that there is some way to hold (and pass) a C address in a Fortran integer. It is also assumed that INTEGER(KIND=MPI_-OFFSET_KIND) can be passed from Fortran to C as MPI_Offset.

2.2.3   Initialization

A call to MPI_INIT or MPI_THREAD_INIT, from any language, initializes MPI for execution in all languages. The function MPI_FINALIZE finalizes the MPI environments for all languages. The function MPI_ABORT kills processes, irrespective of the language used by the caller or by the processes killed.

The global MPI environment is the same in all languages: Thus, the functions MPI_INITIALIZED or MPI_FINALIZED return the same answer in all languages, if called at the same point in the execution; MPI_COMM_WORLD carries the same information regardless of language: same processes, same environmental attributes, same error handlers.

Advice to users.   The use of several languages in one MPI program may require the use of special options at compile and/or link time. ☐

Advice to implementors.   Implementations may selectively link language-specific MPI libraries only to codes that need them, so as not to increase the size of binaries for codes that use only one language. The MPI initialization code needs to perform initialization for a language only if that language library is loaded. ☐

2.2.4   Transfer of Handles

Handles are passed between Fortran and C or C++ by using an explicit C wrapper to convert Fortran handles to C handles. There is no direct access to C or C++ handles in Fortran. Handles are passed between C and C++ using overloaded C++ operators called from C++ code. There is no direct access to C++ objects from C.

C and Fortran.   The type definition MPI_Fint is provided in C/C++ for an integer of the size that matches a Fortran INTEGER; often, MPI_Fint will be equivalent to int.[1]

Functions are provided in C to convert from a Fortran handle (which is an integer) to a C handle, and vice versa. The general form of a Fortran-to-C conversion function is

```
MPI_<CLASS> MPI_<CLASS>_f2c(MPI_Fint handle)
```

The token <CLASS> is used to indicate any valid MPI opaque handle name (e.g., Comm or Group). The function converts valid Fortran handles to valid C handles, null Fortran handles to null C handles; and invalid Fortran handles to invalid C handles.

Thus,

```
MPI_Comm MPI_Comm_f2c(MPI_Fint comm)
```

converts the integer comm to a C handle of type MPI_Comm. If comm is a valid Fortran handle to a communicator, then MPI_Comm_f2c returns a valid C handle to that same communicator; if comm = MPI_COMM_NULL (Fortran value), then MPI_Comm_f2c returns a null C handle (with C value MPI_COMM_NULL); if comm is an invalid Fortran communicator handle, then MPI_Comm_f2c returns an invalid C communicator handle.

The general form of a C-to-Fortran conversion function is

```
MPI_Fint MPI_<CLASS>_c2f(MPI_<CLASS> handle)
```

The function converts valid C handles to valid Fortran handles, null C handles to null Fortran handles; and invalid C handles to invalid Fortran handles.

Thus,

```
MPI_Fint MPI_Comm_c2f(MPI_Comm comm)
```

converts comm into a Fortran handle. If comm is a valid C handle to a communicator, then MPI_Comm_c2f returns a valid Fortran handle to that same communicator; if comm = MPI_COMM_NULL (C value), then MPI_Comm_c2f returns a null Fortran handle; if comm is an invalid C communicator handle, then MPI_Comm_f2c returns an invalid Fortran communicator handle.

---

[1]No MPI::Fint was defined; C++ users should use MPI_Fint. This reflects the fact that the there are no separate Fortran/C++ conversion functions.

The conversion functions for the other types of opaque objects are listed below.

```
MPI_Datatype MPI_Type_f2c(MPI_Fint datatype)
```

```
MPI_Fint MPI_Type_c2f(MPI_Datatype datatype)
```

```
MPI_File MPI_File_f2c(MPI_Fint file)
```

```
MPI_Fint MPI_File_c2f(MPI_File file)
```

```
MPI_Group MPI_Group_f2c(MPI_Fint group)
```

```
MPI_Fint MPI_Group_c2f(MPI_Group group)
```

```
MPI_Info MPI_Info_f2c(MPI_Fint info)
```

```
MPI_Fint MPI_Info_c2f(MPI_Info info)
```

```
MPI_Op MPI_Op_f2c(MPI_Fint op)
```

```
MPI_Fint MPI_Op_c2f(MPI_Op op)
```

```
MPI_Request MPI_Request_f2c(MPI_Fint request)
```

```
MPI_Fint MPI_Request_c2f(MPI_Request request)
```

```
MPI_Win MPI_Win_f2c(MPI_Fint win)
```

```
MPI_Fint MPI_Win_c2f(MPI_Win win)
```

Note that there are no conversion functions defined in MPI-2 for error handlers. This was an oversight of the MPI Forum; vendors are likely (but are not required) to provide the following functions:

```
MPI_Errhandler MPI_Errhandler_f2c(MPI_Fint errhandler)
```

```
MPI_Fint MPI_Errhandler_c2f(MPI_Errhandler errhandler)
```

Example 2.3 The example below illustrates how the Fortran MPI function MPI_TYPE_COMMIT can be implemented by wrapping the C MPI function MPI_Type_commit with a C wrapper to do handle conversions. In this example a Fortran-C interface is assumed where a Fortran function is all uppercase when referred to from C and arguments are passed by addresses.

```
! FORTRAN PROCEDURE
SUBROUTINE MPI_TYPE_COMMIT(DATATYPE, IERR)
```

```
INTEGER DATATYPE, IERR
CALL MPI_X_TYPE_COMMIT(DATATYPE, IERR)
RETURN
END

/* C wrapper */

void MPI_X_TYPE_COMMIT(MPI_Fint *f_handle, MPI_Fint *ierr)
{
MPI_Datatype datatype;

datatype = MPI_Type_f2c(*f_handle);
*ierr = (MPI_Fint)MPI_Type_commit(&datatype);
*f_handle = MPI_Type_c2f(datatype);
return;
}
```

The same approach can be used for all other MPI functions. The call to MPI_-⟨CLASS⟩_f2c (resp. MPI_⟨CLASS⟩_c2f) can be omitted when the handle is an OUT (resp. IN) argument, rather than INOUT.

Rationale. The design here provides a convenient solution for the prevalent case, where a C wrapper is used to allow Fortran code to call a C library, or C code to call a Fortran library. The use of C wrappers is much more likely than the use of Fortran wrappers, because it is much more likely that a variable of type INTEGER can be passed to C than a C handle can be passed to Fortran.

Returning the converted value as a function value rather than through the argument list allows the generation of efficient inlined code when these functions are simple (e.g., the identity). The conversion function in the wrapper does not catch an invalid handle argument. Instead, an invalid handle is passed below to the library function, which, presumably, checks its input arguments. ☐

C and C++. Transfer of opaque objects and handles to opaque objects between C and C++ is supported by the natural casting, construction, and assignment operations. A C++ binding of MPI provides the necessary definitions to allow a C++ program to cast a C++ opaque object or handle to and from the corresponding C opaque object or handle. Assignment and constructors are also provided to create C++ objects from a C MPI handle.

Advice to users. The casting and promotion operators return new handles by value. Using these new handles as INOUT parameters will affect the internal MPI object, but will *not* affect the original handle from which it was cast. Thus, if an MPI object is created in C, and freed in C++, then the original C handle is not set to NULL. ☐

Rationale. Providing conversion from C to C++ via constructors and from C++ to C via casting allows the compiler to make automatic conversions. Calling C from C++ becomes trivial, as does the provision of a C or Fortran interface to a C++ library. ☐

Example 2.4 In order for a C program to use a C++ library, the C++ library must export a C interface that provides appropriate conversions before invoking the underlying C++ library call. This example shows a C interface function that invokes a C++ library call with a C communicator; the communicator is automatically promoted to a C++ handle when the underlying C++ function is invoked.

```
// C++ library function prototype
void cpp_lib_call(MPI::Comm& cpp_comm);

// Exported C function prototype
extern "C" void c_interface(MPI_Comm c_comm);

void c_interface(MPI_Comm c_comm)
{
// the MPI_Comm (c_comm) is automatically promoted to MPI::Comm
cpp_lib_call(c_comm);
}
```

Example 2.5 A C library routine is called from a C++ program. The C library routine is prototyped to take an MPI_Comm as an argument.

```
// C function prototype
extern "C" {
void c_lib_call(MPI_Comm c_comm);
}

void cpp_function()
{
```

```
// Create a C++ communicator, and initialize it with a dup of
//    MPI::COMM_WORLD
MPI::Intracomm cpp_comm(MPI::COMM_WORLD.Dup());
c_lib_call(cpp_comm);
}
```

2.2.5 Status

The following two procedures are provided in C to convert from a Fortran status (which is an array of integers) to a C status (which is a structure), and vice versa. The conversion occurs on all the information in status, including that which is hidden. That is, no status information is lost in the conversion.

```
int MPI_Status_f2c(MPI_Fint *f_status, MPI_Status *c_status)
```

If f_status is a valid Fortran status, but not the Fortran value of MPI_STATUS_IGNORE or MPI_STATUSES_IGNORE, then MPI_Status_f2c returns in c_status a valid C status with the same content. If f_status is the Fortran value of MPI_STATUS_IGNORE or MPI_STATUSES_IGNORE, or if f_status is not a valid Fortran status, then the call is erroneous.

The C status has the same source, tag and error code values as the Fortran status, and returns the same answers when queried for count, elements, and cancellation. The conversion function may be called with a Fortran status argument that has an undefined error field, in which case the value of the error field in the C status argument is undefined.

Two global variables of type MPI_Fint*, MPI_F_STATUS_IGNORE and MPI_F_STATUSES_IGNORE are declared in mpi.h. They can be used to test, in C, whether f_status is the Fortran value of MPI_STATUS_IGNORE or MPI_STATUSES_IGNORE, respectively. These are global variables, not C constant expressions and cannot be used in places where C requires constant expressions. Their value is defined only between the calls to MPI_INIT and MPI_FINALIZE and should not be changed by user code.

To do the conversion in the other direction, we have the following:

```
int MPI_Status_c2f(MPI_Status *c_status, MPI_Fint *f_status)
```

This call converts a C status into a Fortran status, and has a behavior similar to MPI_Status_f2c. That is, the value of c_status must not be either MPI_STATUS_IGNORE or MPI_STATUSES_IGNORE.

Advice to users. There is no separate conversion function for arrays of statuses since one can simply loop through the array, converting each status. ▯

Rationale. The handling of MPI_STATUS_IGNORE is required in order to layer libraries with only a C wrapper: if the Fortran call has passed MPI_STATUS_IGNORE, then the C wrapper must handle this correctly. Note that this constant need not have the same value in Fortran and C. If MPI_Status_f2c were to handle MPI_-STATUS_IGNORE, then the type of its result would have to be MPI_Status**, which was considered an inferior solution. ▯

C and C++. The conversion of an MPI_Status in C to or from an MPI::Status in C++ is carried out by the usual cast, assignment, or construction operations.

2.2.6 MPI Opaque Objects

C, C++ and Fortran MPI opaque objects can be used interchangeably by an application. The behavior is as if there is only one object, accessed via different handles in each language. For example, an application can cache an attribute in C or Fortran on MPI_COMM_WORLD and later retrieve it in C++ from MPI::COMM_WORLD. (In many implementations there actually is only one object for all languages.)

Example 2.6 In the program below, a datatype is constructed and committed in Fortran and and used for communication in C. The C program sends a Fortran string (variable of type CHARACTER). This will work, even if such variables cannot be passed from Fortran to C.

```
! FORTRAN CODE
CHARACTER C(25)
INTEGER TYPE, IERR
INTEGER (KIND=MPI_ADDRESS_KIND) ADDR

! create an absolute datatype for character array C
CALL MPI_GET_ADDRESS(C, ADDR, IERR)
CALL MPI_TYPE_CREATE_STRUCT(1, 25, ADDR, MPI_CHARACTER, TYPE, IERR)
CALL MPI_TYPE_COMMIT(TYPE,IERR)
CALL C_ROUTINE(TYPE)

/* C code */

void C_ROUTINE(MPI_Fint *ftype)
```

```
{
MPI_Send(MPI_BOTTOM, 1, MPI_Type_f2c(*ftype), 1, 0, MPI_COMM_WORLD);
/* the message sent contains the Fortran character array C    */
}
```

We clarify below some issues that arise when objects are transferred across languages.

2.2.7 Attributes

Attribute keys declared in one language are associated with copy and delete functions in that language (the functions provided by the MPI_{TYPE,COMM,WIN}_CREATE_KEYVAL call). When a communicator or datatype is duplicated, for each attribute, the corresponding copy function is called, using the correct calling convention for the language of that function; and similarly, for the delete callback function.

Advice to implementors.   This requires that attributes be tagged either as "C", "C++" or "Fortran", and that the language tag be checked in order to use the right calling convention for the callback function. ⬚

MPI supports two types of attributes: reference (pointer) attributes and integer attributes. Attribute keys created in C and C++ are associated with reference attributes (of type void*). Attribute keys created in Fortran are associated with integer attributes (of type INTEGER(KIND=MPI_ADDRESS_KIND)).

One can associate an integer value with a C-created attribute key by allocating an integer variable to store the value, and by associating the attribute key with a pointer to that variable. This is the mechanism assumed by MPI for access to integer attributes in C or C++: When the value of an integer attribute value is set in C or C++ via a call to MPI_{TYPE,COMM,WIN}_SET_ATTR, then the attribute_val argument should be a pointer to a variable holding the integer value. When the value of an integer attribute value is accessed in C or C++, via a call to MPI_{TYPE,COMM,WIN}_GET_ATTR, then the call returns in attribute_val a pointer to a location where the integer attribute value is stored.

Conversely, one can associate a reference with a Fortran-created attribute key by *interpreting* the integer attribute value as an address. This requires a nonstandard, but fairly common, pointer extension to Fortran—see Section 2.4 and Example 2.7. This is the mechanism assumed by MPI for access to reference attributes in Fortran: When the value of an reference attribute value is set in Fortran, via a call to MPI_{TYPE,COMM,WIN}_SET_ATTR, then the attribute_val argument should be the integer address of the referenced variable. When the value of a reference attribute value is accessed in Fortran via a call to MPI_{TYPE,COMM,WIN}_GET_ATTR, then the call returns in attribute_val the address of the referenced variable.

Predefined integer-valued attributes, such as MPI_TAG_UB, behave as if they were set by a Fortran call. That is, in Fortran, MPI_COMM_GET_ATTR(MPI_COMM-WORLD, MPI_TAG_UB, val, flag, ierr) will return in val the upper bound for tag value; in C, MPI_Comm_get_attr(MPI_COMM_WORLD, MPI_TAG_UB, &p, &flag) will return in p a pointer to an int containing the upper bound for tag value.

Predefined reference attributes, such as MPI_WIN_BASE behave as if they were set by a C call. That is, in Fortran, MPI_WIN_GET_ATTR(win, MPI_WIN_BASE, val, flag, ierror) will return in val the base address of the window, converted to an integer. In C, MPI_Win_get_attr(win, MPI_WIN_BASE, &p, &flag) will return in p a pointer to the window base, cast to (void *).

Rationale.   The design is consistent with the behavior specified in MPI-1 for predefined attributes, and ensures that no information is lost when attributes are passed from language to language. ▯

Advice to implementors.   Implementations should tag attributes either as reference attributes or as integer attributes, according to whether they were set in C or in Fortran. Thus, the right choice can be made when the attribute is retrieved. ▯

Example 2.7
A. Integer attribute, C to Fortran
C code

```
void c_attr_set(MPI_Fint *key)
{
  static MPI_Aint i = 4444;
  void *p;
  p = &i;
  MPI_Comm_set_attr(MPI_COMM_SELF, *key, p);
  return;
}
```

Fortran code

```
PROGRAM TEST
USE MPI
INTEGER key, ierr
```

```
LOGICAL flag
INTEGER(kind = MPI_ADDRESS_KIND) val, xstate

CALL MPI_COMM_CREATE_KEYVAL(MPI_COMM_NULL_COPY_FN, &
          MPI_COMM_NULL_DELETE_FN, key, xstate, ierr)
CALL C_attr_set(key)
CALL MPI_COMM_GET_ATTR(MPI_COMM_SELF, key, val, flag, ierr)
IF(val.NE.4444) CALL ERROR
END
```

B. Integer attribute, Fortran to C

Fortran code

```
PROGRAM TEST
USE MPI
INTEGER key, ierr
INTEGER(kind = MPI_ADDRESS_KIND) val, xstate

CALL MPI_COMM_CREATE_KEYVAL(MPI_COMM_NULL_COPY_FN, &
          MPI_COMM_NULL_DELETE_FN, key, xstate, ierr)
val = 55555
CALL MPI_COMM_SET_ATTR(MPI_COMM_SELF, key, val, ierr)
CALL C_get_attr(key)
END
```

C code

```
void c_get_attr(MPI_Fint *key)
{
  MPI_Aint *p;
  int flag;
  MPI_Comm_get_attr(MPI_COMM_SELF, *key, &p, &flag);
  if (*p != 55555) error();
}
```

The deprecated Fortran attribute-manipulation functions (Section I-5.6.3) use INTEGER attribute values. Attribute values may be truncated by these functions— see Section I-5.6.3.

Callback Functions. MPI calls may associate callback functions with MPI objects: error handlers are associated with communicators and files, attribute copy and delete functions are associated with attribute keys, reduce operations are associated with operation objects, etc. In a multi-language environment, a function passed in an MPI call in one language may be invoked by an MPI call in another language. MPI implementations must make sure that such invocation will use the calling convention of the language the function is bound to.

Advice to implementors. Callback functions need to have a language tag. This tag is set when the callback function is passed in by the library function (which is presumably different for each language), and is used to generate the right calling sequence when the callback function is invoked. □

Error Handlers. `MPI::ERRORS_THROW_EXCEPTIONS` can only be set or retrieved by C++ functions. The result of retrieving `MPI::ERRORS_THROW_EXCEPTIONS` in a non-C++ program is undefined.

If a non-C++ program causes an error that invokes the `MPI::ERRORS_THROW_-EXCEPTIONS` error handler, the exception will pass up the calling stack until C++ code can catch it. If there is no C++ code to catch it, the behavior is undefined. In a multithreaded environment or if a nonblocking MPI call throws an exception while making progress in the background, the behavior is implementation-dependent.

Advice to implementors. Error handlers in C and C++ have a "`stdargs`" argument list. It might be useful to provide to the handler information on the language environment where the error occurred. □

Reduce Operations.

Advice to users. Reduce operations receive as one of their arguments the datatype of the operands. Thus, one can define "polymorphic" reduce operations that work for C, C++, and Fortran datatypes. □

Addresses. Addresses and byte displacements in MPI datatypes are stored internally as address-sized integers. Some of the deprecated MPI datatype constructor and accessor functions are passing addresses and byte displacement via `INTEGER` arguments, in Fortran. When these functions (e.g., MPI_ADDRESS) are used to access addresses or byte displacements then the address may be truncated—see Section I-3.11.

2.2.8   Constants

MPI constants have the same value in all languages, unless specified otherwise. This does not apply to constant handles (MPI_INT, MPI_COMM_WORLD, MPI_ERRORS_-RETURN, MPI_SUM, etc.). These handles need to be converted, as explained in Section 2.2.4. Constants that specify maximum lengths of strings have a value one less in Fortran than C/C++ since in C/C++ the length includes the null terminating character. Thus, these constants represent the amount of space which must be allocated to hold the largest possible such string, rather than the maximum number of printable characters the string could contain.

Advice to users.   This definition means that it is safe in C/C++ to allocate a buffer to receive a string using a declaration like

```
char name [MPI_MAX_NAME_STRING];
```

$\square$

Also, reference constants such as MPI_BOTTOM, MPI_IN_PLACE, MPI_STATUS_-IGNORE, and MPI_STATUSES_IGNORE may have different values in different languages.

Advice to users.   Even though MPI_BOTTOM may have different values in C and Fortran, MPI_GET_ADDRESS will return the same answer in both languages, and absolute addresses in datatypes will designate the same location in both languages. $\square$

Rationale.   A reference constant such as MPI_BOTTOM must be in Fortran the name of a predefined static variable, for example, a variable in an MPI-declared COMMON block. On the other hand, in C, it is natural to take MPI_BOTTOM = 0 (Caveat: Defining MPI_BOTTOM = 0 implies that NULL pointer cannot be distinguished from MPI_BOTTOM; it may be that MPI_BOTTOM = 1 is better . . .). Requiring that the Fortran and C values be the same will imply that these constants cannot be used in C in initialization expressions, and will complicate the initialization process. $\square$

Advice to implementors.   Even if MPI_BOTTOM is different in C and Fortran, one can interpret absolute addresses stored in datatypes in the same way in both languages. MPI_GET_ADDRESS returns the address of the input variable; displacements or absolute addresses provided as inputs to datatype constructors are stored as is in the datatype object. When MPI_BOTTOM is passed as a buffer argument, in C or Fortran, then the buffer address is taken to be 0. $\square$

2.2.9 Interlanguage Communication

The type-matching rules for communications in MPI are not changed: the datatype specification for each item sent should match, in type signature, the datatype specification used to receive this item (unless one of the types is MPI_PACKED). Also, the type of a message item should match the type declaration for the corresponding communication buffer location, unless the type is MPI_BYTE or MPI_PACKED. Interlanguage communication is allowed if it complies with these rules.

Example 2.8 In the example below, a Fortran array is sent from Fortran and received in C.

```
! FORTRAN CODE
REAL R(5)
INTEGER TYPE, IERR, MYRANK
INTEGER(KIND=MPI_ADDRESS_KIND) ADDR

! create an absolute datatype for array R
CALL MPI_GET_ADDRESS(R, ADDR, IERR)
CALL MPI_TYPE_CREATE_STRUCT(1, 5, ADDR, MPI_REAL, TYPE, IERR)
CALL MPI_TYPE_COMMIT(TYPE, IERR)

CALL MPI_COMM_RANK(MPI_COMM_WORLD, MYRANK, IERR)
IF (MYRANK.EQ.0) THEN
    CALL MPI_SEND(MPI_BOTTOM, 1, TYPE, 1, 0, MPI_COMM_WORLD, IERR)
ELSE
    CALL C_ROUTINE(TYPE)
END IF


/* C code */

void C_ROUTINE(MPI_Fint *fhandle)
{
  MPI_Datatype type;
  MPI_Status status;

  type = MPI_Type_f2c(*fhandle);
```

```
  MPI_Recv(MPI_BOTTOM, 1, type, 0, 0, MPI_COMM_WORLD, &status);
}
```

MPI implementors may weaken these type-matching rules, and allow messages to be sent with Fortran types and received with C types, and vice versa, when those types match. That is, if the Fortran type INTEGER is identical to the C type int, then an MPI implementation may allow data to be sent with datatype MPI_INTEGER and be received with datatype MPI_INT. However, such a code is not portable.

2.3   The Info Object

Many of the MPI routines take an info argument. info is an opaque object which consists of (key,value) pairs (both key and value are strings). A key may have only one value. MPI reserves several keys and requires that if an implementation uses a reserved key, it must provide the specified functionality. An implementation is not required to support these keys and may support any others not reserved by MPI. An info object is of type MPI_Info in C, MPI::Info in C++, and INTEGER in Fortran.

If a function does not recognize a key, it will ignore it, unless otherwise specified. If an implementation recognizes a key but does not recognize the format of the corresponding value, the result is undefined.

Keys have an implementation-defined maximum length of MPI_MAX_INFO_KEY (MPI::MAX_INFO_KEY in C++). This is large enough to hold at least least 32 and at most 255 characters (and hence is between 33 and 256 in C/C++, because of the need for the terminating null; see Section 2.2.8). Values have an implementation-defined maximum length of MPI_MAX_INFO_VAL (MPI::MAX_INFO_VAL in C++). In Fortran, leading and trailing spaces are stripped from both. Returned values will never be larger than these maximum lengths. Both key and value are case-sensitive.

Advice to users.   MPI_MAX_INFO_VAL might be very large, so it might not be wise to declare a string of that size. □

Rationale.   It may seem somewhat of an overkill to create a new opaque MPI object, and add eight new functions to MPI, for the mere purpose of manipulating lists of strings. However, neither Fortran nor C provide good support for variable-length lists of variable length strings: one can code them as one string, using a reserved separator character, but then one has to prohibit the use of this character in strings (or provide an escape sequence, further complicating the user interface). Furthermore, such an encoding does not conveniently support the addition, update or deletion of entries. In addition, Fortran implementations may limit string length to 255 or less—this is often insufficient for long lists of optional arguments.

Keys have a maximum length because the set of known keys will always be finite and known to the implementation and because there is no reason for keys to be complex. The small maximum size allows applications to declare keys of size MPI-MAX_INFO_KEY. The limitation on value sizes is so that an implementation is not forced to deal with arbitrarily long strings. ☐

When it is an argument to a nonblocking routine, info is parsed before that routine returns, so that it may be modified or freed immediately after return.

When the descriptions refer to a key or value as being a Boolean, an integer, or a list, they mean the string representation of these types. An implementation may define its own rules for how info value strings are converted to other types, but to ensure portability, every implementation must support the following representations. Legal values for a Boolean must include the strings "true" and "false" (all lower case). For integers, legal values must include string representations of decimal values of integers that are within the range of a standard integer type in the program. (However, it is possible that not every legal integer is a legal value for a given key.) On positive numbers, + signs are optional. No space may appear between a + or − sign and the leading digit of a number. For comma-separated lists, the string must contain legal elements separated by commas. Leading and trailing spaces are stripped automatically from the types of info values described above and for each element of a comma-separated list. These rules apply to all info values of these types. Implementations are free to specify a different interpretation for values of other info keys.

MPI_INFO_CREATE(info)

   OUT   info   info object created (handle)

```
int MPI_Info_create(MPI_Info *info)
```

```
MPI_INFO_CREATE(INFO, IERROR)
    INTEGER INFO, IERROR
```

```
static MPI::Info MPI::Info::Create()
```

MPI_INFO_CREATE creates a new info object. The newly created object contains no key/value pairs.

MPI_INFO_SET(info, key, value)

INOUT	info	info object (handle)
IN	key	key (string)
IN	value	value (string)

```
int MPI_Info_set(MPI_Info info, char *key, char *value)
```

```
MPI_INFO_SET(INFO, KEY, VALUE, IERROR)
    INTEGER INFO, IERROR
    CHARACTER*(*) KEY, VALUE
```

```
void MPI::Info::Set(const char* key, const char* value)
```

MPI_INFO_SET adds the (key,value) pair to info, and overrides the value if a value for the same key was previously set. key and value are null-terminated strings in C. In Fortran, leading and trailing spaces in key and value are stripped. If either key or value are larger than the allowed maxima, the errors MPI_ERR_INFO_KEY or MPI_ERR_INFO_VALUE are raised, respectively.

MPI_INFO_DELETE(info, key)

INOUT	info	info object (handle)
IN	key	key (string)

```
int MPI_Info_delete(MPI_Info info, char *key)
```

```
MPI_INFO_DELETE(INFO, KEY, IERROR)
    INTEGER INFO, IERROR
    CHARACTER*(*) KEY
```

```
void MPI::Info::Delete(const char* key)
```

MPI_INFO_DELETE deletes a (key,value) pair from info. If key is not defined in info, the call raises an error of class MPI_ERR_INFO_NOKEY.

MPI_INFO_GET(info, key, valuelen, value, flag)

IN	info	info object (handle)
IN	key	key (string)
IN	valuelen	length of value arg (integer)
OUT	value	value (string)
OUT	flag	true if key defined (logical)

```
int MPI_Info_get(MPI_Info info, char *key, int valuelen, char *value,
    int *flag)
```

```
MPI_INFO_GET(INFO, KEY, VALUELEN, VALUE, FLAG, IERROR)
    INTEGER INFO, VALUELEN, IERROR
    CHARACTER*(*) KEY, VALUE
    LOGICAL FLAG
```

```
bool MPI::Info::Get(const char* key, int valuelen, char* value)
    const
```

This function retrieves the value associated with key in a previous call to MPI_INFO_SET. If such a key exists, it sets flag to true and returns the value in value, otherwise it sets flag to false and leaves value unchanged. valuelen is the number of characters available in value. If it is less than the actual size of the value, the value is truncated. In C, valuelen should be one less than the amount of allocated space to allow for the null terminator.

If the size of key is larger than MPI_MAX_INFO_KEY, the call is erroneous.

MPI_INFO_GET_VALUELEN(info, key, valuelen, flag)

IN	info	info object (handle)
IN	key	key (string)
OUT	valuelen	length of value arg (integer)
OUT	flag	true if key defined, false if not (logical)

```
int MPI_Info_get_valuelen(MPI_Info info, char *key, int *valuelen,
    int *flag)
```

```
MPI_INFO_GET_VALUELEN(INFO, KEY, VALUELEN, FLAG, IERROR)
    INTEGER INFO, VALUELEN, IERROR
    LOGICAL FLAG
    CHARACTER*(*) KEY
```

```
bool MPI::Info::Get_valuelen(const char* key, int& valuelen) const
```

The function MPI_INFO_GET_VALUELEN retrieves the length of the value associated with key. If key is defined, valuelen is set to the length of its associated value and flag is set to true. If key is not defined, valuelen is not touched and flag is set to false. The length returned in C or C++ does not include the end-of-string character.

If key is longer than MPI_MAX_INFO_KEY, the call is erroneous.

MPI_INFO_GET_NKEYS(info, nkeys)

IN	info	info object (handle)
OUT	nkeys	number of defined keys (integer)

```
int MPI_Info_get_nkeys(MPI_Info info, int *nkeys)
```

```
MPI_INFO_GET_NKEYS(INFO, NKEYS, IERROR)
    INTEGER INFO, NKEYS, IERROR
```

```
int MPI::Info::Get_nkeys() const
```

MPI_INFO_GET_NKEYS returns the number of currently defined keys in info.

MPI_INFO_GET_NTHKEY(info, n, key)

IN	info	info object (handle)
IN	n	key number (integer)
OUT	key	key (string)

```
int MPI_Info_get_nthkey(MPI_Info info, int n, char *key)
```

```
MPI_INFO_GET_NTHKEY(INFO, N, KEY, IERROR)
    INTEGER INFO, N, IERROR
    CHARACTER*(*) KEY
```

```
void MPI::Info::Get_nthkey(int n, char* key) const
```

This function returns the nth defined key in info. Keys are numbered $0 \ldots N-1$ where N is the value returned by MPI_INFO_GET_NKEYS. All keys between 0 and $N-1$ are guaranteed to be defined. The number of a given key does not change as long as info is not modified with MPI_INFO_SET or MPI_INFO_DELETE.

MPI_INFO_DUP(info, newinfo)

| IN | info | info object (handle) |
| OUT | newinfo | info object (handle) |

```
int MPI_Info_dup(MPI_Info info, MPI_Info *newinfo)
```

```
MPI_INFO_DUP(INFO, NEWINFO, IERROR)
    INTEGER INFO, NEWINFO, IERROR
```

```
MPI::Info MPI::Info::Dup() const
```

MPI_INFO_DUP duplicates an existing info object, creating a new object, with the same (key,value) pairs and the same ordering of keys.

MPI_INFO_FREE(info)

| INOUT | info | info object (handle) |

```
int MPI_Info_free(MPI_Info *info)
```

```
MPI_INFO_FREE(INFO, IERROR)
    INTEGER INFO, IERROR
```

```
void MPI::Info::Free()
```

This function frees info and sets it to MPI_INFO_NULL (MPI::INFO_NULL, in C++).

The value of an info argument is interpreted each time the info is passed to a routine. Changes to info after return from the routine do not affect this interpretation.

2.4 Memory Allocation

In some systems, message-passing and remote-memory-access (RMA; see Chapter 4) operations run faster when accessing specially allocated memory (e.g., memory that is shared by the other processes in the communicating group on an SMP). MPI provides a mechanism for allocating and freeing such special memory. The use of such memory for message passing or RMA is not mandatory, and this memory can be used without restrictions as any other dynamically allocated memory. However, implementations may restrict the use of the MPI_WIN_LOCK and MPI_WIN_UNLOCK functions to windows allocated in such memory (see Section 4.4.3.)

MPI_ALLOC_MEM(size, info, baseptr)

IN	size	size of memory segment in bytes
IN	info	info argument (handle)
OUT	baseptr	pointer to beginning of memory segment allocated

```
int MPI_Alloc_mem(MPI_Aint size, MPI_Info info, void *baseptr)
```

```
MPI_ALLOC_MEM(SIZE, INFO, BASEPTR, IERROR)
    INTEGER INFO, IERROR
    INTEGER(KIND=MPI_ADDRESS_KIND) SIZE, BASEPTR
```

```
void* MPI::Alloc_mem(MPI::Aint size, const MPI::Info& info)
```

The info argument can be used to provide directives that control the desired location of the allocated memory. Such a directive does not affect the semantics of the call. Valid info values are implementation-dependent; a null directive value of info = MPI_INFO_NULL is always valid.

The function MPI_ALLOC_MEM may return an error code of class MPI_ERR_NO_MEM to indicate it failed because memory is exhausted.

MPI_FREE_MEM(base)

IN	base	initial address of memory segment allocated by MPI_ALLOC_MEM

```
int MPI_Free_mem(void *base)
```

```
MPI_FREE_MEM(BASE, IERROR)
    <type> BASE(*)
    INTEGER IERROR
```

```
void MPI::Free_mem(void *base)
```

The function MPI_FREE_MEM may return an error code of class MPI_ERR_BASE to indicate an invalid base argument.

Rationale. The C and C++ bindings of MPI_ALLOC_MEM and MPI_FREE_MEM are similar to the bindings for the `malloc` and `free` C library calls: a call to MPI_Alloc_mem(..., &base) should be paired with a call to MPI_Free_mem(base) (one less level of indirection). Both arguments are declared to be of same type void* so as to facilitate type casting. The Fortran binding is consistent with the C and C++ bindings: the Fortran MPI_ALLOC_MEM call returns in baseptr the (integer valued) address of the allocated memory. The base argument of MPI_FREE_MEM is a choice argument, which passes (a reference to) the variable stored at that location. ⬜

Advice to implementors. If MPI_ALLOC_MEM allocates special memory, then a design similar to the design of C `malloc` and `free` functions must be used, in order to find out the size of a memory segment, when the segment is freed. If no special memory is used, MPI_ALLOC_MEM simply invokes `malloc`, and MPI_FREE_MEM invokes `free`.

A call to MPI_ALLOC_MEM can be used in shared memory systems to allocate memory in a shared memory segment. ⬜

Example 2.9   Example of use of MPI_ALLOC_MEM, in Fortran with pointer support. We assume 4-byte REALs, and assume that pointers are address-sized.

```
REAL A
POINTER (P, A(100,100))   ! no memory is allocated
CALL MPI_ALLOC_MEM(4*100*100, MPI_INFO_NULL, P, IERR)
! memory is allocated
...
A(3,5) = 2.71;
...
CALL MPI_FREE_MEM(A, IERR) ! memory is freed
```

Since standard Fortran does not support (C-like) pointers, this code is not Fortran 77 or Fortran 90 code. Some compilers (in particular, at the time of writing, g77 and Fortran compilers for Windows) do not support this code. Even if a Fortran compiler does not support C-like pointers, it is usually possible to allocate memory in C and pass the address of the allocated memory to a Fortran routine.

Example 2.10   Same example, in C:

```
float  (* f)[100][100] ;
MPI_Alloc_mem(sizeof(float)*100*100, MPI_INFO_NULL, &f);
...
```

```
(*f)[5][3] = 2.71;
...
MPI_Free_mem(f);
```

3 Process Creation and Management

In this chapter we present MPI's functions for creating new MPI processes from within an MPI program. We also describe the MPI mechanisms that allow two independently started MPI programs to establish contact and begin to communicate with one another.

3.1 Introduction

MPI-1 provides an interface that allows processes in a parallel program to communicate with one another. MPI-1 specifies neither how the processes are created nor how they establish communication. Moreover, an MPI-1 application is static; no processes can be added to or deleted from an application after it has been started.

MPI users asked that the MPI-1 model be extended to allow process creation and management after an MPI application has been started. A major impetus came from the PVM [8] research effort, which provided a wealth of experience that illustrates the benefits and potential pitfalls of resource control and process management. An early discussion on one possible approach to dynamic processes in MPI is provided in [9].

The MPI Forum decided not to address resource control in MPI-2 because the members were not able to design a portable interface that would be appropriate for the broad spectrum of existing and potential resource and process controllers. Resource control can encompass a wide range of abilities, including adding and deleting nodes from a virtual parallel machine, reserving and scheduling resources, managing compute partitions of an MPP, and returning information about available resources. MPI-2 assumes that resource control is provided externally—probably by computer vendors in the case of tightly coupled systems, or by a third party software package when the environment is a cluster of workstations.

The reasons for adding process management to MPI are both technical and practical. Technically, important classes of message-passing applications require process control. These include task farms, serial applications with parallel modules, and problems that require a runtime assessment of the number and type of processes that should be started. On the practical side, users of workstation clusters who are migrating from PVM to MPI may be accustomed to using PVM's capabilities for process and resource management. The lack of these features is a practical stumbling block to migration.

While process management is essential, all agreed that adding it to MPI should not compromise the portability or performance of MPI applications. In particular, the Forum identified the following requirements:

- The MPI-2 process model must apply to the vast majority of current parallel environments. These include everything from tightly integrated MPPs to heterogeneous networks of workstations.
- MPI must not take over operating system responsibilities. It should instead provide a clean interface between an application and system software.
- MPI must continue to guarantee communication determinism, that is, process management must not introduce unavoidable race conditions.
- MPI-1 programs must work under MPI-2. That is, the MPI-1 static process model must be a special case of the MPI-2 dynamic model.

The MPI-2 process management model addresses these issues in two ways. First, MPI remains primarily a communication library. It does not manage the parallel environment in which a parallel program executes, although it provides a minimal interface between an application and external resource and process managers.

Second, MPI-2 does not change the concept of communicator. Once a communicator is built, it behaves as specified in MPI-1. A communicator is never changed after being created, and it is always created by using deterministic collective operations.

3.2   The MPI-2 Process Model

The MPI-2 process model allows for the creation and cooperative termination of processes after an MPI application has started. It provides a mechanism to establish communication between the newly created processes and the existing MPI application. It also provides a mechanism to establish communication between two existing MPI applications, even when one did not "start" the other.

3.2.1   Starting Processes

MPI applications may start new processes through an interface to an external process manager, which can range from a parallel operating system (CMOST) to layered software (POE) to an rsh command (p4).

MPI_COMM_SPAWN starts MPI processes and establishes communication with them, returning an intercommunicator. MPI_COMM_SPAWN_MULTIPLE starts several different binaries (or the same binary with different arguments), placing them in the same MPI_COMM_WORLD and returning an intercommunicator.

MPI uses the existing group abstraction to represent processes. A process is identified by a (group, rank) pair.

3.2.2   The Runtime Environment

The MPI_COMM_SPAWN and MPI_COMM_SPAWN_MULTIPLE routines provide an interface between MPI and the *runtime environment* of an MPI application. The difficulty is that there is an enormous range of runtime environments and application requirements, and MPI must not be tailored to any particular one. The following are examples of such environments:

- **MPP managed by a batch queuing system**. Batch queuing systems generally allocate resources before an application begins, enforce limits on resource use (CPU time, memory use, etc.), and do not allow a change in resource allocation after a job begins. Moreover, many MPPs have special limitations or extensions, such as a limit on the number of processes that may run on one processor, or the ability to gang-schedule processes of a parallel application.
- **Network of workstations with PVM**. PVM allows a user to create a virtual machine out of a network of workstations. An application may extend the virtual machine or manage processes (create, kill, redirect output, etc.) through the PVM library. Requests to manage the machine or processes may be intercepted and handled by an external resource manager.
- **Network of workstations managed by a load balancing system**. A load balancing system may choose the location of spawned processes based on dynamic quantities, such as load average. The system may transparently migrate processes from one machine to another when a resource becomes unavailable.
- **Large Symmetric Multiprocessor (SMP) with Unix**. On SMPs, applications are run directly by the user. They are scheduled at a low level by the operating system. Processes may have special scheduling characteristics (gang-scheduling, processor affinity, deadline scheduling, processor locking, etc.) and be subject to operating system resource limits (number of processes, amount of memory, etc.).

MPI assumes the existence of a parallel environment in which an application runs. It does not provide operating system services, such as a general ability to query what processes are running, to kill arbitrary processes, or to find out properties of the runtime environment (how many processors, how much memory, etc.).

Complex interaction of an MPI application with its runtime environment should be done through an environment-specific application programming interface (API). An example of such an API would be the PVM task and machine management routines, pvm_addhosts, pvm_config, pvm_tasks, etc., perhaps modified to return an MPI (group,rank) pair when possible. A Condor or PBS API would be another example.

At some low level, obviously, MPI must be able to interact with the runtime system, but the interaction is not visible at the application level, and the details of the interaction are not specified by the MPI standard.

In many cases, environment-specific information cannot be kept out of the MPI interface without seriously compromising MPI functionality. Hence, many MPI routines take an info argument that allows an application to specify environment-specific information. There is a tradeoff between functionality and portability, however: applications that make use of info are not portable.

MPI does not require an underlying virtual machine model, in which there is a consistent global view of an MPI application and an implicit operating system for managing resources and processes. For instance, processes spawned by one task may not be visible to another; additional hosts added to the runtime environment by one process may not be visible in another process; tasks spawned by different processes may not be automatically distributed over available resources.

Interaction between MPI and the runtime environment is limited to the following areas:

• A process may start new processes with MPI_COMM_SPAWN and MPI_COMM_-SPAWN_MULTIPLE.

• When a process spawns a child process, it may optionally use an info argument to tell the runtime environment where or how to start the process. This extra information may be opaque to MPI.

• An attribute MPI_UNIVERSE_SIZE on MPI_COMM_WORLD tells a program how "large" the initial runtime environment is, namely how many processes can usefully be started in all. One can subtract the size of MPI_COMM_WORLD from this value to find out how many processes may usefully be started in addition to those already running.

3.3   Process Manager Interface

In this section we describe the MPI functions by which an MPI program requests that new MPI processes be started. The original processes may or may not subsequently communicate with the new processes.

3.3.1   Processes in MPI

A process is represented in MPI by a (group, rank) pair. A (group, rank) pair specifies a unique process, but a process does not determine a unique (group, rank) pair, since a process may belong to several groups.

3.3.2   Starting Processes and Establishing Communication

The following routine starts a number of MPI processes and establishes communication with them, returning an intercommunicator.

Advice to users.   It is possible in MPI to start a static SPMD or MPMD application by starting one process and having that process start its siblings with MPI_COMM_SPAWN. This practice is discouraged, however, primarily for reasons of performance. If possible, one should start all processes at once, as a single MPI application. 🞎

MPI_COMM_SPAWN(command, argv, maxprocs, info, root, comm, intercomm,
   array_of_errcodes)

IN	command	name of program to be spawned (string, significant only at root)
IN	argv	arguments to command (array of strings, significant only at root)
IN	maxprocs	maximum number of processes to start (integer, significant only at root)
IN	info	a set of key-value pairs telling the runtime system where and how to start the processes (handle, significant only at root)
IN	root	rank of process in which previous arguments are examined (integer)
IN	comm	intracommunicator containing group of spawning processes (handle)
OUT	intercomm	intercommunicator between original group and the newly spawned group (handle)
OUT	array_of_errcodes	one code per process (array of integer)

```
int MPI_Comm_spawn(char *command, char **argv, int maxprocs, MPI_Info
    info, int root, MPI_Comm comm, MPI_Comm *intercomm,
    int *array_of_errcodes)
```

```
MPI_COMM_SPAWN(COMMAND, ARGV, MAXPROCS, INFO, ROOT, COMM, INTERCOMM,
    ARRAY_OF_ERRCODES, IERROR)
    CHARACTER*(*) COMMAND, ARGV(*)
    INTEGER INFO, MAXPROCS, ROOT, COMM, INTERCOMM,
    ARRAY_OF_ERRCODES(*), IERROR
```

```
MPI::Intercomm MPI::Intracomm::Spawn(const char* command,
    const char* argv[], int maxprocs, const MPI::Info& info,
    int root, int array_of_errcodes[]) const
```

```
MPI::Intercomm MPI::Intracomm::Spawn(const char* command,
    const char* argv[], int maxprocs, const MPI::Info& info,
    int root) const
```

MPI_COMM_SPAWN tries to start maxprocs identical copies of the MPI program specified by command, establishing communication with them and returning an intercommunicator. The spawned processes are referred to as *children*, and the processes that spawned them are called the *parents*. The children have their own MPI_COMM_WORLD, which is separate from that of the parents. The routine MPI_COMM_SPAWN is collective over comm and may not return until MPI_INIT has been called in the children. Similarly, MPI_INIT in the children may not return until all parents have called MPI_COMM_SPAWN. In this sense, MPI_COMM_SPAWN in the parents and MPI_INIT in the children form a collective operation over the union of parent and child processes. The intercommunicator returned by MPI_COMM_SPAWN contains the parent processes in the local group and the child processes in the remote group. The ordering of processes in the local and remote groups is the same as the ordering of the group of the comm in the parents and of MPI_COMM_WORLD of the children, respectively. This intercommunicator can be obtained in the children through the function MPI_COMM_GET_PARENT.

Advice to users. An implementation may automatically establish communication before MPI_INIT is called by the children. Thus, completion of MPI_COMM_SPAWN in the parent does not necessarily mean that MPI_INIT has been called in the children (although the returned intercommunicator can be used immediately). ▯

The command **argument.** The command argument is a string containing the name of a program to be spawned. In C, the string is null-terminated. In Fortran, leading and trailing spaces are stripped. MPI does not specify how to find the executable or how to determine the working directory. These rules are implementation-dependent and should be appropriate for the runtime environment. Some of this information can be communicated via the info argument (See Section 3.3.4).

Advice to implementors.   The implementation should use a natural rule for finding executables and determining working directories. For instance, a homogeneous system with a global file system might look first in the working directory of the spawning process or might search the directories in a PATH environment variable, as do Unix shells. An implementation on top of PVM would use PVM's rules for finding executables (usually in `$HOME/pvm3/bin/$`). An MPI implementation running under POE on an IBM SP would use POE's method of finding executables. An implementation should document its rules for finding executables and determining working directories, and a high-quality implementation should give the user some control over these rules. □

If the program named in command does not call MPI_INIT, but instead forks a process that calls MPI_INIT, the results are undefined. Implementations may allow this practice but are not required to.

Advice to users.   MPI does not specify what happens if the program to be started is a shell script and that shell script starts a program that calls MPI_INIT. Although some implementations may allow this practice, they may also have restrictions, such as requiring that arguments supplied to the shell script be supplied to the program, or requiring that certain parts of the environment not be changed. □

The argv **argument.** The argv argument is an array of strings containing arguments that are passed to the program. The first element of argv is the first argument passed to command, not (as is conventional in some contexts) the command itself. The argument list is terminated by NULL in C and C++ and an empty string in Fortran. In Fortran, leading and trailing spaces are always stripped, so that a string consisting of all spaces is considered an empty string. The constant MPI_ARGV_-NULL (MPI::ARGV_NULL in C++) may be used in any language to indicate an empty argument list. In C and C++, this constant is the same as NULL.

Example 3.1   Examples of argv in C and Fortran.
To run the program "ocean" with arguments "-gridfile" and "ocean1.grd" in C:

```
char command[] = "ocean";
char *argv[]   = {"-gridfile", "ocean1.grd", NULL};
MPI_Comm_spawn(command, argv, ...);
```

If not everything is known at compile time:

```
char *command;
char **argv;
command = "ocean";
argv    = (char **)malloc(3 * sizeof(char *));
argv[0] = "-gridfile";
argv[1] = "ocean1.grd";
argv[2] = NULL;
MPI_Comm_spawn(command, argv, ...);
```

In Fortran:

```
CHARACTER*25 command, argv(3)
command = ' ocean '
argv(1) = ' -gridfile '
argv(2) = ' ocean1.grd'
argv(3) = ' '
call MPI_COMM_SPAWN(command, argv, ...)
```

Arguments are supplied to the program if this procedure is allowed by the operating system. In C, the MPI_COMM_SPAWN argument argv differs from the argv argument of main in two respects. First, it is shifted by one element. Specifically, argv[0] of main is provided by the implementation and conventionally contains the name of the program (given by command). The second argument, argv[1], of main corresponds to argv[0] in MPI_COMM_SPAWN, argv[2] of main corresponds to argv[1] of MPI_COMM_SPAWN, and so on. Second, argv of MPI_COMM_SPAWN must be null-terminated, so that its length can be determined. Passing an argv of MPI_ARGV_NULL to MPI_COMM_SPAWN results in main receiving argc of 1 and an argv whose element 0 is (conventionally) the name of the program.

If a Fortran implementation supplies routines that allow a program to obtain its arguments, the arguments may be available through that mechanism. In C, if the operating system does not support arguments appearing in argv of main(), the MPI implementation may add the arguments to the argv that is passed to MPI_INIT.

The maxprocs **argument.** MPI tries to spawn maxprocs processes. If it is unable to do so, it raises an error of class MPI_ERR_SPAWN.

An implementation may allow the info argument to change the default behavior such that, if the implementation is unable to spawn all maxprocs processes, it may spawn a smaller number of processes instead of raising an error. In principle, the info argument may specify an arbitrary set $\{m_i : 0 \leq m_i \leq \text{maxprocs}\}$ of allowed values for the number of processes spawned. The set $\{m_i\}$ does not necessarily include the value maxprocs. If an implementation is able to spawn one of these allowed numbers of processes, MPI_COMM_SPAWN returns successfully and the number of spawned processes, m, is given by the size of the remote group of intercomm. If m is less than maxprocs, reasons why the other processes were not spawned are given in array_of_errcodes as described below. If it is not possible to spawn one of the allowed numbers of processes, MPI_COMM_SPAWN raises an error of class MPI_ERR_SPAWN.

A spawn call with the default behavior is called *hard*. A spawn call for which fewer than maxprocs processes may be returned is called *soft*. See Section 3.3.4 for more information on the soft key for info.

Advice to users. By default, requests are hard and MPI errors are fatal. Hence, by default, there will be a fatal error if MPI cannot spawn all the requested processes. To obtain the behavior "spawn as many processes as possible, up to N," the user should do a soft spawn, where the set of allowed values $\{m_i\}$ is $\{0 \ldots N\}$. However, this strategy is not completely portable, since implementations are not required to support soft spawning. □

The info **argument.** The info argument to all of the routines in this chapter is an opaque handle of type MPI_Info in C, MPI::Info in C++, and INTEGER in Fortran. It is a container for a number of user-specified (key,value) pairs, where key and value are strings (null-terminated char* in C, character*(*) in Fortran). Routines that create and manipulate the info argument are described in Section 2.3.

For the SPAWN calls, info provides additional (and possibly implementation-dependent) instructions to MPI and the runtime system on how to start processes. An application may pass MPI_INFO_NULL in C or Fortran, or MPI::INFO_NULL in C++. Portable programs not requiring detailed control over process locations should use MPI_INFO_NULL.

MPI does not specify the content of the info argument, except to reserve a number of special key values (see Section 3.3.4). The info argument is quite flexible and can even be used, for example, to specify the executable and its command-line arguments. In this case the command argument to MPI_COMM_SPAWN can be empty. This capability follows from the fact that MPI does not specify how an executable is found, and the info argument can tell the runtime system where to "find" the executable "" (empty string). Of course, such a program will not be portable across MPI implementations.

The root argument. All arguments before the root argument are examined only on the process whose rank in comm is equal to root. The value of these arguments on other processes is ignored.

The array_of_errcodes argument. The array_of_errcodes is an array of length max-procs in which MPI reports the status of each process that MPI was requested to start. If all maxprocs processes were spawned, array_of_errcodes is filled in with the value MPI_SUCCESS. If only m $(0 \leq m <$ maxprocs) processes are spawned, m of the entries will contain MPI_SUCCESS and the rest will contain an implementation-specific error code indicating the reason MPI could not start the process. MPI does not specify which entries correspond to failed processes. An implementation may, for instance, fill in error codes in one-to-one correspondence with a detailed specification in the info argument. These error codes all belong to the error class MPI_ERR_SPAWN if there was no error in the argument list. In C or Fortran, an application may pass MPI_ERRCODES_IGNORE if it is not interested in the error codes. In C++ this constant does not exist, and the array_of_errcodes argument may be omitted from the argument list.

Advice to implementors. MPI_ERRCODES_IGNORE in Fortran is a special type of constant, like MPI_BOTTOM. See the discussion in Section 1.5.4. □

MPI_COMM_GET_PARENT(parent)

    OUT   parent   the parent communicator (handle)

```
int MPI_Comm_get_parent(MPI_Comm *parent)
```

```
MPI_COMM_GET_PARENT(PARENT, IERROR)
    INTEGER PARENT, IERROR
```

```
static MPI::Intercomm MPI::Comm::Get_parent()
```

If a process was started with MPI_COMM_SPAWN or MPI_COMM_SPAWN_-MULTIPLE, MPI_COMM_GET_PARENT returns the "parent" intercommunicator of the current process. This parent intercommunicator is created implicitly inside of MPI_INIT and is the same intercommunicator returned by SPAWN in the parents.

If the process was not started by MPI_COMM_SPAWN, MPI_COMM_GET_-PARENT returns MPI_COMM_NULL.

After the parent communicator is freed or disconnected, the function MPI_-COMM_GET_PARENT returns MPI_COMM_NULL.

Advice to users.   MPI_COMM_GET_PARENT returns a handle to a single intercommunicator. Calling MPI_COMM_GET_PARENT a second time returns a handle to the same intercommunicator. Freeing the handle with MPI_COMM_-DISCONNECT or MPI_COMM_FREE will cause other references to the intercommunicator to become invalid. Note that calling MPI_COMM_FREE on the parent communicator is not useful. ☐

Rationale.   The Forum wished to create a constant MPI_COMM_PARENT similar to MPI_COMM_WORLD. Unfortunately, such a constant cannot be used (syntactically) as an argument to MPI_COMM_DISCONNECT, which is explicitly allowed. ☐

3.3.3   Starting Multiple Executables and Establishing Communication

While MPI_COMM_SPAWN is sufficient for most cases, it does not allow the spawning of multiple binaries or of the same binary with multiple sets of arguments. The following routine spawns multiple binaries or the same binary with multiple sets of arguments, establishing communication with them and placing them in the same MPI_COMM_WORLD.

MPI_COMM_SPAWN_MULTIPLE(count, array_of_commands,
    array_of_argv, array_of_maxprocs, array_of_info, root, comm, intercomm,
    array_of_errcodes)

IN	count	number of commands (positive integer, significant to MPI only at root—see advice to users)
IN	array_of_commands	programs to be executed (array of strings, significant only at root)
IN	array_of_argv	arguments for **commands** (array of array of strings, significant only at root)
IN	array_of_maxprocs	maximum number of processes to start for each command (array of integer, significant only at root)
IN	array_of_info	info objects telling the runtime system where and how to start processes (array of handles, significant only at root)

IN	root	rank of process in which previous arguments are examined (integer)
IN	comm	intracommunicator containing group of spawning processes (handle)
OUT	intercomm	intercommunicator between original group and newly spawned group (handle)
OUT	array_of_errcodes	one error code per process (array of integer)

```
int MPI_Comm_spawn_multiple(int count, char **array_of_commands,
    char ***array_of_argv, int *array_of_maxprocs,
    MPI_Info *array_of_info, int root, MPI_Comm comm,
    MPI_Comm *intercomm, int *array_of_errcodes)
```

```
MPI_COMM_SPAWN_MULTIPLE(COUNT, ARRAY_OF_COMMANDS, ARRAY_OF_ARGV,
    ARRAY_OF_MAXPROCS, ARRAY_OF_INFO, ROOT, COMM, INTERCOMM,
    ARRAY_OF_ERRCODES, IERROR)
    INTEGER COUNT, ARRAY_OF_INFO(*), ARRAY_OF_MAXPROCS(*), ROOT,
    COMM, INTERCOMM, ARRAY_OF_ERRCODES(*), IERROR
    CHARACTER*(*) ARRAY_OF_COMMANDS(*), ARRAY_OF_ARGV(COUNT, *)
```

```
MPI::Intercomm MPI::Intracomm::Spawn_multiple(int count,
    const char* array_of_commands[], const char** array_of_argv[],
    const int array_of_maxprocs[], const MPI::Info array_of_info[],
    int root, int array_of_errcodes[])
```

```
MPI::Intercomm MPI::Intracomm::Spawn_multiple(int count,
    const char* array_of_commands[], const char** array_of_argv[],
    const int array_of_maxprocs[], const MPI::Info array_of_info[],
    int root)
```

MPI_COMM_SPAWN_MULTIPLE is identical to MPI_COMM_SPAWN except that there are multiple executable specifications. The first argument, count, gives the number of specifications. The next four arguments are simply arrays of the corresponding arguments in MPI_COMM_SPAWN. For the Fortran version of array_of_argv, the element array_of_argv(i,j) is the jth argument to the ith command.

Rationale. This approach may seem backwards to Fortran programmers who are familiar with Fortran's column-major ordering. However, it is necessary in order to allow MPI_COMM_SPAWN to sort out arguments. Note that the leading dimension of array_of_argv *must* be the same as count. □

Advice to users. The argument count is interpreted by MPI only at the root, as is array_of_argv. Since the leading dimension of array_of_argv is count, a nonpositive value of count at a nonroot node could theoretically cause a runtime bounds check error, even though array_of_argv should be ignored by the subroutine. If such an error happens, the user should explicitly supply a reasonable value of count on the nonroot nodes. ☐

In any language, an application may use the constant MPI_ARGVS_NULL (MPI::-ARGVS_NULL in C++) to specify that no arguments should be passed to any commands. This constant is likely to be (char ***)0 in C. The effect of setting individual elements of array_of_argv to MPI_ARGV_NULL is not defined. To specify arguments for some commands but not others, the commands without arguments should have a corresponding argv whose first element is null ((char *)0 in C and empty string in Fortran).

All of the spawned processes have the same MPI_COMM_WORLD. Their ranks in MPI_COMM_WORLD correspond directly to the order in which the commands are specified in MPI_COMM_SPAWN_MULTIPLE. Assume that m_1 processes are generated by the first command, m_2 by the second, etc. The processes corresponding to the first command have ranks $0, 1, \ldots, m_1 - 1$. The processes in the second command have ranks $m_1, m_1 + 1, \ldots, m_1 + m_2 - 1$. The processes in the third have ranks $m_1 + m_2, m_1 + m_2 + 1, \ldots, m_1 + m_2 + m_3 - 1$, etc.

Advice to users. Calling MPI_COMM_SPAWN multiple times would create many sets of children with different MPI_COMM_WORLDs, whereas MPI_-COMM_SPAWN_MULTIPLE creates children with a single MPI_COMM_WORLD. Hence the two methods are not completely equivalent. For performance reasons, the user should call MPI_COMM_SPAWN_MULTIPLE instead of calling MPI_COMM_SPAWN several times. Spawning several things at once may be faster than spawning them sequentially. Moreover, in some implementations, communication between processes spawned at the same time may be faster than communication between processes spawned separately. ☐

The array_of_errcodes argument is a one-dimensional array of size $\sum_{i=1}^{count} n_i$, where n_i is the ith element of array_of_maxprocs. Command number i corresponds to the n_i contiguous slots in this array from element $\sum_{j=1}^{i-1} n_j$ to $\left[\sum_{j=1}^{i} n_j\right] - 1$. Error codes are treated as for MPI_COMM_SPAWN.

Example 3.2   Examples of array_of_argv in C and Fortran
To run the program "ocean" with arguments "-gridfile" and "ocean1.grd" and the
program "atmos" with argument "atmos.grd" in C:

```
char *array_of_commands[2] = {"ocean", "atmos"};
char **array_of_argv[2];
char *argv0[] = {"-gridfile", "ocean1.grd", (char *)0};
char *argv1[] = {"atmos.grd", (char *)0};
array_of_argv[0] = argv0;
array_of_argv[1] = argv1;
MPI_Comm_spawn_multiple(2, array_of_commands, array_of_argv,
                        ...);
```

In Fortran:

```
CHARACTER*25 commands(2), array_of_argv(2, 3)
commands(1) = ' ocean '
array_of_argv(1, 1) = ' -gridfile '
array_of_argv(1, 2) = ' ocean1.grd'
array_of_argv(1, 3) = ' '

commands(2) = ' atmos '
array_of_argv(2, 1) = ' atmos.grd '
array_of_argv(2, 2) = ' '

call MPI_COMM_SPAWN_MULTIPLE(2, commands, array_of_argv, ...)
```

3.3.4   Reserved info Keys

The MPI Forum decided, after some effort, not to try to define a universal process
manager interface, because of the great variety of process managers. Instead, the
info argument to MPI_SPAWN is used to communicate information to the process
manager, thus allowing nonstandard (and hence nonportable) parameters. Nevertheless, to encourage as much portability as possible, the following small set of info
keys is reserved. An implementation is not required to interpret these keys; but if
it does, it must provide the functionality described.

host: Value is a hostname. The format of the hostname is determined by the implementation.

arch: Value is an architecture name. Valid architecture names and their meanings
are determined by the implementation.

wdir: Value is the name of a directory on a machine on which the spawned process(es) execute(s). This directory is made the working directory of the executing process(es). The format of the directory name is determined by the implementation.

path: Value is a directory or set of directories where the implementation should look for the executable. The format of path is determined by the implementation.

file: Value is the name of a file in which additional information is specified. The format of the filename and internal format of the file are determined by the implementation.

soft: Value specifies a set of numbers which are allowed values for the number of processes that MPI_COMM_SPAWN and other such routines may create. The format of the value is a comma-separated list of Fortran-90 triplets each of which specifies a set of integers and which together specify the set formed by the union of these sets. Negative values in this set and values greater than maxprocs are ignored. MPI will spawn the largest number of processes it can, consistent with some number in the set. The order in which triplets are given is not significant.

By Fortran-90 triplets, we mean the following:

1. a means a.

2. a:b means $a, a + 1, a + 2, \ldots, b$.

3. a:b:c means $a, a + c, a + 2c, \ldots, a + ck$, where for $c > 0$, k is the largest integer for which $a + ck \leq b$ and for $c < 0$, k is the largest integer for which $a + ck \geq b$. If $b > a$, then c must be positive. If $b < a$, then c must be negative.

Examples:

1. a:b gives a range between a and b.

2. 0:N gives full "soft" functionality.

3. 1,2,4,8,16,32,64,128,256,512,1024,2048,4096 allows a power of two number of processes.

4. 2:10000:2 allows an even number of processes.

5. 2:10:2,7 allows 2, 4, 6, 7, 8, or 10 processes.

3.3.5 Manager-Worker Example, Using MPI_SPAWN

```
/* manager */
#include "mpi.h"
int main(int argc, char **argv)
{
```

```
int world_size, universe_size, *universe_sizep, flag;
MPI_Comm everyone;              /* intercommunicator */
char worker_program[100];

MPI_Init(&argc, &argv);
MPI_Comm_size(MPI_COMM_WORLD, &world_size);

if (world_size != 1)
    error("Top heavy with management");

MPI_Comm_get_attr(MPI_COMM_WORLD, MPI_UNIVERSE_SIZE,
            &universe_sizep, &flag);
if (!flag) {
    printf("This MPI does not support UNIVERSE_SIZE.");
    printf("How many processes total? ");
    scanf("%d", &universe_size);
} else
    universe_size = *universe_sizep;
if (universe_size == 1)
    error("No room to start workers");

/*
 * Now spawn the workers. Note that there is a runtime
 * determination of what type of worker to spawn, and presumably
 * this calculation must be done at run time and cannot be
 * calculated before starting the program. If everything is
 * known when the application is first started, it is generally
 * better to start them all at once in a single MPI_COMM_WORLD.
 */

choose_worker_program(worker_program);
MPI_Comm_spawn(worker_program, MPI_ARGV_NULL, universe_size-1,
        MPI_INFO_NULL, 0, MPI_COMM_SELF, &everyone,
        MPI_ERRCODES_IGNORE);
/*
 * Parallel code here. The communicator "everyone" can be used
 * to communicate with the spawned processes, which have ranks
 * 0,...,MPI_UNIVERSE_SIZE-1 in the remote group of the
```

```
 * intercommunicator "everyone".  An MPI_Bcast using this
 * communicator will broadcast just to the workers.
 */

    MPI_Finalize();
    return 0;
}

/* worker */

#include "mpi.h"
int main(int argc, char **argv)
{
    int size;
    MPI_Comm parent;
    MPI_Init(&argc, &argv);
    MPI_Comm_get_parent(&parent);
    if (parent == MPI_COMM_NULL) error("No parent!");
    MPI_Comm_remote_size(parent, &size);
    if (size != 1) error("Something's wrong with the parent");

    /*
     * Parallel code here.
     * The manager is represented as the process with rank 0 in (the
     * remote group of) MPI_COMM_PARENT.  If the workers need to
     * communicate among themselves, they can use MPI_COMM_WORLD.
     */

    MPI_Finalize();
    return 0;
}
```

3.4   Establishing Communication

This section discusses functions that establish communication between two sets of
MPI processes that do not share a communicator.

Some situations in which these functions are useful are the following:

- Two parts of an application that are started independently need to communicate.
- A visualization tool wants to attach to a running process.
- A server wants to accept connections from multiple clients. Both clients and server may be parallel programs.

In each of these situations, MPI must establish communication channels where none existed before and where no parent/child relationship exists. The routines described in this section establish communication between the two sets of processes by creating an MPI intercommunicator, where the two groups of the intercommunicator are the original sets of processes.

Establishing contact between two groups of processes that do not share an existing communicator is a collective but asymmetric process. One group of processes indicates its willingness to accept connections from other groups of processes. We call this group the (parallel) *server*, even if this is not a client/server type of application. The other group connects to the server; we call it the *client*.

Advice to users. While the names *client* and *server* are used throughout this section, MPI does not guarantee the traditional robustness of client/server systems. The functionality described in this section is intended to allow two cooperating parts of the same application to communicate with one another. For instance, a client that gets a segmentation fault and dies or one that doesn't participate in a collective operation may cause a server to crash or hang. □

3.4.1   Names, Addresses, Ports, and All That

Almost all of the complexity in MPI client/server routines addresses the question How does the client find out how to contact the server? The difficulty, of course, is that no communication channel exists between them, yet they must somehow agree on a rendezvous point where they will establish communication—Catch 22.

Agreeing on a rendezvous point always involves a third party. The third party may itself provide the rendezvous point or may communicate rendezvous information from server to client. Complicating matters might be the fact that a client may not really care which server it contacts, only that it be able to get in touch with one that can handle its request.

Ideally, MPI can accommodate a wide variety of runtime systems while retaining the ability to write simple portable code. The following should be compatible with MPI:

- The server resides at a well-known Internet address host:port.
- The server prints out an address to the terminal, and the user gives this address to the client program.
- The server places the address information on a nameserver,
- The server to which the client connects is actually a broker, acting as a middleman between the client and the real server.

Since MPI does not require a nameserver, not all implementations will be able to support all of the above scenarios. However, MPI provides an optional nameserver interface and is compatible with external nameservers.

A port_name is a *system-supplied* string that encodes a low-level network address at which a server can be contacted. Typically this is an IP address and a port number, but an implementation is free to use any protocol. The server establishes a port_name with the MPI_OPEN_PORT routine. It accepts a connection to a given port with MPI_COMM_ACCEPT. A client uses port_name to connect to the server.

By itself, the port_name mechanism is completely portable, but it may be clumsy to use because of the necessity to communicate port_name to the client. It is more convenient if a server can specify that it is known by an *application-supplied* service_-name so that the client can connect to that service_name without knowing the port_-name.

An MPI implementation may allow the server to publish a (port_name, service_-name) pair with MPI_PUBLISH_NAME and may allow the client to retrieve the port name from the service name with MPI_LOOKUP_NAME. This approach allows three levels of portability, with increasing levels of functionality.

1. Applications that do not rely on the ability to publish names are the most portable. Typically, the port_name must be transferred "by hand" from server to client.

2. Applications that use the MPI_PUBLISH_NAME mechanism are completely portable among implementations that provide this service. To be portable among all implementations, these applications should have a fall-back mechanism that can be used when names are not published.

3. Applications may ignore MPI's name publishing functionality and use their own mechanism (possibly system supplied) to publish names. This approach allows arbitrary flexibility but is not portable.

3.4.2 Server Routines

A server makes itself available with two routines. First, it must call MPI_OPEN_-
PORT to establish a port at which it may be contacted. Second, it must call
MPI_COMM_ACCEPT to accept connections from clients.

MPI_OPEN_PORT(info, port_name)

IN	info	implementation-specific information on how to establish an address (handle)
OUT	port_name	newly established port (string)

```
int MPI_Open_port(MPI_Info info, char *port_name)
```

```
MPI_OPEN_PORT(INFO, PORT_NAME, IERROR)
    CHARACTER*(*) PORT_NAME
    INTEGER INFO, IERROR
```

```
void MPI::Open_port(const MPI::Info& info, char* port_name)
```

This function establishes a network address, encoded in the port_name string, at
which the server will be able to accept connections from clients. The port_name is
supplied by the system, possibly using information in the info argument.

MPI copies a system-supplied port name into port_name. The port_name argument
identifies the newly opened port and can be used by a client to contact the server.
The maximum size string that may be supplied by the system is MPI_MAX_PORT_-
NAME (MPI::MAX_PORT_NAME in C++).

Advice to users.   The system copies the port name into port_name. The application must pass a buffer of sufficient size to hold this value. □

The port name is essentially a network address. It is unique within the communication universe to which it belongs (determined by the implementation) and may
be used by any client within that communication universe. For instance, if it is an
Internet (host:port) address, it will be unique on the Internet. If it is a low-level
switch address on an IBM SP, it will be unique to that SP.

Advice to implementors.   These examples are not meant to constrain implementations. A port_name could, for instance, contain a user name or the name of a batch
job, as long as it is unique within some well-defined communication domain. The

larger the communication domain, the more useful MPI's client/server functionality will be. ☐

The precise form of the address is implementation defined. For instance, an Internet address may be a host name or IP address or anything that the implementation can decode into an IP address. A port name may be reused after it is freed with MPI_CLOSE_PORT and released by the system.

Advice to implementors. Since the user may type in port_name by hand, it is useful to choose a form that is easily readable and does not have embedded spaces. ☐

One can use info to tell the implementation how to establish the address. It may, and usually will, be MPI_INFO_NULL in order to get the implementation defaults. There are no reserved keys.

MPI_CLOSE_PORT(port_name)

IN	port_name	a port (string)

```
int MPI_Close_port(char *port_name)
```

```
MPI_CLOSE_PORT(PORT_NAME, IERROR)
    CHARACTER*(*) PORT_NAME
    INTEGER IERROR
```

```
void MPI::Close_port(const char* port_name)
```

This function releases the network address represented by port_name.

MPI_COMM_ACCEPT(port_name, info, root, comm, newcomm)

IN	port_name	port name (string, used only on root)
IN	info	implementation-dependent information (handle, used only on root)
IN	root	rank in comm of root node (integer)
IN	comm	intracommunicator over which call is collective (handle)
OUT	newcomm	intercommunicator with client as remote group (handle)

```
int MPI_Comm_accept(char *port_name, MPI_Info info, int root,
    MPI_Comm comm, MPI_Comm *newcomm)
```

```
MPI_COMM_ACCEPT(PORT_NAME, INFO, ROOT, COMM, NEWCOMM, IERROR)
    CHARACTER*(*) PORT_NAME
    INTEGER INFO, ROOT, COMM, NEWCOMM, IERROR
```

```
MPI::Intercomm MPI::Intracomm::Accept(const char* port_name,
    const MPI::Info& info, int root) const
```

MPI_COMM_ACCEPT establishes communication with a client. It is collective over the calling communicator. It returns an intercommunicator that allows communication with the client.

The port_name must have been established through a call to MPI_OPEN_PORT.

The argument info is an implementation-defined string that may allow fine control over the MPI_COMM_ACCEPT call.

Note that MPI_COMM_ACCEPT is a blocking call. A user may implement a nonblocking accept by issuing an MPI_COMM_ACCEPT in a separate thread.

3.4.3 Client Routines

The client side has only one routine.

MPI_COMM_CONNECT(port_name, info, root, comm, newcomm)

IN	port_name	network address (string, used only on root)
IN	info	implementation-dependent information (handle, used only on root)
IN	root	rank in comm of root node (integer)
IN	comm	intracommunicator over which call is collective (handle)
OUT	newcomm	intercommunicator with server as remote group (handle)

```
int MPI_Comm_connect(char *port_name, MPI_Info info, int root,
    MPI_Comm comm, MPI_Comm *newcomm)
```

```
MPI_COMM_CONNECT(PORT_NAME, INFO, ROOT, COMM, NEWCOMM, IERROR)
    CHARACTER*(*) PORT_NAME
    INTEGER INFO, ROOT, COMM, NEWCOMM, IERROR
```

```
MPI::Intercomm MPI::Intracomm::Connect(const char* port_name,
    const MPI::Info& info, int root) const
```

This routine establishes communication with a server specified by port_name. It is collective over the calling communicator and returns an intercommunicator in which the remote group participated in an MPI_COMM_ACCEPT.

If the named port does not exist (or has been closed), MPI_COMM_CONNECT raises an error of class MPI_ERR_PORT.

If the port exists but does not have a pending MPI_COMM_ACCEPT, the connection attempt will eventually time out after an implementation-defined time or succeed when the server calls MPI_COMM_ACCEPT. In the case of a time out, MPI_COMM_CONNECT raises an error of class MPI_ERR_PORT.

Advice to implementors.   The time out period may be arbitrarily short or long. However, a high-quality implementation will try to queue connection attempts so that a server can handle simultaneous requests from several clients. A high-quality implementation may also provide a mechanism, through the info arguments to MPI_-OPEN_PORT, MPI_COMM_ACCEPT and/or MPI_COMM_CONNECT, for the user to control timeout and queuing behavior. □

MPI provides no guarantee of fairness in servicing connection attempts. That is, connection attempts are not necessarily satisfied in the order they were initiated, and competition from other connection attempts may prevent a particular connection attempt from being satisfied.

The port_name argument is the address of the server. It must be the same as the name returned by MPI_OPEN_PORT on the server. Some freedom is allowed here: an implementation may accept equivalent forms of port_name. For instance, if port_name is (hostname:port), an implementation may accept (*ip_address*:port) as well.

3.4.4 Name Publishing

The routines in this section provide a mechanism for publishing names. A pair, (service_name, port_name), is published by the server and may be retrieved by a client using the service_name only. An MPI implementation defines the *scope* of the service_name, that is, the domain over which the service_name can be retrieved. If the domain is the empty set (i.e., if no client can retrieve the information), we say that name publishing is not supported. Implementations should document how the scope is determined. High-quality implementations will give some control to users through the info arguments to name-publishing functions. Examples are given in the descriptions of individual functions.

MPI_PUBLISH_NAME(service_name, info, port_name)

IN	service_name	a service name to associate with the port (string)
IN	info	implementation-specific information (handle)
IN	port_name	a port name (string)

```
int MPI_Publish_name(char *service_name, MPI_Info info,
    char *port_name)
```

```
MPI_PUBLISH_NAME(SERVICE_NAME, INFO, PORT_NAME, IERROR)
    INTEGER INFO, IERROR
    CHARACTER*(*) SERVICE_NAME, PORT_NAME
```

```
void MPI::Publish_name(const char* service_name,
    const MPI::Info& info, const char* port_name)
```

This routine publishes the pair (port_name, service_name) so that an application may retrieve a system-supplied port_name using a well-known service_name.

The implementation must define the scope of a published service name, that is, the domain over which the service name is unique and, conversely, the domain over which the (port name, service name) pair may be retrieved. For instance, a service name may be unique to a job (where job is defined by a distributed operating system or batch scheduler), unique to a machine, or unique to a Kerberos realm. The scope may depend on the info argument to MPI_PUBLISH_NAME.

MPI permits publishing more than one service_name for a single port_name. On the other hand, if service_name has already been published within the scope determined by info, the behavior of MPI_PUBLISH_NAME is undefined. An MPI implementation may, through a mechanism in the info argument to MPI_PUBLISH_NAME, provide a way to allow multiple servers with the same service in the same scope. In this case, an implementation-defined policy will determine which of several port names is returned by MPI_LOOKUP_NAME.

Note that while service_name has a limited scope, determined by the implementation, port_name always has global scope within the communication universe used by the implementation (i.e., it is globally unique).

The port_name argument should be the name of a port established by MPI_OPEN_PORT and not yet deleted by MPI_CLOSE_PORT. If it is not, the result is undefined.

Advice to implementors.   In some cases, an MPI implementation may use a name service that a user can also access directly. In this case, a name published by MPI could easily conflict with a name published by a user. In order to avoid such conflicts, MPI implementations should mangle service names so that they are unlikely to conflict with user code that makes use of the same service. Such name mangling will, of course, be completely transparent to the user.

The following situation is problematic but unavoidable if we wish to allow implementations to use nameservers. Suppose multiple instances of "ocean" are running on a machine. If the scope of a service name is confined to a job, multiple oceans can coexist. If an implementation provides site-wide scope, however, multiple instances are not possible, because all calls to MPI_PUBLISH_NAME after the first may fail. There is no universal solution to this problem. To handle these situations, a high-quality implementation should make it possible to limit the domain over which names are published. ☐

MPI_UNPUBLISH_NAME(service_name, info, port_name)

IN	service_name	a service name (string)
IN	info	implementation-specific information (handle)
IN	port_name	a port name (string)

```
int MPI_Unpublish_name(char *service_name, MPI_Info info,
    char *port_name)
```

```
MPI_UNPUBLISH_NAME(SERVICE_NAME, INFO, PORT_NAME, IERROR)
    INTEGER INFO, IERROR
    CHARACTER*(*) SERVICE_NAME, PORT_NAME
```

```
void MPI::Unpublish_name(const char* service_name,
    const MPI::Info& info, const char* port_name)
```

This routine unpublishes a service name that has been previously published. Attempting to unpublish a name that has not been published or has already been unpublished raises an error of class MPI_ERR_SERVICE.

All published names must be unpublished before the corresponding port is closed and before the publishing process exits. The behavior of MPI_UNPUBLISH_NAME is implementation-dependent when a process tries to unpublish a name that it did not publish.

If the info argument was used with MPI_PUBLISH_NAME to tell the implementation how to publish names, the implementation may require that info passed to MPI_UNPUBLISH_NAME contain information to tell the implementation how to unpublish a name.

MPI_LOOKUP_NAME(service_name, info, port_name)

IN	service_name	a service name (string)
IN	info	implementation-specific information (handle)
OUT	port_name	a port name (string)

```
int MPI_Lookup_name(char *service_name, MPI_Info info,
    char *port_name)
```

```
MPI_LOOKUP_NAME(SERVICE_NAME, INFO, PORT_NAME, IERROR)
    CHARACTER*(*) SERVICE_NAME, PORT_NAME
    INTEGER INFO, IERROR
```

```
void MPI::Lookup_name(const char* service_name,
    const MPI::Info& info, char* port_name)
```

This function retrieves a port_name published by MPI_PUBLISH_NAME with service_name. If service_name has not been published, it raises an error of class MPI_ERR_NAME. The application must supply a port_name buffer large enough to hold the largest possible port name (see the preceding discussion under MPI_OPEN_PORT).

If an implementation allows multiple entries with the same service_name within the same scope, a particular port_name is chosen in a way determined by the implementation.

If the info argument was used with MPI_PUBLISH_NAME to tell the implementation how to publish names, a similar info argument may be required for MPI_LOOKUP_NAME.

3.4.5   Reserved Key Values

The following key values are reserved. An implementation is not required to interpret these key values; but if it does, it must provide the functionality described.

ip_port: Value contains IP port number at which to establish a port. (Reserved for MPI_OPEN_PORT only.)

ip_address: Value contains IP address at which to establish a port. If the address is not a valid IP address of the host on which the MPI_OPEN_PORT call is made, the results are undefined. (Reserved for MPI_OPEN_PORT only.)

3.4.6 Client/Server Examples

Example 3.3   The following example shows the simplest way to use the client/server interface. It does not use service names at all.

On the server side:

```
char myport[MPI_MAX_PORT_NAME];
MPI_Comm intercomm;
/* ... */
MPI_Open_port(MPI_INFO_NULL, myport);
printf("port name is: %s\n", myport);

MPI_Comm_accept(myport, MPI_INFO_NULL, 0, MPI_COMM_SELF,
                &intercomm);
/* do something with intercomm */
```

The server prints out the port name to the terminal, and the user must type it in when starting up the client (assuming the MPI implementation supports stdin such that this works).

On the client side:

```
MPI_Comm intercomm;
char name[MPI_MAX_PORT_NAME];
printf("enter port name: ");
gets(name);
MPI_Comm_connect(name, MPI_INFO_NULL, 0, MPI_COMM_SELF,
                 &intercomm);
```

Example 3.4   In this example, the "ocean" application is the "server" side of a coupled ocean-atmosphere climate model. It assumes that the MPI implementation publishes names.

```
MPI_Open_port(MPI_INFO_NULL, port_name);
MPI_Publish_name("ocean", MPI_INFO_NULL, port_name);

MPI_Comm_accept(port_name, MPI_INFO_NULL, 0, MPI_COMM_SELF,
```

```
                            &intercomm);
        /* do something with intercomm */
        MPI_Unpublish_name("ocean", MPI_INFO_NULL, port_name);
```

On the client side:

```
        MPI_Lookup_name("ocean", MPI_INFO_NULL, port_name);
        MPI_Comm_connect( port_name, MPI_INFO_NULL, 0, MPI_COMM_SELF,
                          &intercomm);
```

Example 3.5   This is a simple client-server example. The server accepts only a single connection at a time and serves that connection until it receives a message with tag 1, that is, until the client requests to be disconnected. A message with tag 0 tells the server to exit. The server is a single process.

```
#include "mpi.h"
int main( int argc, char **argv )
{
    MPI_Comm client;
    MPI_Status status;
    char port_name[MPI_MAX_PORT_NAME];
    double buf[MAX_DATA];
    int     size, again;

    MPI_Init( &argc, &argv );
    MPI_Comm_size(MPI_COMM_WORLD, &size);
    if (size != 1) error(FATAL, "Server too big");
    MPI_Open_port(MPI_INFO_NULL, port_name);
    printf("server available at %s\n",port_name);
    while (1) {
        MPI_Comm_accept( port_name, MPI_INFO_NULL, 0, MPI_COMM_WORLD,
                         &client );
        again = 1;
        while (again) {
            MPI_Recv( buf, MAX_DATA, MPI_DOUBLE,
                      MPI_ANY_SOURCE, MPI_ANY_TAG, client, &status );
            switch (status.MPI_TAG) {
                case 0: MPI_Comm_free( &client );
                        MPI_Close_port(port_name);
```

```
                               MPI_Finalize();
                               return 0;
                case 1: MPI_Comm_disconnect( &client );
                               again = 0;
                               break;
                case 2: /* do something */
                ...
                default:
                               /* Unexpected message type */
                               MPI_Abort( MPI_COMM_WORLD, 1 );
                }
            }
        }
}
```

Here is the client.

```c
#include "mpi.h"
int main( int argc, char **argv )
{
    MPI_Comm server;
    double buf[MAX_DATA];
    char port_name[MPI_MAX_PORT_NAME];

    MPI_Init( &argc, &argv );
    strcpy(port_name, argv[1] );/* assume server's name is
                                   cmd-line arg */

    MPI_Comm_connect( port_name, MPI_INFO_NULL, 0, MPI_COMM_WORLD,
                      &server );

    while (!done) {
        tag = 2; /* Action to perform */
        MPI_Send( buf, n, MPI_DOUBLE, 0, tag, server );
        /* etc */
        }
    MPI_Send( buf, 0, MPI_DOUBLE, 0, 1, server );
    MPI_Comm_disconnect( &server );
    MPI_Finalize();
```

```
    return 0;
}
```

3.5   Other Functionality

In this section we discuss the remaining MPI features for dynamic process management.

3.5.1   Universe Size

Many "dynamic" MPI applications are expected to exist in a static runtime environment, in which resources have been allocated before the application is run. When one of these quasi-static applications is run, the user (or possibly a batch system) will usually specify a number of processes to start and a total number of processes that are expected. An application needs to know how many slots there are, that is, how many processes it should spawn.

MPI provides the attribute MPI_UNIVERSE_SIZE (MPI::UNIVERSE_SIZE in C++) on MPI_COMM_WORLD that allows the application to obtain this information in a portable manner. This attribute indicates the total number of processes that are expected. In Fortran, the attribute is the integer value. In C, the attribute is a pointer to the integer value. An application typically subtracts the size of MPI_COMM_WORLD from MPI_UNIVERSE_SIZE to find out how many processes it should spawn. MPI_UNIVERSE_SIZE is initialized in MPI_INIT and is not changed by MPI. If defined, it has the same value on all processes of MPI_COMM_WORLD. MPI_UNIVERSE_SIZE is determined by the application startup mechanism in a way not specified by MPI. (The size of MPI_COMM_WORLD is another example of such a parameter.)

Possibilities for how MPI_UNIVERSE_SIZE might be set include

• A -universe_size argument to a program that starts MPI processes, such as mpiexec (see Section I-7.1).
• Automatic interaction with a batch scheduler to figure out how many processors have been allocated to an application.
• An environment variable set by the user.
• Extra information passed to MPI_COMM_SPAWN through the info argument.

An implementation must document how MPI_UNIVERSE_SIZE is set. If an implementation does not support the ability to set MPI_UNIVERSE_SIZE, the attribute MPI_UNIVERSE_SIZE is not set.

MPI_UNIVERSE_SIZE is a recommendation, not necessarily a hard limit. For instance, some implementations may allow an application to spawn 50 processes per processor, if requested. However, the user probably only wants to spawn only one process per processor.

MPI_UNIVERSE_SIZE is assumed to have been specified when an application was started and is, in essence, a portable mechanism to allow the user to pass to the application (through the MPI process startup mechanism, such as `mpiexec`) a piece of critical runtime information. Note that no interaction with the runtime environment is required. If the runtime environment changes size while an application is running, MPI_UNIVERSE_SIZE is not updated, and the application must find out about the change through direct communication with the runtime system.

3.5.2 Singleton MPI_INIT

A high-quality implementation will allow any process (including those not started with a "parallel application" mechanism) to become an MPI process by calling MPI_INIT. Such a process can then connect to other MPI processes by using the MPI_COMM_ACCEPT and MPI_COMM_CONNECT routines, or spawn other MPI processes. MPI does not mandate that this facility (a program can become a single-process MPI program, no matter how it was originally started), but strongly encourages it where technically feasible.

Advice to implementors.   To start an MPI-1 application with more than one process requires special coordination. The processes must be started at the "same" time; they also must have a mechanism to establish communication. Either the user or the operating system must take special steps beyond simply starting processes.

When an application enters MPI_INIT, clearly it must be able to determine whether these special steps were taken. MPI-1 does not say what happens if these special steps were not taken; presumably this situation is treated as an error in starting the MPI application. MPI-2 recommends the following behavior.

If a process enters MPI_INIT and determines that no special steps were taken (i.e., it has not been given the information to form an MPI_COMM_WORLD with other processes), it succeeds and forms a singleton MPI program (i.e., one in which MPI_COMM_WORLD has size 1).

In some implementations, MPI may not be able to function without an "MPI environment." For example, MPI may require that demons be running, or MPI may not be able to work at all on the front-end of an MPP. In this case, an MPI implementation may either

1. create the environment (e.g., start a demon) or

2. raise an error if it cannot create the environment and the environment has not been started independently.

A high-quality implementation will try to create a singleton MPI process and not raise an error. ⬚

3.5.3   MPI_APPNUM

MPI has a predefined attribute MPI_APPNUM (MPI::APPNUM in C++) of MPI_COMM_WORLD. In Fortran, the attribute is an integer value. In C, the attribute is a pointer to an integer value. If a process was spawned with MPI_COMM_SPAWN_MULTIPLE, the command number MPI_APPNUM generated the current process. Numbering starts from zero. If a process was spawned with MPI_COMM_SPAWN, it will have MPI_APPNUM equal to zero.

If the process was started not by a spawn call, but by an implementation-specific startup mechanism that can handle multiple process specifications, MPI_APPNUM should be set to the number of the corresponding process specification. In particular, if it is started with

```
mpiexec spec0 : spec1 : spec2
```

MPI_APPNUM should be set to the number of the corresponding specification.

If an application was not spawned with MPI_COMM_SPAWN or MPI_COMM_SPAWN_MULTIPLE, and if MPI_APPNUM doesn't make sense in the context of the implementation-specific startup mechanism, MPI_APPNUM is not set.

MPI implementations may optionally provide a mechanism to override the value of MPI_APPNUM through the info argument. MPI reserves the following key for all SPAWN calls.

appnum: Value contains an integer that overrides the default value for MPI_APPNUM in the child.

Rationale.   When a single application is started, it is able to figure out how many processes there are by looking at the size of MPI_COMM_WORLD. On the other hand, an application consisting of multiple subapplications, each of which is a single-program-multiple-data parallel (SPMD) program, has no general mechanism to find out how many subapplications there are and to which subapplication the process belongs. ⬚

3.5.4 Releasing Connections

Before a client and server connect, they are independent MPI applications. An error in one does not affect the other. After a connection is established with MPI_COMM_CONNECT and MPI_COMM_ACCEPT, however, an error in one may affect the other. Hence, it is desirable that a client and server be able to disconnect so that an error in one will not affect the other. Similarly, it might be desirable for a parent and child to disconnect so that errors in the child do not affect the parent, or vice versa.

- Two processes are **connected** if there is a communication path (direct or indirect) between them. More precisely:

    1. Two processes are connected if

        (a) they both belong to the same communicator (inter- or intra-, including MPI_COMM_WORLD),

        (b) they have previously belonged to a communicator that was freed with MPI_COMM_FREE instead of MPI_COMM_DISCONNECT, or

        (c) they both belong to the group of the same window or filehandle.

    2. If A is connected to B and B to C, then A is connected to C.

- Two processes are **disconnected** (also **independent**) if they are not connected.
- By the above definitions, connectivity is a transitive property, and divides the universe of MPI processes into disconnected (independent) sets (equivalence classes) of processes.
- Processes that are connected but don't share the same MPI_COMM_WORLD may become disconnected (independent) if the communication path between them is broken by using MPI_COMM_DISCONNECT.

The following additional rules apply to MPI functions:

- MPI_FINALIZE is collective over a set of connected processes.
- MPI_ABORT does not abort independent processes. As in MPI-1, it may abort all processes in MPI_COMM_WORLD (ignoring its comm argument). Additionally, it may abort connected processes, though it makes a "best attempt" to abort only the processes in comm.
- If a process terminates without calling MPI_FINALIZE, independent processes are not affected, but the effect on connected processes is not defined.

MPI_COMM_DISCONNECT(comm)

INOUT   comm   communicator (handle)

```
int MPI_Comm_disconnect(MPI_Comm *comm)
```

```
MPI_COMM_DISCONNECT(COMM, IERROR)
    INTEGER COMM, IERROR
```

```
void MPI::Comm::Disconnect()
```

This function waits for all pending communication on comm to complete internally, deallocates the communicator object, and sets the handle to MPI_COMM_-NULL. It is a collective operation. It may not be called with the communicator MPI_COMM_WORLD or MPI_COMM_SELF.

MPI_COMM_DISCONNECT may be called only if all communication is complete and matched, so that buffered data can be delivered to its destination. This requirement is the same as for MPI_FINALIZE.

MPI_COMM_DISCONNECT has the same action as MPI_COMM_FREE, except that it waits for pending communication to finish internally and enables the guarantee about the behavior of disconnected processes.

Advice to users.   To disconnect two processes the user may need to call MPI_-COMM_DISCONNECT, MPI_WIN_FREE, and MPI_FILE_CLOSE to remove all communication paths between the two processes. Note that it may be necessary to disconnect several communicators (or to free several windows or files) before two processes are completely independent. □

Rationale.   It would be nice to be able to use MPI_COMM_FREE instead, but that function explicitly does not wait for pending communication to complete. □

3.5.5   Another Way to Establish MPI Communication

If two MPI programs do not share a communicator but have established non-MPI communication via a socket, the socket can be used to "bootstrap" MPI communication.

MPI_COMM_JOIN(fd, intercomm)

IN	fd	socket file descriptor
OUT	intercomm	new intercommunicator (handle)

```
int MPI_Comm_join(int fd, MPI_Comm *intercomm)
```

```
MPI_COMM_JOIN(FD, INTERCOMM, IERROR)
    INTEGER FD, INTERCOMM, IERROR
```

```
static MPI::Intercomm MPI::Comm::Join(const int fd)
```

MPI_COMM_JOIN is intended for MPI implementations that exist in an environment supporting the Berkeley Socket interface [18, 21]. Implementations that exist in an environment not supporting Berkeley Sockets should provide the entry point for MPI_COMM_JOIN and should return MPI_COMM_NULL.

This call creates an intercommunicator from the union of two MPI processes that are connected by a socket. MPI_COMM_JOIN should succeed if the local and remote processes have access to the same implementation-defined MPI communication universe.

Advice to users. An MPI implementation may require a specific communication medium for MPI communication, such as a shared-memory segment or a special switch. In this case, it may not be possible for two processes to successfully join even if there is a socket connecting them and they are using the same MPI implementation. □

Advice to implementors. A high-quality implementation will attempt to establish communication over a slow medium if its preferred one is not available. If implementations do not do so, they must document why they cannot do MPI communication over the medium used by the socket (especially if the socket is a TCP connection). □

fd is a file descriptor representing a socket of type SOCK_STREAM (a two-way reliable byte-stream connection). Nonblocking I/O and asynchronous notification via SIGIO must not be enabled for the socket. The socket must be in a connected state. The socket must be quiescent when MPI_COMM_JOIN is called (see below). The application must create the socket by using standard socket API calls.

MPI_COMM_JOIN must be called by the process at each end of the socket. It does not return until both processes have called MPI_COMM_JOIN. The two processes are referred to as the local and remote processes.

MPI uses the socket to bootstrap creation of the intercommunicator, and for nothing else. Upon return from MPI_COMM_JOIN, the file descriptor will be open and quiescent (see below).

If MPI is unable to create an intercommunicator, but is able to leave the socket in its original state with no pending communication, it succeeds and sets intercomm to MPI_COMM_NULL.

The socket must be quiescent before MPI_COMM_JOIN is called and after MPI_-COMM_JOIN returns. More specifically, on entry to MPI_COMM_JOIN, a read on the socket will not read any data that was written to the socket before the remote process called MPI_COMM_JOIN. On exit from MPI_COMM_JOIN, a read will not read any data that was written to the socket before the remote process returned from MPI_COMM_JOIN. It is the responsibility of the application to ensure the first condition, and the responsibility of the MPI implementation to ensure the second. In a multithreaded application, either the application must ensure that one thread does not access the socket while another is calling MPI_COMM_JOIN, or it must call MPI_COMM_JOIN concurrently.

Advice to implementors.   MPI is free to use any available communication path(s) for MPI messages in the new communicator; the socket is used only for the initial handshaking. ☐

MPI_COMM_JOIN uses non-MPI communication to do its work. The interaction of non-MPI communication with pending MPI communication is not defined. Therefore, the result of calling MPI_COMM_JOIN on two connected processes (see Section 3.5.4 for the definition of "connected") is undefined.

The returned communicator may be used to establish MPI communication with additional processes, through the usual MPI communicator-creation mechanisms.

4 One-Sided Communication

In this chapter we describe the extension that most dramatically modifies the programming model of MPI-1. One-sided communication significantly expands the set of parallel algorithms that can be expressed in MPI.

4.1 Introduction

Remote Memory Access (RMA) extends the communication mechanisms of MPI by allowing one process to specify all communication parameters, both for the sending side and for the receiving side. This mode of communication facilitates the coding of some applications with dynamically changing data access patterns where the data distribution is fixed or slowly changing. In such a case, each process can compute what data it needs to access or update at other processes. However, processes may not know which data items in their own memories need to be accessed or updated by remote processes, and may not even know the identity of these processes. Thus, the transfer parameters are all available only on one side. Regular send/receive communication requires matching operations by sender and receiver. In order to issue the matching operations, an application needs to distribute the transfer parameters. This may require all processes to participate in a time-consuming global computation, or to periodically poll for potential communication requests to receive and act upon. The use of RMA communication mechanisms avoids the need for global computations or explicit polling. A generic example of this nature is the execution of an assignment of the form A = B(map), where map is a permutation vector, and A, B and map are distributed in the same manner.

Message-passing communication achieves two effects: *communication* of data from sender to receiver and *synchronization* of sender with receiver. The RMA design separates these two functions. Three communication calls are provided: MPI_PUT (remote write), MPI_GET (remote read), and MPI_ACCUMULATE (remote update). A larger number of synchronization calls are provided that support different synchronization styles. The design is similar to that of weakly coherent memory systems: correct ordering of memory accesses has to be imposed by the user, using synchronization calls; the implementation can delay communication operations until the synchronization calls occur, for efficiency.

The design of the RMA functions allows implementors to take advantage, in many cases, of fast communication mechanisms provided by various platforms, such as coherent or noncoherent shared memory, DMA engines, hardware-supported put/get operations, communication coprocessors, etc.

It is important to note that the MPI one-sided operations do *not* provide a shared-memory programming model or support for direct shared-memory programming.

This chapter is organized as follows. First, the concept of a memory window is introduced, along with the routines used to create and free the MPI object representing a collection of windows. Next, the RMA communication routines are described, along with some examples of their use. All RMA communication routines are nonblocking. This is followed by the RMA synchronization calls (recall that with RMA, we wish to synchronize many RMA communication calls with a single synchronization step, so the send/receive completion routines such as MPI_WAIT are not appropriate). Finally, a careful description of the semantics and correct use of the RMA operations is described; this makes precise what happens when, for example, several processes access the same remote window.

The major new concepts in this chapter are those of a window (Section 4.2), access and exposure epochs of windows, and RMA synchronization (both in Section 4.4).

We shall denote by **origin** the process that performs the RMA call, and by **target** the process in which the memory is accessed. Thus, in a put operation, source=origin and destination=target; in a get operation, source=target and destination=origin.

4.2   Initialization

Before any RMA operation may be used, MPI must be informed what parts of a process's memory will be used with RMA operations and what other processes may access that memory. Just as an MPI communicator is used to identify both the processes, as well as providing a separate context, in send-receive operations, a *window object* (MPI_Win in C) identifies the memory and processes that one-sided operations may act on. Just as for communicators, the user may define many overlapping window objects.

4.2.1   Window Creation

The initialization operation allows each process in an intracommunicator group to specify, in a collective operation, a "window" in its memory that is made accessible to accesses by remote processes. The call returns an opaque object that represents the group of processes that own and access the set of windows, and the attributes of each window, as specified by the initialization call.

MPI_WIN_CREATE(base, size, disp_unit, info, comm, win)

IN	base	initial address of window (choice)
IN	size	size of window in bytes (nonnegative integer)
IN	disp_unit	local unit size for displacements, in bytes (positive integer)
IN	info	info argument (handle)
IN	comm	communicator (handle)
OUT	win	window object returned by the call (handle)

```
int MPI_Win_create(void *base, MPI_Aint size, int disp_unit,
    MPI_Info info, MPI_Comm comm, MPI_Win *win)
```

```
MPI_WIN_CREATE(BASE, SIZE, DISP_UNIT, INFO, COMM, WIN, IERROR)
    <type> BASE(*)
    INTEGER(KIND=MPI_ADDRESS_KIND) SIZE
    INTEGER DISP_UNIT, INFO, COMM, WIN, IERROR
```

```
static MPI::Win MPI::Win::Create(const void* base, MPI::Aint size,
    int disp_unit, const MPI::Info& info, const MPI::Intracomm& comm)
```

This is a collective call executed by all processes in the group of comm. It returns a window object that can be used by these processes to perform RMA operations. Each process specifies a window of existing memory that it exposes to RMA accesses by the processes in the group of comm. The window consists of size bytes, starting at address base. A process may elect to expose no memory by specifying size = 0.

The displacement unit argument is provided to facilitate address arithmetic in RMA operations: the target displacement argument of an RMA operation is scaled by the factor disp_unit specified by the target process, at window creation.

Note that the object represented by MPI_Win is a collection of windows, not an individual window.

Rationale.   The window size is specified using an address-sized integer, so as to allow windows that span more than 4 GB of address space. (Even if the physical memory size is less than 4 GB, the address range may be larger than 4 GB, if addresses are not contiguous.) □

Advice to users.   Common choices for disp_unit are 1 (no scaling), and (C syntax) sizeof(type), for a window that consists of an array of elements of type type. The latter choice will allow one to use array indices in RMA calls, and have those scaled correctly to byte displacements, even in a heterogeneous environment. □

The info argument provides optimization hints to the runtime system about the expected usage pattern of the window. The following info key is predefined:

no_locks: if set to true, then the implementation may assume that the local window is never locked (by a call to MPI_WIN_LOCK). This implies that this window is not used for 3-party communication, and RMA can be implemented with no (or less) asynchronous agent activity at this process.

The various processes in the group of comm may specify completely different target windows, in location, size, displacement units and info arguments. As long as all the get, put, and accumulate accesses to a particular process fit their specific target window this should pose no problem. The same area in memory may appear in multiple windows, each associated with a different window object. However, concurrent communications to distinct, overlapping windows may lead to erroneous results. See Section 4.7 for more details.

Advice to users. A window can be created in any part of the process memory. However, on some systems, the performance of windows in memory allocated by MPI_ALLOC_MEM (Section 2.4) will be better. Also, on some systems, performance is improved when window boundaries are aligned at "natural" boundaries (word, double-word, cache line, page frame, etc.). ☐

Advice to implementors. In cases where RMA operations use different mechanisms in different memory areas (e.g., load/store in a shared-memory segment, and an asynchronous handler in private memory), the MPI_WIN_CREATE call needs to figure out which type of memory is used for the window. To do so, MPI maintains, internally, the list of memory segments allocated by MPI_ALLOC_MEM, or by other, implementation specific, mechanisms, together with information on the type of memory segment allocated. When a call to MPI_WIN_CREATE occurs, MPI checks which segment contains each window, and decides, accordingly, which mechanism to use for RMA operations.

Vendors may provide additional, implementation-specific mechanisms to allow such memory to be used for static variables.

Implementors should document any performance impact of window alignment. ☐

MPI_WIN_FREE(win)

    INOUT win   window object (handle)

```
int MPI_Win_free(MPI_Win *win)
```

```
MPI_WIN_FREE(WIN, IERROR)
    INTEGER WIN, IERROR
```

```
void MPI::Win::Free()
```

MPI_WIN_FREE frees the window object win and returns a null handle (equal to MPI_WIN_NULL in C and Fortran and MPI::WIN_NULL in C++). This is a collective call executed by all processes in the group associated with win. MPI_WIN_FREE(win) can be invoked by a process only after it has completed its involvement in RMA communications on window object win: that is, the process has called MPI_WIN_FENCE, or called MPI_WIN_WAIT to match a previous call to MPI_WIN_POST, or called MPI_WIN_COMPLETE to match a previous call to MPI_WIN_START, or called MPI_WIN_UNLOCK to match a previous call to MPI_WIN_LOCK. When the call returns, the window memory can be freed.

Advice to implementors. MPI_WIN_FREE requires a barrier synchronization: no process can return from free until all processes in the group of win have called free. This requirement ensures that no process will attempt to access a remote window (e.g., with lock/unlock) after it was freed. □

4.2.2 Window Attributes

The following three attributes are cached with a window object when the window object is created. The values of these attributes refer to the local window.

MPI_WIN_BASE: window base address

MPI_WIN_SIZE: window size, in bytes

MPI_WIN_DISP_UNIT: displacement unit associated with the window

The C++ names for these constants begin with MPI::WIN instead of MPI_WIN.

In C, calls to MPI_Win_get_attr(win, MPI_WIN_BASE, &base, &flag), MPI_Win_get_attr(win, MPI_WIN_SIZE, &size, &flag) and MPI_Win_get_attr(win, MPI_WIN_DISP_UNIT, &disp_unit, &flag) will return in base a pointer to the start of the window win, and will return in size and disp_unit pointers to the size and displacement unit of the window, respectively, and similarly in C++.

In Fortran, calls to MPI_WIN_GET_ATTR(win, MPI_WIN_BASE, base, flag, ierror), MPI_WIN_GET_ATTR(win, MPI_WIN_SIZE, size, flag, ierror) and MPI_WIN_GET_ATTR(win, MPI_WIN_DISP_UNIT, disp_unit, flag, ierror) will return in base, size and disp_unit the (integer representation of) the base address, the size and the displacement unit of the window win, respectively. (The window attribute access functions are defined in Section 6.7.)

The other "window attribute," namely the group of processes attached to the window, can be retrieved using the call below.

MPI_WIN_GET_GROUP(win, group)

| IN | win | window object (handle) |
| OUT | group | group of processes which share access to the window (handle) |

```
int MPI_Win_get_group(MPI_Win win, MPI_Group *group)
```

```
MPI_WIN_GET_GROUP(WIN, GROUP, IERROR)
    INTEGER WIN, GROUP, IERROR
```

```
MPI::Group MPI::Win::Get_group() const
```

MPI_WIN_GET_GROUP returns a duplicate of the group of the communicator used to create the window object associated with win. The group is returned in group.

4.3   Communication Calls

MPI supports three RMA communication calls: MPI_PUT transfers data from the caller's memory (origin) to the target memory; MPI_GET transfers data from the target memory to the caller's memory; and MPI_ACCUMULATE updates locations in the target memory, for example, by adding to these locations values sent from the caller's memory. These operations are *nonblocking*: the call initiates the transfer, but the transfer may continue after the call returns. The transfer is completed, both at the origin and at the target, when a subsequent *synchronization* call is issued by the caller on the involved window object. These synchronization calls are described in Section 4.4.

The local communication buffer of an RMA call should not be updated, and the local communication buffer of a get call should not be accessed after the RMA call, until the subsequent synchronization call completes.

Rationale.   The rule above is more lenient than for message passing, where we do not allow two concurrent sends, with overlapping send buffers. Here, we allow two concurrent puts with overlapping send buffers. The reasons for this relaxation are

1.   Users do not like that restriction, which is not very natural (it prohibits concurrent reads).

2.   Weakening the rule does not prevent efficient implementation, as far as we know.

3.   Weakening the rule is important for performance of RMA: we want to associate one synchronization call with as many RMA operations as possible. If puts from overlapping buffers cannot be concurrent, then we need to needlessly add synchronization points in the code.

☐

It is erroneous to have concurrent conflicting accesses to the same memory location in a window; if a location is updated by a put or accumulate operation, then this location cannot be accessed by a load or another RMA operation until the updating operation has completed at the target. There is one exception to this rule; namely, the same location can be updated by several concurrent accumulate calls, the outcome being as if these updates occurred in some order. In addition, a window cannot concurrently be updated by a put or accumulate operation and by a local store operation, even if these two updates access different locations in the window. The last restriction enables more efficient implementations of RMA operations on many systems. These restrictions are described in more detail in Section 4.7.

The calls use general datatype arguments to specify communication buffers at the origin and at the target. Thus, a transfer operation may also gather data at the source and scatter it at the destination. However, all arguments specifying both communication buffers are provided by the caller.

For all three calls, the target process may be identical with the origin process; that is, a process may use an RMA operation to move data in its memory.

Rationale.   The choice of supporting "self-communication" is the same as for message passing. It simplifies some coding, and is very useful with accumulate operations, to allow atomic updates of local variables. ☐

4.3.1   Put

The execution of a put operation is similar to the execution of a send by the origin process and a matching receive by the target process. The obvious difference is that all arguments are provided by one call—the call executed by the origin process.

MPI_PUT(origin_addr, origin_count, origin_datatype, target_rank, target_disp,
   target_count, target_datatype, win)

IN	origin_addr	initial address of origin buffer (choice)
IN	origin_count	number of entries in origin buffer (nonnegative integer)
IN	origin_datatype	datatype of each entry in origin buffer (handle)
IN	target_rank	rank of target (nonnegative integer)
IN	target_disp	displacement from start of window to target buffer (nonnegative integer)
IN	target_count	number of entries in target buffer (nonnegative integer)
IN	target_datatype	datatype of each entry in target buffer (handle)
IN	win	window object used for communication (handle)

```
int MPI_Put(void *origin_addr, int origin_count, MPI_Datatype
    origin_datatype, int target_rank, MPI_Aint target_disp, int
    target_count, MPI_Datatype target_datatype, MPI_Win win)
```

```
MPI_PUT(ORIGIN_ADDR, ORIGIN_COUNT, ORIGIN_DATATYPE, TARGET_RANK,
    TARGET_DISP, TARGET_COUNT, TARGET_DATATYPE, WIN, IERROR)
    <type> ORIGIN_ADDR(*)
    INTEGER(KIND=MPI_ADDRESS_KIND) TARGET_DISP
    INTEGER ORIGIN_COUNT, ORIGIN_DATATYPE, TARGET_RANK, TARGET_COUNT,
    TARGET_DATATYPE, WIN, IERROR
```

```
void MPI::Win::Put(const void* origin_addr, int origin_count, const
    MPI::Datatype& origin_datatype, int target_rank, MPI::Aint
    target_disp, int target_count, const MPI::Datatype&
    target_datatype) const
```

MPI_PUT transfers origin_count successive entries of the type specified by the origin_datatype, starting at address origin_addr on the origin node to the target node specified by the win, target_rank pair. The data are written in the target buffer at address target_addr = window_base + target_disp×disp_unit, where window_base and disp_unit are the base address and window displacement unit specified at window object initialization, by the target process.

The target buffer is specified by the arguments target_count and target_datatype.

The data transfer is the same as that which would occur if the origin process executed a send operation with arguments origin_addr, origin_count, origin_datatype, target_rank, tag, comm, and the target process executed a receive operation with arguments target_addr, target_count, target_datatype, source, tag, comm, where target_addr is the target buffer address computed as explained above, and comm is a communicator for the group of win.

The communication must satisfy the same constraints as for a similar message-passing communication. The target_datatype may not specify overlapping entries in the target buffer. The message sent must fit, without truncation, in the target buffer. Furthermore, the target buffer must fit in the target window.

The target_datatype argument is a handle to a datatype object defined at the origin process. However, this object is interpreted at the target process: the outcome is as if the target datatype object was defined at the target process, by the same sequence of calls used to define it at the origin process. The target datatype must contain only relative displacements, not absolute addresses. The same holds for get and accumulate.

Advice to users.   The target_datatype argument is a handle to a datatype object that is defined at the origin process, even though it defines a data layout in the target process memory. This causes no problems in a homogeneous environment, or in a heterogeneous environment, if only portable datatypes are used (portable datatypes are defined in Section 1.4).

The performance of a put transfer can be significantly affected, on some systems, by the choice of window location and the shape and location of the origin and target buffer: transfers to a target window in memory allocated by MPI_ALLOC_MEM may be much faster on shared memory systems; transfers from contiguous buffers will be faster on most, if not all, systems; the alignment of the communication buffers may also impact performance. ☐

Advice to implementors.   A high-quality implementation will attempt to prevent remote accesses to memory outside the window that was exposed by the process, both for debugging purposes and for protection with client-server codes that use RMA. That is, a high-quality implementation will check, if possible, window bounds on each RMA call, and raise an MPI exception at the origin call if an out-of-bound situation occurred. Note that the condition can be checked at the origin. Of course, the added safety achieved by such checks must be weighed against the added cost of such checks. ☐

4.3.2 Get

MPI_GET(origin_addr, origin_count, origin_datatype, target_rank, target_disp,
  target_count, target_datatype, win)

OUT	origin_addr	initial address of origin buffer (choice)
IN	origin_count	number of entries in origin buffer (nonnegative integer)
IN	origin_datatype	datatype of each entry in origin buffer (handle)
IN	target_rank	rank of target (nonnegative integer)
IN	target_disp	displacement from window start to the beginning of the target buffer (nonnegative integer)
IN	target_count	number of entries in target buffer (nonnegative integer)
IN	target_datatype	datatype of each entry in target buffer (handle)
IN	win	window object used for communication (handle)

```
int MPI_Get(void *origin_addr, int origin_count, MPI_Datatype
    origin_datatype, int target_rank, MPI_Aint target_disp, int
    target_count, MPI_Datatype target_datatype, MPI_Win win)
```

```
MPI_GET(ORIGIN_ADDR, ORIGIN_COUNT, ORIGIN_DATATYPE, TARGET_RANK,
    TARGET_DISP, TARGET_COUNT, TARGET_DATATYPE, WIN, IERROR)
    <type> ORIGIN_ADDR(*)
    INTEGER(KIND=MPI_ADDRESS_KIND) TARGET_DISP
    INTEGER ORIGIN_COUNT, ORIGIN_DATATYPE, TARGET_RANK, TARGET_COUNT,
    TARGET_DATATYPE, WIN, IERROR
```

```
void MPI::Win::Get(void *origin_addr, int origin_count,
    const MPI::Datatype& origin_datatype, int target_rank,
    MPI::Aint target_disp, int target_count,
    const MPI::Datatype& target_datatype) const
```

MPI_GET is similar to MPI_PUT, except that the direction of data transfer is reversed. Data are copied from the target memory to the origin. The origin_datatype may not specify overlapping entries in the origin buffer. The target buffer must be contained within the target window, and the copied data must fit, without truncation, in the origin buffer.

4.3.3 Examples

Example 4.1 We show how to implement the generic indirect assignment A = B(map), where A, B and map have the same distribution, and map is a permutation.

To simplify, we assume a block distribution with equal size blocks. That is, we assume that the arrays A, B, and map are represented by subranges on each processor. Process 0 has the first n/size entries, process 1 has the second n/size entries, and so on (size is the size of the communicator and n is the "global" size of the vector). In order to emphasize that the arrays in each process contain only the "local" part, the variable names Alocal, Blocal, and mapLocal are used.

These examples use MPI_WIN_FENCE to complete the RMA operations. The reason for the fence before the get is discussed in Section 4.4.

```
SUBROUTINE MAPVALS(Alocal, Blocal, mapLocal, m, comm, p)
USE MPI
INTEGER m, mapLocal(m), comm, p
REAL    Alocal(m), Blocal(m)

INTEGER otype(p), oindex(m),   & ! used to construct origin datatypes
        ttype(p), tindex(m),   & ! used to construct target datatypes
        count(p), total(p),    &
        win, ierr
INTEGER(KIND=MPI_ADDRESS_KIND) sizeofreal

! This part does the work that depends on the locations of B.
! Can be reused while this does not change

CALL MPI_TYPE_SIZE(MPI_REAL, sizeofreal, ierr)
CALL MPI_WIN_CREATE(Blocal, m*sizeofreal, sizeofreal, &
                    MPI_INFO_NULL, comm, win, ierr)

! This part does the work that depends on the value of mapLocal and
! the locations of the arrays.
! Can be reused while these do not change

! Compute number of entries to be received from each process

DO i=1,p
  count(i) = 0
END DO
DO i=1,m
  j = mapLocal(i)/m+1
```

```fortran
    count(j) = count(j)+1
END DO

total(1) = 0
DO i=2,p
  total(i) = total(i-1) + count(i-1)
END DO

DO i=1,p
  count(i) = 0
END DO


! compute origin and target indices of entries.
! entry i at current process is received from location
! k at process (j-1), j = 1..p and k = 1..m,
! and mapLocal(i) = (j-1)*m + (k-1).

DO i=1,m
  j = mapLocal(i)/m+1
  k = MOD(mapLocal(i),m)+1
  count(j) = count(j)+1
  oindex(total(j) + count(j)) = i
  tindex(total(j) + count(j)) = k
END DO

! create origin and target datatypes for each get operation
DO i=1,p
  CALL MPI_TYPE_INDEXED_BLOCK(count(i), 1, oindex(total(i)+1),    &
                           MPI_REAL, otype(i), ierr)
  CALL MPI_TYPE_COMMIT(otype(i), ierr)
  CALL MPI_TYPE_INDEXED_BLOCK(count(i), 1, tindex(total(i)+1),    &
                           MPI_REAL, ttype(i), ierr)
  CALL MPI_TYPE_COMMIT(ttype(i), ierr)
END DO

! this part does the assignment itself
CALL MPI_WIN_FENCE(0, win, ierr)
DO i=1,p
```

```
  CALL MPI_GET(Alocal, 1, otype(i), i-1, 0, 1, ttype(i), win, ierr)
END DO
CALL MPI_WIN_FENCE(0, win, ierr)

CALL MPI_WIN_FREE(win, ierr)
DO i=1,p
  CALL MPI_TYPE_FREE(otype(i), ierr)
  CALL MPI_TYPE_FREE(ttype(i), ierr)
END DO
RETURN
END
```

Example 4.2 A simpler version can be written that does not require that a datatype be built for the target buffer by using a separate get call for each entry. This code is much simpler, but usually much less efficient, for large arrays.

```
SUBROUTINE MAPVALS(Alocal, Blocal, mapLocal, m, comm, p)
USE MPI
INTEGER m, mapLocal(m), comm, p
REAL    Alocal(m), Blocal(m)
INTEGER win, ierr
INTEGER(KIND=MPI_ADDRESS_KIND) sizeofreal

CALL MPI_TYPE_SIZE(MPI_REAL, sizeofreal, ierr)
CALL MPI_WIN_CREATE(Blocal, m*sizeofreal, sizeofreal, &
                    MPI_INFO_NULL, comm, win, ierr)

CALL MPI_WIN_FENCE(0, win, ierr)
DO i=1,m
  j = mapLocal(i)/p
  k = MOD(mapLocal(i),p)
  CALL MPI_GET(Alocal(i), 1, MPI_REAL, j, k, 1, MPI_REAL, win, ierr)
END DO
CALL MPI_WIN_FENCE(0, win, ierr)
CALL MPI_WIN_FREE(win, ierr)
RETURN
END
```

4.3.4   Accumulate Function

It is often useful in a put operation to combine the data moved to the target process with the data that resides at that process, rather then replacing the data there. This allows, for example, the accumulation of a sum by having all involved processes add their contribution to the sum variable in the memory of one process.

MPI_ACCUMULATE(origin_addr, origin_count, origin_datatype, target_rank,
   target_disp, target_count, target_datatype, op, win)

IN	origin_addr	initial address of buffer (choice)
IN	origin_count	number of entries in buffer (nonnegative integer)
IN	origin_datatype	datatype of each buffer entry (handle)
IN	target_rank	rank of target (nonnegative integer)
IN	target_disp	displacement from start of window to beginning of target buffer (nonnegative integer)
IN	target_count	number of entries in target buffer (nonnegative integer)
IN	target_datatype	datatype of each entry in target buffer (handle)
IN	op	reduce operation (handle)
IN	win	window object (handle)

```
int MPI_Accumulate(void *origin_addr, int origin_count,
    MPI_Datatype origin_datatype, int target_rank,
    MPI_Aint target_disp, int target_count,
    MPI_Datatype target_datatype, MPI_Op op, MPI_Win win)
```

```
MPI_ACCUMULATE(ORIGIN_ADDR, ORIGIN_COUNT, ORIGIN_DATATYPE,
    TARGET_RANK, TARGET_DISP, TARGET_COUNT, TARGET_DATATYPE, OP, WIN,
    IERROR)
    <type> ORIGIN_ADDR(*)
    INTEGER(KIND=MPI_ADDRESS_KIND) TARGET_DISP
    INTEGER ORIGIN_COUNT, ORIGIN_DATATYPE,TARGET_RANK, TARGET_COUNT,
    TARGET_DATATYPE, OP, WIN, IERROR
```

```
void MPI::Win::Accumulate(const void* origin_addr, int origin_count,
    const MPI::Datatype& origin_datatype, int target_rank, MPI::Aint
    target_disp, int target_count,
    const MPI::Datatype& target_datatype, const MPI::Op& op) const
```

This function accumulates the contents of the origin buffer (as defined by origin_-addr, origin_count and origin_datatype) to the buffer specified by arguments target_-count and target_datatype, at offset target_disp, in the target window specified by target_rank and win, using the operation op. This is like MPI_PUT except that data is combined into the target area instead of overwriting it.

Any of the predefined operations for MPI_REDUCE can be used. User-defined functions cannot be used. For example, if op is MPI_SUM, each element of the origin buffer is added to the corresponding element in the target, replacing the former value in the target.

Each datatype argument must be either a predefined datatype or a derived datatype, where all basic components are of the same predefined datatype. Both origin and target datatype arguments must be constructed from the same predefined datatype. The operation op applies to elements of that predefined type. target_datatype must not specify overlapping entries, and the target buffer must fit in the target window.

In addition, a new predefined operation, MPI_REPLACE (MPI::REPLACE in C++), is defined. It corresponds to the associative function $f(a, b) = b$; that is, the current value in the target memory is replaced by the value supplied by the origin.

Advice to users.   In the simplest case, MPI_PUT is a special case of MPI_-ACCUMULATE, with the operation MPI_REPLACE. Note, however, that MPI_PUT and MPI_ACCUMULATE have different constraints on concurrent updates (see Section 4.7). □

Example 4.3   We want to compute $B(j) = \sum_{i:\text{map}(i)=j} A(i)$. The arrays A, B and map are distributed in the same manner. We write the simple version.

```
SUBROUTINE SUM(Alocal, Blocal, mapLocal, m, comm, p)
USE MPI
INTEGER m, mapLocal(m), comm, p, win, ierr
INTEGER(KIND=MPI_ADDRESS_KIND) sizeofreal
REAL    Alocal(m), Blocal(m)

CALL MPI_TYPE_SIZE(MPI_REAL, sizeofreal, ierr)
CALL MPI_WIN_CREATE(Blocal, m*sizeofreal, sizeofreal, &
                    MPI_INFO_NULL, comm, win, ierr)

CALL MPI_WIN_FENCE(0, win, ierr)
DO i=1,m
```

```
      j = mapLocal(i)/p
      k = MOD(mapLocal(i),p)
      CALL MPI_ACCUMULATE(Alocal(i), 1, MPI_REAL, j, k, 1, MPI_REAL,  &
                          MPI_SUM, win, ierr)
END DO
CALL MPI_WIN_FENCE(0, win, ierr)

CALL MPI_WIN_FREE(win, ierr)
RETURN
END
```

This code is identical to the code in Example 4.2 except that a call to get has been replaced by a call to accumulate. (Note that, if `mapLocal` is one-to-one, then the code computes $B = A(map^{-1})$, which is the reverse assignment to the one computed in that previous example.) In a similar manner, in Example 4.1, we can replace the call to get by a call to accumulate, thus performing the computation with only one communication between any two processes.

4.4 Synchronization Calls

RMA communications fall in two categories:

• **active target** communication, where data is moved from the memory of one process to the memory of another, and both are explicitly involved in the communication. This communication pattern is similar to message passing, except that all the data transfer arguments are provided by one process, and the second process only participates in the synchronization.

• **passive target** communication, where data is moved from the memory of one process to the memory of another, and only the origin process is explicitly involved in the transfer. Thus, two origin processes may communicate by accessing the same location in a target window. The process that owns the target window may be distinct from the two communicating processes, in which case it does not participate explicitly in the communication. This communication paradigm is closest to a shared-memory model, where shared data can be accessed by all processes, irrespective of location.

RMA communication calls with argument win must occur at a process only within an **access epoch** for win. Such an epoch starts with an RMA synchronization call on win; it proceeds with zero or more RMA communication calls (MPI_PUT, MPI_GET or MPI_ACCUMULATE) on win; it completes with another synchronization call on win. This allows users to amortize one synchronization with multiple data transfers and provide implementors more flexibility in the implementation of RMA operations.

Distinct access epochs for win at the same process must be disjoint. On the other hand, epochs pertaining to different win arguments may overlap.

In active target communication, a target window can be accessed by RMA operations only within an **exposure epoch**. Such an epoch is started and completed by RMA synchronization calls executed by the target process. Distinct exposure epochs at a process on the same window must be disjoint, but such an exposure epoch may overlap with exposure epochs on other windows or with access epochs for the same or other win arguments. There is a one-to-one matching between access epochs at origin processes and exposure epochs on target processes: RMA operations issued by an origin process for a target window will access that target window during the same exposure epoch if and only if they were issued during the same access epoch.

In passive target communication the target process does not execute RMA synchronization calls, and there is no concept of an exposure epoch.

Local operations or other MPI calls may also occur during an epoch.

MPI provides three synchronization mechanisms:

1.   The MPI_WIN_FENCE collective synchronization call supports a simple synchronization pattern that is often used in parallel computations: namely a loosely synchronous model, where global computation phases alternate with global communication phases. This mechanism is most useful for loosely synchronous algorithms where the graph of communicating processes changes very frequently, or where each process communicates with many others.

 This call is used for active target communication. An access epoch at an origin process or an exposure epoch at a target process are started and completed by calls to MPI_WIN_FENCE. A process can access windows at all processes in the group of win during such an access epoch, and the local window can be accessed by all processes in the group of win during such an exposure epoch.

2.   The four functions MPI_WIN_START, MPI_WIN_COMPLETE, MPI_WIN_POST and MPI_WIN_WAIT can be used to restrict synchronization to the minimum: only pairs of communicating processes synchronize, and they do so only when a synchronization is needed to correctly order RMA accesses to a window with respect to local accesses to that same window. This

mechanism may be more efficient when each process communicates with few (logical) neighbors, and the communication graph is fixed or changes infrequently.

These calls are used for active target communication. An access epoch is started at the origin process by a call to MPI_WIN_START and is terminated by a call to MPI_WIN_COMPLETE. The start call has a group argument that specifies the group of target processes for that epoch. An exposure epoch is started at the target process by a call to MPI_WIN_POST and is completed by a call to MPI_WIN_WAIT. The post call has a group argument that specifies the set of origin processes for that epoch.

3. Finally, shared and exclusive locks are provided by the two functions MPI_WIN_LOCK and MPI_WIN_UNLOCK. Lock synchronization is useful for MPI applications that emulate a shared-memory model via MPI calls; for example, in a "billboard" model, where processes can, at random times, access or update different parts of the billboard.

These two calls provide passive target communication. An access epoch is started by a call to MPI_WIN_LOCK and terminated by a call to MPI_WIN_UNLOCK. Only one target window can be accessed during that epoch with win.

Figure 4.1 illustrates the general synchronization pattern for active target communication. The synchronization between post and start ensures that the put call of the origin process does not start until the target process exposes the window (with the post call); the target process will expose the window only after preceding local accesses to the window have completed. The synchronization between complete and wait ensures that the put call of the origin process completes before the window is unexposed (with the wait call). The target process will execute following local accesses to the target window only after the wait returned.

Figure 4.1 shows operations occurring in the natural temporal order implied by the synchronizations: the post occurs before the matching start, and complete occurs before the matching wait. However, such **strong** synchronization is more than needed for correct ordering of window accesses. The semantics of MPI calls allow **weak** synchronization, as illustrated in Figure 4.2. The access to the target window is delayed until the window is exposed, after the post. However, the start may complete earlier; the put and complete may also terminate earlier, if put data is buffered by the implementation. The synchronization calls order correctly window accesses, but do not necessarily synchronize other operations. This weaker synchronization semantic allows for more efficient implementations.

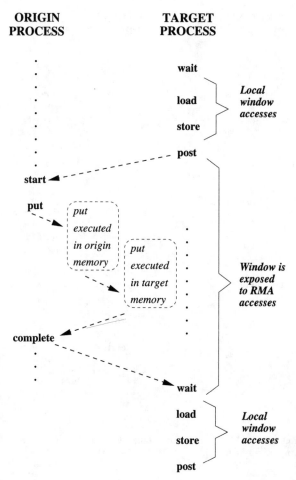

Figure 4.1
Active target communication. Dashed arrows represent synchronizations (ordering of events).

Figure 4.3 illustrates the general synchronization pattern for passive target communication. The first origin process communicates data to the second origin process, through the memory of the target process; the target process is not explicitly involved in the communication. The `lock` and `unlock` calls ensure that the two RMA accesses do not occur concurrently. However, they do *not* ensure that the `put` by origin 1 will precede the `get` by origin 2.

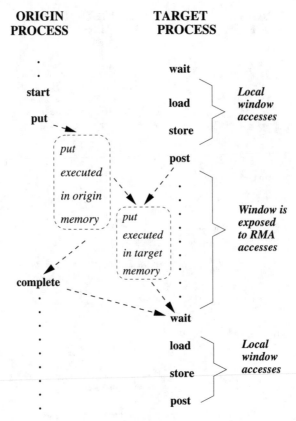

ORIGIN PROCESS

TARGET PROCESS

Figure 4.2
Active target communication, with weak synchronization. Dashed arrows represent synchronizations (ordering of events).

4.4.1   Fence

MPI_WIN_FENCE(assert, win)
IN	assert	program assertion (integer)
IN	win	window object (handle)

```
int MPI_Win_fence(int assert, MPI_Win win)
```

```
MPI_WIN_FENCE(ASSERT, WIN, IERROR)
    INTEGER ASSERT, WIN, IERROR
```

```
void MPI::Win::Fence(int assert) const
```

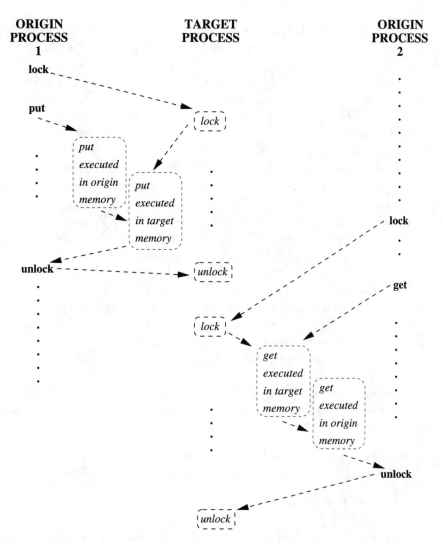

Figure 4.3
Passive target communication. Dashed arrows represent synchronizations (ordering of events).

The MPI call MPI_WIN_FENCE(assert, win) synchronizes RMA calls on win. The call is collective on the group of win. All RMA operations on win originating at a given process and started before the fence call will complete at that process before the fence call returns. They will be completed at their target before the fence call returns at the target. RMA operations on win started by a process after the fence call returns will access their target window only after MPI_WIN_FENCE has been called by the target process.

The call completes an RMA access epoch if it was preceded by another fence call and the local process issued RMA communication calls on win between these two calls. The call completes an RMA exposure epoch if it was preceded by another fence call and the local window was the target of RMA accesses between these two calls. The call starts an RMA access epoch if it is followed by another fence call and by RMA communication calls issued between these two fence calls. The call starts an exposure epoch if it is followed by another fence call and the local window is the target of RMA accesses between these two fence calls. Thus, the fence call is equivalent to calls to a subset of post, start, complete, wait.

A fence call usually entails a barrier synchronization: a process completes a call to MPI_WIN_FENCE only after all other processes in the group entered their matching call. However, a call to MPI_WIN_FENCE that is known not to end any epoch (in particular, a call with assert = MPI_MODE_NOPRECEDE) does not necessarily act as a barrier.

The assert argument is used to provide assertions on the context of the call that may be used for various optimizations. This is described in Section 4.4.4. A value of assert = 0 is always valid.

Advice to users. Calls to MPI_WIN_FENCE should both precede and follow calls to put, get or accumulate that are synchronized with fence calls. ☐

4.4.2   General Active Target Synchronization

MPI_WIN_START(group, assert, win)

IN	group	group of target processes (handle)
IN	assert	program assertion (integer)
IN	win	window object (handle)

```
int MPI_Win_start(MPI_Group group, int assert, MPI_Win win)
```

```
MPI_WIN_START(GROUP, ASSERT, WIN, IERROR)
```

```
      INTEGER GROUP, ASSERT, WIN, IERROR
```

```
void MPI::Win::Start(const MPI::Group& group, int assert) const
```

MPI_WIN_START starts an RMA access epoch for win. RMA calls issued on win during this epoch must access only windows at processes in group. Each process in group must issue a matching call to MPI_WIN_POST. RMA accesses to each target window will be delayed, if necessary, until the target process executed the matching call to MPI_WIN_POST. MPI_WIN_START is allowed to block until the corresponding MPI_WIN_POST calls are executed, but is not required to.

The assert argument is used to provide assertions on the context of the call that may be used for various optimizations. This is described in Section 4.4.4. A value of assert = 0 is always valid.

MPI_WIN_COMPLETE(win)

IN	win	window object (handle)

```
int MPI_Win_complete(MPI_Win win)
```

```
MPI_WIN_COMPLETE(WIN, IERROR)
    INTEGER WIN, IERROR
```

```
void MPI::Win::Complete() const
```

MPI_WIN_COMPLETE completes an RMA access epoch on win started by a call to MPI_WIN_START. All RMA communication calls issued on win during this epoch will have completed at the origin when the call returns.

MPI_WIN_COMPLETE enforces completion of preceding RMA calls at the origin, but not at the target. A put or accumulate call may not have completed at the target when it has completed at the origin.

Consider the sequence of calls in the example below.

Example 4.4

```
MPI_Win_start(group, flag, win);
MPI_Put(...,win);
MPI_Win_complete(win);
```

The call to MPI_WIN_COMPLETE does not return until the put call has completed at the origin; and the target window will be accessed by the put operation only after the call to MPI_WIN_START has matched a call to MPI_WIN_POST by the target process. This still leaves much choice to implementors. The call to MPI_WIN_START can block until the matching call to MPI_WIN_POST occurs at all target processes. One can also have implementations where the call to MPI_-WIN_START is nonblocking, but the call to MPI_PUT blocks until the matching call to MPI_WIN_POST occurred; or implementations where the first two calls are nonblocking, but the call to MPI_WIN_COMPLETE blocks until the call to MPI_-WIN_POST occurred; or even implementations where all three calls can complete before any target process called MPI_WIN_POST—the data put must be buffered, in this last case, so as to allow the put to complete at the origin ahead of its completion at the target. However, once the call to MPI_WIN_POST is issued, the sequence above must complete, without further dependencies.

MPI_WIN_POST(group, assert, win)

IN	group	group of origin processes (handle)
IN	assert	program assertion (integer)
IN	win	window object (handle)

```
int MPI_Win_post(MPI_Group group, int assert, MPI_Win win)
```

```
MPI_WIN_POST(GROUP, ASSERT, WIN, IERROR)
    INTEGER GROUP, ASSERT, WIN, IERROR
```

```
void MPI::Win::Post(const MPI::Group& group, int assert) const
```

MPI_WIN_POST starts an RMA exposure epoch for the local window associated with win. Only processes in group should access the window with RMA calls on win during this epoch. Each process in group must issue a matching call to MPI_WIN_-START. MPI_WIN_POST does not block.

MPI_WIN_WAIT(win)

| IN | win | window object (handle) |

```
int MPI_Win_wait(MPI_Win win)
```

```
MPI_WIN_WAIT(WIN, IERROR)
    INTEGER WIN, IERROR
```

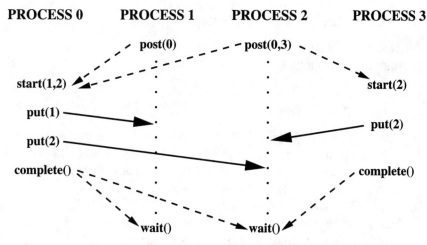

Figure 4.4
Active target communication. Dashed arrows represent synchronizations and solid arrows
represent data transfer.

```
void MPI::Win::Wait() const
```

Completes an RMA exposure epoch started by a call to MPI_WIN_POST on win.
This call matches calls to MPI_WIN_COMPLETE(win) issued by each of the origin
processes that were granted access to the window during this epoch. The call to
MPI_WIN_WAIT will block until all matching calls to MPI_WIN_COMPLETE have
occurred. This guarantees that all these origin processes have completed their RMA
accesses to the local window. When the call returns, all these RMA accesses will
have completed at the target window.

Figure 4.4 illustrates the use of these four functions. Process 0 puts data in the
windows of processes 1 and 2 and process 3 puts data in the window of process 2.
Each start call lists the ranks of the processes whose windows will be accessed;
each post call lists the ranks of the processes that access the local window. The
figure illustrates a possible timing for the events, assuming strong synchronization;
in a weak synchronization, the start, put or complete calls may occur ahead of the
matching post calls.

MPI_WIN_TEST(win, flag)

IN	win	window object (handle)
OUT	flag	success flag (logical)

```
int MPI_Win_test(MPI_Win win, int *flag)
```

```
MPI_WIN_TEST(WIN, FLAG, IERROR)
    INTEGER WIN, IERROR
    LOGICAL FLAG
```

```
bool MPI::Win::Test() const
```

This is the nonblocking version of MPI_WIN_WAIT. It returns flag = true if MPI_-WIN_WAIT would return, flag = false otherwise. The effect of return of MPI_WIN_-TEST with flag = true is the same as the effect of a return of MPI_WIN_WAIT. If flag = false is returned, then the call has no visible effect.

MPI_WIN_TEST should be invoked only where MPI_WIN_WAIT can be invoked.

Once the call has returned flag = true on a window object, it must not be invoked on that window until that window object is posted again.

The rules for matching of post and start calls and for matching complete and wait call can be derived from the rules for matching sends and receives, by considering the following (partial) model implementation. Assume that window win is associated with a "hidden" communicator wincomm, used for communication by the processes of win.

MPI_WIN_POST(group,0,win): initiate a nonblocking send with tag tag0 to each process in group, using wincomm. No need to wait for the completion of these sends.

MPI_WIN_START(group,0,win): initiate a nonblocking receive with tag tag0 from each process in group, using wincomm. An RMA access to a window in target process i is delayed until the receive from i is completed.

MPI_WIN_COMPLETE(win): initiate a nonblocking send with tag tag1 to each process in the group of the preceding start call. No need to wait for the completion of these sends.

MPI_WIN_WAIT(win): initiate a nonblocking receive with tag tag1 from each process in the group of the preceding post call. Wait for the completion of all receives.

No races can occur in a correct program: each of the sends matches a unique receive, and vice versa.

Rationale.   The design for general active target synchronization requires the user to provide complete information on the communication pattern, at each end of a communication link: each origin specifies a list of targets, and each target specifies a list of origins. This provides maximum flexibility (hence, efficiency) for the implementor: each synchronization can be initiated by either side, since each "knows" the identity of the other. This also provides maximum protection from possible races. On the other hand, the design requires more information than RMA needs, in general: in general, it is sufficient for the origin to know the rank of the target, but not vice versa. Users that want more "anonymous" communication will be required to use the fence or lock mechanisms. □

Advice to users. Assume a communication pattern that is represented by a directed graph $G = < V, E >$, with the vertices $V = \{0, \ldots, n-1\}$ and edges E defined by $ij \in E$ if origin process i accesses the window at target process j. Then each process i issues a call to MPI_WIN_POST($ingroup_i$, ...), followed by a call to MPI_WIN_START($outgroup_i$, ...), where $outgroup_i = \{j \ : \ ij \in E\}$ and $ingroup_i = \{j \ : \ ji \in E\}$. A call is a no-op, and can be skipped, if the group argument is empty. After the communications calls, each process that issued a start will issue a complete. Finally, each process that issued a post will issue a wait.

Note that each process may call MPI_WIN_POST or MPI_WIN_START with a group argument that has different members. □

4.4.3 Lock

The most general window synchronization mechanism is provided by the following two routines.

MPI_WIN_LOCK(lock_type, rank, assert, win)

IN	lock_type	either MPI_LOCK_EXCLUSIVE or MPI_LOCK_SHARED (state)
IN	rank	rank of locked window (nonnegative integer)
IN	assert	program assertion (integer)
IN	win	window object (handle)

```
int MPI_Win_lock(int lock_type, int rank, int assert, MPI_Win win)

MPI_WIN_LOCK(LOCK_TYPE, RANK, ASSERT, WIN, IERROR)
    INTEGER LOCK_TYPE, RANK, ASSERT, WIN, IERROR

void MPI::Win::Lock(int lock_type, int rank, int assert) const
```

Starts an RMA access epoch. Only the window at the process with rank rank can be accessed by RMA operations on win during that epoch.

MPI_WIN_UNLOCK(rank, win)

IN	rank	rank of window (nonnegative integer)
IN	win	window object (handle)

```
int MPI_Win_unlock(int rank, MPI_Win win)
```

```
MPI_WIN_UNLOCK(RANK, WIN, IERROR)
    INTEGER RANK, WIN, IERROR
```

```
void MPI::Win::Unlock(int rank) const
```

MPI_WIN_UNLOCK completes an RMA access epoch started by a call to MPI_-WIN_LOCK(...,win). RMA operations issued during this period will have completed both at the origin and at the target when the call returns.

Locks are used to protect accesses to the locked target window effected by RMA calls issued between the lock and unlock call, and to protect local load/store accesses to a locked local window executed between the lock and unlock call. Accesses that are protected by an exclusive lock will not be concurrent at the window site with other accesses to the same window that are lock protected. Accesses that are protected by a shared lock will not be concurrent at the window site with accesses protected by an exclusive lock to the same window.

It is erroneous to have a window locked and exposed (in an exposure epoch) concurrently. That is, a process may not call MPI_WIN_LOCK to lock a target window if the target process has called MPI_WIN_POST and has not yet called MPI_WIN_WAIT; it is erroneous to call MPI_WIN_POST while the local window is locked. Similarly, it is erroneous to call MPI_WIN_FENCE while a window is locked, or to lock a window while it is exposed as a result of a call to MPI_WIN_FENCE.

Rationale. An alternative is to require MPI to enforce mutual exclusion between exposure epochs and locking periods. But this would entail additional overheads when locks or active target synchronization do not interact in support of those rare interactions between the two mechanisms. The programming style that we encourage here is that a window object (set of windows) is used with only one synchronization mechanism at a time, with shifts from one mechanism to another being rare and involving global synchronization. □

Advice to users.   Users need to use explicit synchronization code in order to enforce mutual exclusion between locking periods and exposure epochs on a window.▯

Implementations may restrict the use of RMA communication that is synchronized by lock calls to windows in memory allocated by MPI_ALLOC_MEM (Section 2.4). Locks can be used portably only with such memory.

Rationale.   The implementation of passive target communication when memory is not shared requires an asynchronous agent. Such an agent can be implemented more easily, and can achieve better performance, if restricted to specially allocated memory. It can be avoided altogether if shared memory is used. It seems natural to impose restrictions that allow one to use shared memory for third-party communication in shared-memory machines.

The downside of this decision is that passive target communication cannot be used without taking advantage of nonstandard Fortran features: namely, the availability of C-like pointers; these are not supported by some Fortran compilers (g77 and Windows/NT compilers, at the time of writing). Also, passive target communication cannot be portably targeted to COMMON blocks, or other statically declared Fortran arrays. ▯

Consider the sequence of calls in the example below.

Example 4.5

```
MPI_Win_lock(MPI_LOCK_EXCLUSIVE, rank, assert, win)
MPI_Put(..., rank, ..., win)
MPI_Win_unlock(rank, win)
```

The call to MPI_WIN_UNLOCK will not return until the put transfer has completed at the origin and at the target. This still leaves much freedom to implementors. The call to MPI_WIN_LOCK may block until an exclusive lock on the window is acquired; or, the call MPI_WIN_LOCK may not block, while the call to MPI_PUT blocks until a lock is acquired; or, the first two calls may not block, while MPI_WIN_UNLOCK blocks until a lock is acquired—the update of the target window is then postponed until the call to MPI_WIN_UNLOCK occurs. However, if the call to MPI_WIN_LOCK is used to lock a local window, then the call must block until the lock is acquired, since the lock may protect local load/store accesses to the window issued after the lock call returns.

Example 4.6   Using lock to update a shared array.

In this example, one process (`rank = 0`) has an array of `size` entries. All processes in the communicator update values in this array, reading the next entry in the array.

This first program fragment shows how the process owning the array `Local` defines its window.

```
int     *Local;
MPI_Win win;
...
MPI_Alloc_mem( size * sizeof(int), MPI_INFO_NULL, &Local );
for (i=0; i<size; i++)
    Local[i] = 0;
MPI_Win_create( Local, size*sizeof(int), sizeof(int),
                MPI_INFO_NULL, comm, &win );
MPI_Win_free( &win );
MPI_Free_mem( Local );
```

Note that this process will wait in MPI_Win_free until all of the other processes have called MPI_Win_free. Also note the use of MPI_Alloc_mem to acquire the memory that the window uses; this is necessary for portability though some implementations may not require it.

The following code is executed by all of the other processes in communicator `comm`. Each process computes a value `myresult` and adds this into the array `Local` on process zero. The process then fetches a new value from the array `Local` and goes to the next iteration of the loop. Note that the value obtained with MPI_Get cannot be used until the end of the access epoch that was started with MPI_Win_lock. This code also uses MPI_LOCK_EXCLUSIVE to ensure that only one process is accessing `Local` (the memory on process 0 attached to the window) at a time. Finally, the code takes care not to execute an accumulate and a get to the same location in memory within the access epoch. This would be a conflicting access and is prohibited.

```
MPI_Win win;
int     i, myrank, curval;
...
MPI_Win_create( MPI_BOTTOM, 0, sizeof(int), MPI_INFO_NULL, comm,
                &win );
for (i=0; i<size; i++) {
```

```
    myresult = function_to_compute( i );
    MPI_Win_lock( MPI_LOCK_EXCLUSIVE, 0, 0, win );
    /* Add myresult into the ith location of Local on process 0 */
    MPI_Accumulate( &myresult, 1, MPI_INT,
                    0, i, 1, MPI_INT, MPI_SUM, win );
    /* Get Local[myrank] */
    if (i != myrank)
        MPI_Get( &curval, 1, MPI_INT, 0, myrank, 1, MPI_INT, win );
    MPI_Win_unlock( 0, win );
    /* After the unlock we can use the data that
       we have fetched with get */
    if (i != myrank)
        printf( "Current value of Local[%d] is %d\n",
                myrank, curval );
}
MPI_Win_free( &win );
```

4.4.4 Assertions

The assert argument in the calls MPI_WIN_POST, MPI_WIN_START, MPI_WIN-FENCE and MPI_WIN_LOCK is used to provide assertions on the context of the call that may be used to optimize performance. The assert argument does not change program semantics if it provides correct information about the program—it is erroneous to provide incorrect information. Users may always specify assert = 0 to indicate a general case to indicate that no guarantees are made.

Advice to users.   Many implementations may not take advantage of the information in assert; some of the information is relevant only for noncoherent, shared-memory machines. Users should consult their implementation manual to find which information is useful on each system. On the other hand, applications that provide correct assertions whenever applicable are portable and will take advantage of assertion specific optimizations, whenever available. □

Advice to implementors.   Implementations can always ignore the assert argument. Implementors should document which assert values are significant on their implementation. □

assert is the bit-vector OR of zero or more of the following integer constants: MPI_MODE_NOCHECK, MPI_MODE_NOSTORE, MPI_MODE_NOPUT,

MPI_MODE_NOPRECEDE and MPI_MODE_NOSUCCEED. The significant options are listed below, for each call.

Advice to users.   C/C++ users can use bit vector or (|) to combine these constants; Fortran 90 users can use the bit-vector IOR intrinsic. Fortran 77 users can use (nonportably) bit vector IOR on systems that support it. Alternatively, Fortran users can portably use integer addition to OR the constants (each constant should appear at most once in the addition!). □

MPI_WIN_START:

MPI_MODE_NOCHECK: the matching calls to MPI_WIN_POST have already completed on all target processes when the call to MPI_WIN_START is made. The nocheck option can be specified in a start call if and only if it is specified in each matching post call. This is similar to the optimization of "ready-send" that may save a handshake when the handshake is implicit in the code. (However, ready-send is matched by a regular receive, whereas both start and post must specify the nocheck option.)

MPI_WIN_POST:

MPI_MODE_NOCHECK: the matching calls to MPI_WIN_START have not yet occurred on any origin processes when the call to MPI_WIN_POST is made. The nocheck option can be specified by a post call if and only if it is specified by each matching start call.

MPI_MODE_NOSTORE: the local window was not updated by local stores (or local get or receive calls) since the last synchronization. This may avoid the need for cache synchronization at the post call.

MPI_MODE_NOPUT: the local window will not be updated by put or accumulate calls after the post call, until the next (wait) synchronization. This may avoid the need for cache synchronization at the wait call.

MPI_WIN_FENCE:

MPI_MODE_NOSTORE: the local window was not updated by local stores (or local get or receive calls) since the last synchronization.

MPI_MODE_NOPUT: the local window will not be updated by put or accumulate calls after the fence call, until the ensuing (fence) synchronization.

MPI_MODE_NOPRECEDE: the fence does not complete any sequence of locally issued RMA calls. If this assertion is given by any process in the window group, then it must be given by all processes in the group.

MPI_MODE_NOSUCCEED: the fence does not start any sequence of locally issued RMA calls. If the assertion is given by any process in the window group, then it must be given by all processes in the group.

MPI_WIN_LOCK:

MPI_MODE_NOCHECK: no other process holds, or will attempt to acquire a conflicting lock, while the caller holds the window lock. This is useful when mutual exclusion is achieved by other means, but the coherence operations that may be attached to the lock and unlock calls are still required.

The C++ names of the above-defined constants begin with MPI::MODE instead of MPI_MODE.

Advice to users.   Note that the nostore and noprecede flags provide information on what happened *before* the call; the noput and nosucceed flags provide information on what will happen *after* the call. □

4.4.5   Miscellaneous Clarifications

Once an RMA routine completes, it is safe to free any opaque objects passed as argument to that routine. For example, the datatype argument of a MPI_PUT call can be freed as soon as the call returns, even though the communication may not be complete.

As in message passing, datatypes must be committed before they can be used in RMA communication.

4.5   Examples

Example 4.7   The following example shows a generic loosely synchronous, iterative code that uses fence synchronization. The window at each process consists of array A, which contains the origin and target buffers of the put calls.

```
...
while(!converged(A)){
  update(A);
  MPI_Win_fence(MPI_MODE_NOPRECEDE, win);
```

```
for(i=0; i < toneighbors; i++)
  MPI_Put(&frombuf[i], 1, fromtype[i], toneighbor[i],
                     todisp[i], 1, totype[i], win);
  MPI_Win_fence((MPI_MODE_NOSTORE | MPI_MODE_NOSUCCEED), win);
  }
```

The same code could be written with get, rather than put. Note that, during the communication phase, each window is concurrently read (as origin buffer of puts) and written (as target buffer of puts). This is permissible, provided that there is no overlap between the target buffer of a put and another communication buffer.

Example 4.8   This is the same generic example, with more overlap of computation and communication. We assume that the update phase is broken in two subphases: the first, where the "boundary," which is involved in communication, is updated, and the second, where the "core," which neither use nor provide communicated data, is updated.

```
...
while(!converged(A)){
  update_boundary(A);
  MPI_Win_fence((MPI_MODE_NOPUT | MPI_MODE_NOPRECEDE), win);
  for(i=0; i < fromneighbors; i++)
    MPI_Get(&tobuf[i], 1, totype[i], fromneighbor[i],
                      fromdisp[i], 1, fromtype[i], win);
  update_core(A);
  MPI_Win_fence(MPI_MODE_NOSUCCEED, win);
  }
```

The get communication can be concurrent with the core update, since they do not access the same locations, and the local update of the origin buffer by the get call can be concurrent with the local update of the core by the update_core call. In order to get similar overlap with put communication we would need to use separate windows for the core and for the boundary. This is required because we do not allow local stores to be concurrent with puts on the same, or on overlapping, windows.

Example 4.9   This is the same code as in Example 4.7, rewritten using post-start-complete-wait.

```
...
while(!converged(A)){
```

```
  update(A);
  MPI_Win_post(fromgroup, 0, win);
  MPI_Win_start(togroup, 0, win);
  for(i=0; i < toneighbors; i++)
    MPI_Put(&frombuf[i], 1, fromtype[i], toneighbor[i],
                          todisp[i], 1, totype[i], win);
  MPI_Win_complete(win);
  MPI_Win_wait(win);
  }
```

Example 4.10   This is the same example, with split phases, as in Example 4.8.

```
...
while(!converged(A)){
  update_boundary(A);
  MPI_Win_post(togroup, MPI_MODE_NOPUT, win);
  MPI_Win_start(fromgroup, 0, win);
  for(i=0; i < fromneighbors; i++)
    MPI_Get(&tobuf[i], 1, totype[i], fromneighbor[i],
                      fromdisp[i], 1, fromtype[i], win);
  update_core(A);
  MPI_Win_complete(win);
  MPI_Win_wait(win);
  }
```

Example 4.11   A checkerboard, or double-buffer communication pattern, that allows more computation/communication overlap. Array A0 is updated using values of array A1, and vice versa. We assume that communication is symmetric: if process A gets data from process B, then process B gets data from process A. Window win$i$ consists of array Ai.

```
...
if (!converged(A0,A1))
  MPI_Win_post(neighbors, (MPI_MODE_NOCHECK | MPI_MODE_NOPUT),
              win0);
MPI_Barrier(comm0);
/* the barrier is needed because the start call inside the
loop uses the nocheck option */
while(!converged(A0, A1)){
```

```
/* communication on A0 and computation on A1 */
update2(A1, A0); /* local update of A1 that depends on
                    A0 (and A1) */
MPI_Win_start(neighbors, MPI_MODE_NOCHECK, win0);
for(i=0; i < neighbors; i++)
  MPI_Get(&tobuf0[i], 1, totype0[i], neighbor[i],
            fromdisp0[i], 1, fromtype0[i], win0);
update1(A1); /* local update of A1 that is
                concurrent with communication that updates A0 */
MPI_Win_post(neighbors, (MPI_MODE_NOCHECK | MPI_MODE_NOPUT),
            win1);
MPI_Win_complete(win0);
MPI_Win_wait(win0);

/* communication on A1 and computation on A0 */
update2(A0, A1); /* local update of A0 that depends on
                    A1 (and A0)*/
MPI_Win_start(neighbors, MPI_MODE_NOCHECK, win1);
for(i=0; i < neighbors; i++)
  MPI_Get(&tobuf1[i], 1, totype1[i], neighbor[i],
            fromdisp1[i], 1, fromtype1[i], win1);
update1(A0); /* local update of A0 that depends on A0 only,
                concurrent with communication that updates A1 */
if (!converged(A0,A1))
  MPI_Win_post(neighbors, (MPI_MODE_NOCHECK | MPI_MODE_NOPUT),
              win0);
MPI_Win_complete(win1);
MPI_Win_wait(win1);
}
```

A process posts the local window associated with win0 before it completes RMA accesses to the remote windows associated with win1. When the wait(win1) call returns, then all neighbors of the calling process have posted the windows associated with win0. Conversely, when the wait(win0) call returns, then all neighbors of the calling process have posted the windows associated with win1. Therefore, the nocheck option can be used with the calls to MPI_WIN_START.

Put calls can be used, instead of get calls, if the area of array A0 (resp. A1) used by the update(A1, A0) (resp. update(A0, A1)) call is disjoint from the area modified by the RMA communication. On some systems, a put call may be more efficient than a get call, as it requires information exchange only in one direction.

4.6 Error Handling

4.6.1 Error Handlers

Errors occurring during calls to MPI_WIN_CREATE(...,comm,...) cause the error handler currently associated with comm to be invoked. All other RMA calls have an input win argument. When an error occurs during such a call, the error handler currently associated with win is invoked.

The default error handler associated with win is MPI_ERRORS_ARE_FATAL. Users may change this default by explicitly associating a new error handler with win (see Section I-7.5.1).

4.6.2 Error Classes

The following new error classes are defined:

MPI_ERR_WIN	invalid win argument
MPI_ERR_BASE	invalid base argument
MPI_ERR_SIZE	invalid size argument
MPI_ERR_DISP	invalid disp argument
MPI_ERR_LOCKTYPE	invalid locktype argument
MPI_ERR_ASSERT	invalid assert argument
MPI_ERR_RMA_CONFLICT	conflicting accesses to window
MPI_ERR_RMA_SYNC	wrong synchronization of RMA calls

4.7 Semantics and Correctness

The description of one-sided operations has not yet addressed exactly what happens when, for example, several processes access the same target window. This section provides a more precise description of the semantics of RMA operations, and is particularly important for understanding exactly what happens (and what is allowed in MPI-1) with several processes accessing the same window, both with and without MPI-2 RMA operations.

The semantics of RMA operations are best understood by assuming that the system maintains a separate *public* copy of each window, in addition to the original location in process memory (the *private* window copy). There is only one instance of each variable in process memory, but a distinct *public* copy of the variable for

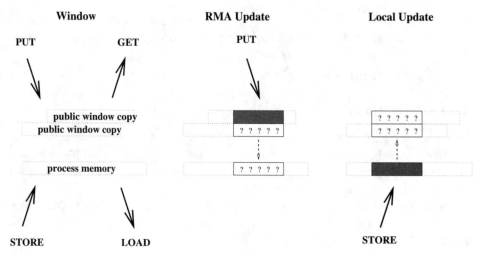

Figure 4.5
Schematic description of window

each window that contains it. A load accesses the instance in process memory (this includes MPI sends). A store accesses and updates the instance in process memory (this includes MPI receives), but the update may affect other public copies of the same locations. A get on a window accesses the public copy of that window. A put or accumulate on a window accesses and updates the public copy of that window, but the update may affect the private copy of the same locations in process memory, and public copies of other overlapping windows. This is illustrated in Figure 4.5.

The following rules specify the latest time at which an operation must complete at the origin or the target. The update performed by a get call in the origin process memory is visible when the get operation is complete at the origin (or earlier); the update performed by a put or accumulate call in the public copy of the target window is visible when the put or accumulate has completed at the target (or earlier). The rules also specify the latest time at which an update of one window copy becomes visible in another overlapping copy.

1. An RMA operation is completed at the origin by the ensuing call to MPI_WIN_COMPLETE, MPI_WIN_FENCE or MPI_WIN_UNLOCK that synchronizes this access at the origin.

2. If an RMA operation is completed at the origin by a call to MPI_WIN_FENCE then the operation is completed at the target by the matching call to MPI_WIN_FENCE by the target process.

3. If an RMA operation is completed at the origin by a call to MPI_WIN_-COMPLETE then the operation is completed at the target by the matching call to MPI_WIN_WAIT by the target process.

4. If an RMA operation is completed at the origin by a call to MPI_WIN_-UNLOCK then the operation is completed at the target by that same call to MPI_-WIN_UNLOCK.

5. An update of a location in a private window copy in process memory becomes visible in the public window copy at the latest when an ensuing call to MPI_WIN_-POST, MPI_WIN_FENCE, or MPI_WIN_UNLOCK is executed on that window by the window owner.

6. An update by a put or accumulate call to a public window copy becomes visible in the private copy in process memory at the latest when an ensuing call to MPI_WIN_WAIT, MPI_WIN_FENCE, or MPI_WIN_LOCK is executed on that window by the window owner.

The MPI_WIN_FENCE or MPI_WIN_WAIT call that completes the transfer from public copy to private copy (6) is the same call that completes the put or accumulate operation in the window copy (2, 3). If a put or accumulate access was synchronized with a lock, then the update of the public window copy is complete as soon as the updating process executed MPI_WIN_UNLOCK. On the other hand, the update of private copy in the process memory may be delayed until the target process executes a synchronization call on that window (6). Thus, updates to process memory can always be delayed until the process executes a suitable synchronization call. Updates to a public window copy can also be delayed until the window owner executes a synchronization call, if fences or post-start-complete-wait synchronization are used. Only when lock synchronization is used does it becomes necessary to update the public window copy, even if the window owner does not execute any related synchronization call.

The rules above also define, by implication, when an update to a public window copy becomes visible in another overlapping public window copy. Consider, for example, two overlapping windows, win1 and win2. A call to MPI_WIN_FENCE(0, win1) by the window owner makes visible in the process memory previous updates to window win1 by remote processes. A subsequent call to MPI_WIN_FENCE(0, win2) makes these updates visible in the public copy of win2.

A correct program must obey the following rules.

1. A location in a window must not be accessed locally once an update to that location has started, until the update becomes visible in the private window copy in process memory.

2. A location in a window must not be accessed as a target of an RMA operation once an update to that location has started, until the update becomes visible in the public window copy. There is one exception to this rule, in the case where the same variable is updated by two concurrent accumulates that use the same operation, with the same predefined datatype, on the same window.

3. A put or accumulate must not access a target window once a local update or a put or accumulate update to another (overlapping) target window have started on a location in the target window, until the update becomes visible in the public copy of the window. Conversely, a local update in process memory to a location in a window must not start once a put or accumulate update to that target window has started, until the put or accumulate update becomes visible in process memory. In both cases, the restriction applies to operations even if they access disjoint locations in the window.

A program is erroneous if it violates these rules.

Rationale.   The last constraint on correct RMA accesses may seem unduly restrictive, as it forbids concurrent accesses to nonoverlapping locations in a window. The reason for this constraint is that, on some architectures, explicit coherence restoring operations may be needed at synchronization points. A different operation may be needed for locations that were locally updated by stores and for locations that were remotely updated by put or accumulate operations. Without this constraint, the MPI library will have to track precisely which locations in a window were updated by a put or accumulate call. The additional overhead of maintaining such information is considered prohibitive. □

Advice to users.   A user can write correct programs by following the following rules:

fence: During each period between fence calls, each window is either updated by put or accumulate calls, or updated by local stores, but not both. Locations updated by put or accumulate calls should not be accessed during the same period (with the exception of concurrent updates to the same location by accumulate calls). Locations accessed by get calls should not be updated during the same period.

post-start-complete-wait: A window should not be updated locally while being posted, if it is being updated by put or accumulate calls. Locations updated by put or accumulate calls should not be accessed while the window is posted (with the exception of concurrent updates to the same location by accumulate calls). Locations accessed by get calls should not be updated while the window is posted.

With the post-start synchronization, the target process can tell the origin process that its window is now ready for RMA access; with the complete-wait synchronization, the origin process can tell the target process that it has finished its RMA accesses to the window.

lock: Updates to the window are protected by exclusive locks if they may conflict. Nonconflicting accesses (such as read-only accesses or accumulate accesses) are protected by shared locks, both for local accesses and for RMA accesses.

changing window or synchronization mode: One can change synchronization mode, or change the window used to access a location that belongs to two overlapping windows, when the process memory and the window copy are guaranteed to have the same values. This is true after a local call to MPI_WIN_FENCE, if RMA accesses to the window are synchronized with fences; after a local call to MPI_WIN_WAIT, if the accesses are synchronized with post-start-complete-wait; after the call at the origin (local or remote) to MPI_WIN_UNLOCK, if the accesses are synchronized with locks.

In addition, a process should not access the local buffer of a get operation until the operation is complete, and should not update the local buffer of a put or accumulate operation until that operation is complete. □

4.7.1   Atomicity

The outcome of concurrent accumulates to the same location, with the same operation and predefined datatype, is as if the accumulates were done at that location in some serial order. On the other hand, if two locations are both updated by two accumulate calls, then the updates may occur in reverse order at the two locations. Thus, there is no guarantee that the entire call to MPI_ACCUMULATE is executed atomically. The effect of this lack of atomicity is limited: the previous correctness conditions imply that a location updated by a call to MPI_ACCUMULATE cannot be accessed by load or an RMA call other than accumulate, until the MPI_ACCUMULATE call has completed (at the target). Different interleavings can lead to different results only to the extent that computer arithmetics are not truly associative or commutative.

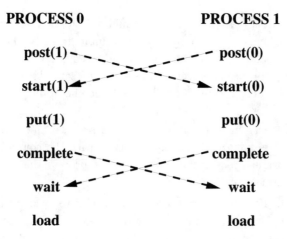

Figure 4.6
Symmetric communication

4.7.2 Progress

One-sided communication has the same progress requirements as point-to-point communication: once a communication is enabled, then it is guaranteed to complete. RMA calls must have local semantics, except when required for synchronization with other RMA calls.

There is some fuzziness in the definition of the time when a RMA communication becomes enabled. This fuzziness provides to the implementor more flexibility than with point-to-point communication. Access to a target window becomes enabled once the corresponding synchronization (such as MPI_WIN_FENCE or MPI_WIN_POST) has executed. On the origin process, an RMA communication may become enabled as soon as the corresponding put, get or accumulate call has executed, or as late as when the ensuing synchronization call is issued. Once the communication is enabled both at the origin and at the target, the communication must complete.

Consider the code fragment in Example 4.4. Some of the calls may block if the target window is not posted. However, if the target window is posted, then the code fragment must complete. The data transfer may start as soon as the put call occurs, but may be delayed until the ensuing complete call occurs.

Consider the code fragment in Example 4.5. Some of the calls may block if another process holds a conflicting lock. However, if no conflicting lock is held, then the code fragment must complete.

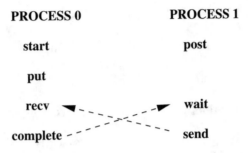

Figure 4.7
Deadlock situation

Consider the code illustrated in Figure 4.6. Each process updates the window of the other process using a put operation, then accesses its own window. The post calls are nonblocking, and should complete. Once the post calls occur, RMA access to the windows is enabled, so that each process should complete the sequence of calls start-put-complete. Once these are done, the wait calls should complete at both processes. Thus, this communication should not deadlock, irrespective of the amount of data transferred.

Assume, in the last example, that the order of the post and start calls is reversed, at each process. Then, the code may deadlock, as each process may block on the start call, waiting for the matching post to occur. Similarly, the program will deadlock, if the order of the complete and wait calls is reversed, at each process.

The following two examples illustrate the fact that the synchronization between complete and wait is not symmetric: the wait call blocks until the complete executes, but not vice versa. Consider the code illustrated in Figure 4.7. This code will deadlock: the wait of process 1 blocks until process 0 calls complete, and the receive of process 0 blocks until process 1 calls send. Consider, on the other hand, the code illustrated in Figure 4.8. This code will not deadlock. Once process 1 calls post, then the sequence start, put, complete on process 0 can proceed to completion. Process 0 will reach the send call, allowing the receive call of process 1 to complete.

Rationale.   MPI implementations must guarantee that a process makes progress on all enabled communications it participates in, while blocked on an MPI call. This is true for send-receive communication and applies to RMA communication as well. Thus, in the example in Figure 4.8, the put and complete calls of process 0 should complete while process 1 is blocked on the receive call. This may require the

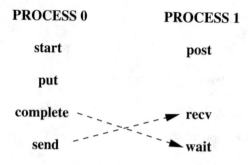

Figure 4.8
No deadlock

involvement of process 1, for example, to transfer the data put, while it is blocked on the receive call.

A similar issue is whether such progress must occur while a process is busy computing, or blocked in a non-MPI call. Suppose that in the last example the send-receive pair is replaced by a write-to-socket/read-from-socket pair. Then MPI does not specify whether deadlock is avoided. Suppose that the blocking receive of process 1 is replaced by a very long compute loop. Then, according to one interpretation of the MPI standard, process 0 must return from the complete call after a bounded delay, even if process 1 does not reach any MPI call in this period of time. According to another interpretation, the complete call may block until process 1 reaches the wait call, or reaches another MPI call. The qualitative behavior is the same, under both interpretations, unless a process is caught in an infinite compute loop, in which case the difference may not matter. However, the quantitative expectations are different. Different MPI implementations reflect these different interpretations. While this ambiguity is unfortunate, it does not seem to affect many real codes. The MPI Forum decided not to decide which interpretation of the standard is the correct one, since the issue is very contentious, and a decision would have much impact on implementors but less impact on users. ☐

4.7.3 Registers and Compiler Optimizations

Advice to users.   All the material in this section is advice to users. ☐

A coherence problem exists between variables kept in registers and the memory value of these variables. An RMA call may access a variable in memory (or cache), while the up-to-date value of this variable is in a register. A get will not return the latest variable value, and a put may be overwritten when the register is stored back in memory.

The problem is illustrated by the following code:

Source of Process 1	**Source of Process 2**	**Executed in Process 2**
`bbbb = 777`	`buff = 999`	`reg_A:=999`
`call MPI_WIN_FENCE`	`call MPI_WIN_FENCE`	
`call MPI_PUT(bbbb`		`stop appl. thread`
`into buff of process 2)`		`buff:=777 in PUT`
		`    handler`
		`continue appl. thread`
`call MPI_WIN_FENCE`	`call MPI_WIN_FENCE`	
	`ccc = buff`	`ccc:=reg_A`

In this example, variable `buff` is allocated in the register `reg_A` and therefore `ccc` will have the old value of `buff` and not the new value 777.

This problem, which also afflicts in some cases send/receive communication, is discussed more at length in Section 8.2.2.

MPI implementations will avoid this problem for standard-conforming C programs. Many Fortran compilers will avoid this problem, without disabling compiler optimizations. However, in order to avoid register-coherence problems in a completely portable manner, users should restrict their use of RMA windows to variables stored in COMMON blocks, or to variables that were declared VOLATILE (while VOLATILE is not a standard Fortran declaration, it is supported by many Fortran compilers). Details and an additional solution are discussed in Section 8.2.2. See also Section 8.2.2 for additional Fortran problems.

5 Intercommunicator Collective Operations

In Chapter 4 of Book 1, collective operations were described only for intracommunicators. Indeed, the MPI-1 standard defined collective operations only for intracommunicators. However, most MPI collective operations can be generalized to intercommunicators. This generalization has several uses: for example, in pipelined algorithms, one often needs to move data from one group of processes to another group. The two groups may have different sizes, and data may need to reorganized during the transfer. This type of communication is expressed naturally as a collective operation on an intercommunicator. The extension of collective operations to intercommunicators was done in MPI-2.

5.1 Introduction

We can view most MPI intracommunicator collective operations as fitting one of the following three categories:

All-to-all: All processes contribute data, and all processes receive data.

- MPI_Allgather, MPI_Allgatherv
- MPI_Alltoall, MPI_Alltoallv, MPI_Alltoallw
- MPI_Allreduce, MPI_Reduce_scatter

Rooted: Either all processes contribute data and one process receives data (all-to-one) or one process contributes data and all processes receive data (one-to-all).

- MPI_Gather, MPI_Gatherv
- MPI_Reduce
- MPI_Bcast
- MPI_Scatter, MPI_Scatterv

Other: Collective operations that do not fit into one of the above categories.

- MPI_Scan, MPI_Exscan
- MPI_Barrier

The MPI_Barrier operation does not fit into this classification since no data is being moved. The data movement pattern of MPI_Scan does not fit this taxonomy.

An intercommunicator has two groups, A and B. When collective communications are extended to intracommunicators, then all data sent by processes in one group

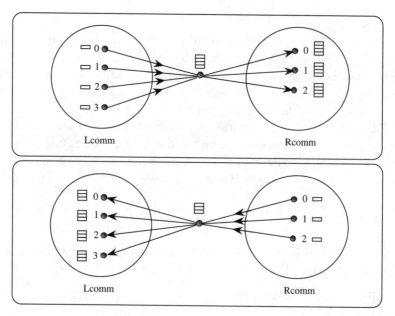

Figure 5.1
Intercommunicator allgather.

are received by processes in the other group. Communication is **duplex** for all-to-all operations: data sent by processes in group A is received by processes in group B, and data sent by processes in group B is received by processes in group A. This is illustrated in Figure 5.1, for MPI_ALLGATHER (the figure indicates an implementation where data is gathered at one process, next broadcast to all processes in the other group; this is for illustrative purposes only, as other implementations are possible).

Communication is **simplex** for rooted operations. One group (either A or B) contains the root process. Data moves from the root to all processes in the other group (one-to-all) or vice-versa (all-to-one). This is illustrated in Figure 5.2 for MPI_SCATTER.

When rooted operations are executed on intracommunicators, the root is specified by having all processes pass as argument the root rank. This does not work for intercommunicators, as one needs to specify which of the two groups contains the root. In this case, for the group containing the root process (the **root group**), all processes in the group must call the routine using a special argument for the root. The root process uses the special root value MPI_ROOT (MPI::ROOT in C++); all

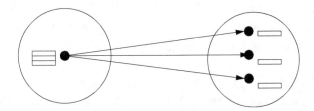

Figure 5.2
Intercommunicator scatter.

other processes in the root group use MPI_PROC_NULL. All processes in the other group (the **leaf group**) must call the collective routine and provide the rank of the root.

Note that the "in place" option for intracommunicators does not apply to intercommunicators since in the intercommunicator case there is no communication from a process to itself.

Rationale.   Rooted operations are unidirectional by nature, and there is a clear way of specifying direction. The calling scheme ensures that the root identity is passed as an argument by all processes that communicate with the root.

All-to-all, nonrooted operations will often occur as part of an exchange, where it makes sense to communicate in both directions at once. □

Advice to users.   When a rooted collective operation executes on an intercommunicator, then all processes in the root group, with the exclusion of the root process, neither send nor receive data. Nevertheless, all these processes must participate in the collective call. The implementation may actually involve some or all of these processes in the collective communication. □

5.2   Collective Operations

We describe now the semantics of collective operations on intercommunicators. We do not repeat the bindings for these functions, as these are identical to the bindings presented in Chapter I-4. Note, however, that the functions should be passed a comm argument that represents an intercommunicator. In C++, they should be invoked as methods on objects of type MPI::Intercomm.

MPI_BARRIER(comm)
All processes in group A may exit the barrier when all of the processes in group B
have entered the barrier, and vice-versa.

MPI_BCAST(buffer, count, datatype, root, comm)
The root process passes the value MPI_ROOT in root. All other processes in the
root group pass the value MPI_PROC_NULL in root. All processes in the leaf group
pass the same value in argument root, which is the rank of the root process in the
root group. Data is broadcast from the root to all processes in the leaf group. The
receive buffer arguments of the processes in the leaf group must be consistent with
the send buffer argument of the root process. The arguments buffer and count are
not significant at the processes of the root group, except at the root process.

MPI_GATHER(sendbuf, sendcount, sendtype, recvbuf, recvcount, recvtype, root,
comm)
MPI_GATHERV(sendbuf, sendcount, sendtype, recvbuf, recvcounts, displs, recvtype,
root, comm)
The root process passes the value MPI_ROOT in root. All other processes in the root
group pass the value MPI_PROC_NULL in root. All processes in the leaf group pass
the same value in argument root, which is the rank of the root process in the root
group. Data is gathered from all processes in the leaf group to the root process. The
send buffer arguments of the processes in the leaf group must be consistent with the
receive buffer argument of the root process. The sendbuf, sendcount and sendtype
arguments are significant only at processes of the leaf group. The recvbuf, recvcount,
and recvtype (recvbuf, recvcounts, displs and recvtype) arguments are significant only
at the root process.

MPI_SCATTER(sendbuf, sendcount, sendtype, recvbuf, recvcount, recvtype, root,
comm)
MPI_SCATTERV(sendbuf, sendcounts, displs, sendtype, recvbuf, recvcount, recvtype,
root, comm)
The root process passes the value MPI_ROOT in root. All other processes in the root
group pass the value MPI_PROC_NULL in root. All processes in the leaf group pass
the same value in argument root, which is the rank of the root process in the root
group. Data is scattered from the root process to all processes in the leaf group.
The receive buffer arguments of the processes in the leaf group must be consistent
with the send buffer argument of the root process. The sendbuf, sendcount and

sendtype (sendbuf, sendcounts, displs and sendtype) arguments are significant only at the root process. The recvbuf, recvcount, and recvtype arguments are significant only at the processes of the leaf group.

MPI_ALLGATHER(sendbuf, sendcount, sendtype, recvbuf, recvcount, recvtype, comm)
MPI_ALLGATHERV(sendbuf, sendcount, sendtype, recvbuf, recvcounts, displs, recvtype, comm)

Each process in group A contributes a data item; these items are concatenated and the result is stored at each process in group B. Conversely the concatenation of the contributions of the processes in group B is stored at each process in group A. The send buffer arguments in group A must be consistent with the receive buffer arguments in group B, and vice versa.

Advice to users. The communication pattern of MPI_ALLGATHER executed on an intercommunication domain need not be symmetric. The number of items sent by processes in group A (as specified by the arguments sendcount, sendtype in group A and the arguments recvcount, recvtype in group B), need not equal the number of items sent by processes in group B (as specified by the arguments sendcount, sendtype in group B and the arguments recvcount, recvtype in group A). In particular, one can move data in only one direction by specifying sendcount = 0 for the communication in the reverse direction. ☐

MPI_ALLTOALL(sendbuf, sendcount, sendtype, recvbuf, recvcount, recvtype, comm)
MPI_ALLTOALLV(sendbuf, sendcounts, sdispls, sendtype, recvbuf, recvcounts, rdispls, recvtype, comm)
MPI_ALLTOALLW(sendbuf, sendcounts, sdispls, sendtypes, recvbuf, recvcounts, rdispls, recvtypes, comm)

The outcome is as if each process in group A sends a message to each process in group B, and vice versa. The j-th send buffer of process i in group A should be consistent with the i-th receive buffer of process j in group B, and vice versa.

Advice to users. When all-to-all is executed on an intercommunication domain, then the number of data items sent from processes in group A to processes in group B need not equal the number of items sent in the reverse direction. In particular, one can have unidirectional communication by specifying sendcount = 0 in the reverse direction. ☐

MPI_REDUCE(sendbuf, recvbuf, count, datatype, op, root, comm)

The root process passes the value MPI_ROOT in root. All other processes in the root group pass the value MPI_PROC_NULL in root. All processes in the leaf group pass the same value in argument root, which is the rank of the root process in the root group. The result of the reduction of the data provided by processes in the leaf group is stored at the root process. The argument sendbuf is not significant at processes in the root group; the argument recvbuf is significant only at the root process.

MPI_ALLREDUCE(sendbuf, recvbuf, count, datatype, op, comm)

The result of the reduction of the data provided by processes in group A is stored at each process in group B, and vice versa. Both groups should provide the same count value.

MPI_REDUCE_SCATTER(sendbuf, recvbuf, recvcounts, datatype, op, comm)

The result of the reduction of the data provided by processes in group A is scattered among processes in group B, and vice versa. Within each group, all processes provide the same recvcounts argument, and the sum of the recvcounts entries should be the same for the two groups.

Rationale.   The last restriction is needed so that the length of the send buffer can be determined by the sum of the local recvcounts entries. Otherwise, a communication is needed to figure out how many elements are reduced. □

MPI_SCAN(sendbuf, recvbuf, count, datatype, op, comm)

This operation is illegal for intercommunicators.

MPI_EXSCAN(sendbuf, recvbuf, count, datatype, op, comm)

This operation is illegal for intercommunicators.

6 External Interfaces

Although MPI-2 provides extensions to MPI-1 in critical areas (e.g., process management, one-sided communication, and I/O), true flexibility comes from being able to extend MPI in as yet unforeseen ways. The functions described here provide this facility—to extend MPI within the MPI framework. These extensions fall into three areas: creation of new nonblocking operations (or new libraries using nonblocking operations), debugger and profiler support, and layering of significant parts of MPI-2 on top of the rest of MPI. This chapter is primarily targeted towards "low-level" developers, and, as such, can be safely skipped by all but the most sophisticated users of MPI.

6.1 Introduction

This chapter begins with calls used to create **generalized requests**. The objective of this MPI-2 addition is to allow users of MPI to be able to create new nonblocking operations whose interface is similar to that of MPI nonblocking operations. Generalized requests can be used to layer new functionality on top of MPI. Next, Section 6.3 deals with setting the information found in status. This is needed for generalized requests as well as layering.

Section 6.4 allows users to associate names with communicators, windows, and datatypes. This will allow debuggers and profilers to identify communicators, windows, and datatypes with more useful labels; common objects are given useful default names. Section 6.5 allows users to add error codes, classes, and strings to MPI. With users being able to layer functionality on top of MPI, it is desirable for them to use the same error mechanisms found in MPI. Keep in mind, however, that the default error behavior (except for I/O) is errors are fatal.

Section 6.6 deals with decoding datatypes. The opaque datatype object has found a number of uses outside MPI, and the ability to decode datatypes is a key feature required for layering. Furthermore, a number of tools wish to display internal information about datatypes.

Section 6.7 has information on attribute caching on datatypes and windows, similar to the attribute caching on communicators that was introduced in Section I-5.6. Permitting caching on "heavy weight" objects facilitates all three areas of extension.

6.2   Generalized Requests

The goal of this MPI-2 extension is to allow users to define new nonblocking operations. Such outstanding nonblocking operations are represented by (generalized) requests. A fundamental property of a nonblocking operation is that progress toward its completion occurs asynchronously, that is, concurrently with normal program execution. Typically, this requires execution of code concurrently with the execution of the user code, for example, in a separate thread or in a signal handler. Operating systems provide a variety of mechanisms in support of concurrent execution. MPI does not attempt to standardize or replace these mechanisms: it is assumed programmers who wish to define new asynchronous operations will use the mechanisms provided by the underlying operating system. Thus, the calls in this section only provide a means for defining the effect of MPI calls such as MPI_WAIT or MPI_CANCEL when they apply to generalized requests, and for signaling to MPI the completion of a generalized operation.

Rationale.   It is tempting to also define an MPI standard mechanism for achieving concurrent execution of user-defined nonblocking operations. However, it is very difficult to define such a mechanism without consideration of the specific mechanisms used in the operating system. The Forum felt that concurrency mechanisms are a proper part of the underlying operating system and should not be standardized by MPI; the MPI standard should only deal with the interaction of such mechanisms with MPI. □

For a regular request, the operation associated with the request is performed by the MPI implementation, and the operation completes without intervention by the application. For a generalized request, the operation associated with the request is performed by the application; therefore, the application must notify MPI when the operation completes. This is done by making a call to MPI_GREQUEST_- COMPLETE. MPI maintains the "completion" status of generalized requests. Any other request state has to be maintained by the user.

A new generalized request is started with

MPI_GREQUEST_START(query_fn, free_fn, cancel_fn, extra_state, request)

IN	query_fn	callback function invoked when request status is queried (function)
IN	free_fn	callback function invoked when request is freed (function)

IN	cancel_fn	callback function invoked when request is cancelled (function)
IN	extra_state	extra state
OUT	request	generalized request (handle)

```
int MPI_Grequest_start(MPI_Grequest_query_function *query_fn,
    MPI_Grequest_free_function *free_fn, MPI_Grequest_cancel_function
    *cancel_fn, void *extra_state, MPI_Request *request)
```

```
MPI_GREQUEST_START(QUERY_FN, FREE_FN, CANCEL_FN, EXTRA_STATE, REQUEST,
    IERROR)
    INTEGER REQUEST, IERROR
    EXTERNAL QUERY_FN, FREE_FN, CANCEL_FN
    INTEGER (KIND=MPI_ADDRESS_KIND) EXTRA_STATE
```

```
static MPI::Grequest
    MPI::Grequest::Start(const MPI::Grequest::Query_function
    query_fn, const MPI::Grequest::Free_function free_fn,
    const MPI::Grequest::Cancel_function cancel_fn,
    void* extra_state)
```

Advice to users. Note that a generalized request belongs, in C++, to the class MPI::Grequest, which is a derived class of MPI::Request. It is of the same type as regular requests in C and Fortran. □

The call starts a generalized request and returns a handle to it in request.

The syntax and meaning of the callback functions are listed below. All callback functions are passed the extra_state argument that was associated with the request by the starting call MPI_GREQUEST_START. This can be used to maintain user-defined state for the request. In C, the query function is

```
typedef int MPI_Grequest_query_function(void *extra_state,
    MPI_Status *status);
```

in Fortran

```
SUBROUTINE GREQUEST_QUERY_FUNCTION(EXTRA_STATE, STATUS, IERROR)
    INTEGER STATUS(MPI_STATUS_SIZE), IERROR
    INTEGER(KIND=MPI_ADDRESS_KIND) EXTRA_STATE
```

and in C++

```
typedef int MPI::Grequest::Query_function(void* extra_state,
    MPI::Status& status);
```

The query_fn function computes the status that should be returned for the generalized request. The status also includes information about successful/unsuccessful cancellation of the request (result to be returned by MPI_TEST_CANCELLED).

The query_fn callback is invoked by the MPI_{WAIT|TEST}{ANY|SOME|ALL} call that completed the generalized request associated with this callback. The callback function is also invoked by calls to MPI_REQUEST_GET_STATUS, if the request is complete when the call occurs. In both cases, the callback is passed a reference to the corresponding status variable passed by the user to the MPI call; the status set by the callback function is returned by the MPI call. Even if the user provided MPI_STATUS_IGNORE or MPI_STATUSES_IGNORE to the MPI function that causes query_fn to be called, MPI will pass a valid status object to query_fn, but ignore it upon return of the callback function. Note that query_fn is invoked only after MPI_GREQUEST_COMPLETE is called on the request; it may be invoked several times for the same generalized request, for example, if the user calls MPI_REQUEST_GET_STATUS several times for this request. Note also that a call to MPI_{WAIT|TEST}{SOME|ALL} may cause multiple invocations of query_fn callback functions, one for each generalized request that is completed by the MPI call. The order of these invocations is not specified by MPI.

In C, the free function is

```
typedef int MPI_Grequest_free_function(void *extra_state);
```

and in Fortran

```
SUBROUTINE GREQUEST_FREE_FUNCTION(EXTRA_STATE, IERROR)
    INTEGER IERROR
    INTEGER(KIND=MPI_ADDRESS_KIND) EXTRA_STATE
```

and in C++

```
typedef int MPI::Grequest::Free_function(void* extra_state);
```

The free_fn function is invoked to clean up user-allocated resources when the generalized request is freed.

The free_fn callback is invoked by the MPI_{WAIT|TEST}{ANY|SOME|ALL} call that completed the generalized request associated with this callback. free_fn is invoked after the call to query_fn for the same request. However, if the MPI call completed multiple generalized requests, the order in which free_fn callback functions are invoked is not specified by MPI.

The free_fn callback is also invoked for generalized requests that are freed by a call to MPI_REQUEST_FREE (no call to MPI_{WAIT|TEST}{_ANY|SOME|ALL} will occur for such a request). In this case, the callback function will be called either in the MPI call MPI_REQUEST_FREE(request), or in the MPI call MPI_GREQUEST_COMPLETE(request), whichever happens last. That is, in this case the actual freeing code is executed as soon as both calls MPI_REQUEST_FREE and MPI_GREQUEST_COMPLETE have occurred. The request is not deallocated until after free_fn completes. Note that free_fn will be invoked only once per request by a correct program.

Advice to users.   Calling MPI_REQUEST_FREE(request) will cause the request handle to be set to MPI_REQUEST_NULL. This handle to the generalized request is no longer valid. However, other user copies of this handle are valid until after free_fn completes since MPI does not deallocate the object until then. Since free_fn is not called until after MPI_GREQUEST_COMPLETE, the user copy of the handle can be used to make this call. Users should note that MPI will deallocate the object after free_fn executes. At this point, user copies of the request handle no longer point to a valid request. MPI will not set user copies to MPI_REQUEST_NULL in this case, so it is up to the user to avoid accessing this stale handle. This is a special case where MPI defers deallocating the object until a later time that is known by the user. □

In C, the cancel function is

```
typedef int MPI_Grequest_cancel_function(void *extra_state, int
    complete);
```

in Fortran

```
SUBROUTINE GREQUEST_CANCEL_FUNCTION(EXTRA_STATE, COMPLETE, IERROR)
    INTEGER IERROR
    INTEGER(KIND=MPI_ADDRESS_KIND) EXTRA_STATE
    LOGICAL COMPLETE
```

and in C++

```
typedef int MPI::Grequest::Cancel_function(void* extra_state,
    bool complete);
```

The cancel_fn function is invoked to start the cancellation of a generalized request. It is called by MPI_REQUEST_CANCEL(request). MPI passes to the callback function complete=true if MPI_GREQUEST_COMPLETE was already called on the request, and complete=false otherwise.

All callback functions return an error code. The code is passed back to the MPI function that invoked the callback function, and dealt with as appropriate for the error code. For example, if error codes are returned then the error code returned by the callback function will be returned by the MPI function that invoked the callback function. In the case of MPI_{WAIT|TEST}_ANY call that invokes both query_fn and free_fn, the MPI call will return the error code returned by the last callback, namely free_fn. If one or more of the requests in a call to MPI_{WAIT|TEST}{SOME|ALL} failed, then the MPI call will return MPI_ERR_IN_STATUS. In such a case, if the MPI call was passed an array of statuses, then MPI will return in each of the statuses that correspond to a completed generalized request the error code returned by the corresponding invocation of its free_fn callback function. However, if the MPI function was passed MPI_STATUSES_IGNORE, then the individual error codes returned by each callback functions will be lost.

Advice to users.   query_fn must *not* set the error field of status since query_fn may be called by MPI_WAIT or MPI_TEST, in which case the error field of status should not change. The MPI library knows the "context" in which query_fn is invoked and can decide correctly when to put in the error field of status the returned error code. ▯

MPI_GREQUEST_COMPLETE(request)

    INOUT   request   generalized request (handle)

```
int MPI_Grequest_complete(MPI_Request request)
```

```
MPI_GREQUEST_COMPLETE(REQUEST, IERROR)
    INTEGER REQUEST, IERROR
```

```
void MPI::Grequest::Complete()
```

The call informs MPI that the operations represented by the generalized request request are complete. (See definitions in Section 1.4.) A call to MPI_WAIT(request, status) will return and a call to MPI_TEST(request, flag, status) will return flag=true only after a call to MPI_GREQUEST_COMPLETE has declared that these operations are complete.

However, new nonblocking operations should be defined so that the general MPI imposes no restrictions on the code executed by the callback functions. semantic rules about MPI calls such as MPI_TEST, MPI_REQUEST_FREE, or MPI_CANCEL still hold. For example, all these calls are supposed to be local and nonblocking. Therefore, the callback functions query_fn, free_fn, or cancel_fn should invoke blocking MPI communication calls only if the context is such that these calls are guaranteed to return in finite time. Once MPI_CANCEL is invoked, the cancelled operation should complete in finite time, irrespective of the state of other processes (the operation has acquired "local" semantics). It should either succeed, or fail without side-effects. The user should guarantee these same properties for newly defined operations.

Advice to implementors.   A call to MPI_GREQUEST_COMPLETE may unblock a blocked user process/thread. The MPI library should ensure that the blocked user computation will resume. □

6.2.1 Examples

Example 6.1   This example shows the code for a user-defined reduce operation on an int using a binary tree: each nonroot node receives two messages, sums them, and sends them up. It is assumed that no status is returned and that the operation cannot be cancelled.

```
typedef struct {
    MPI_Comm comm;
    int tag;
    int root;
    int valin;
    int *valout;
    MPI_Request request;
    } ARGS;


int myreduce(MPI_Comm comm, int tag, int root,
            int valin, int *valout, MPI_Request *request)
{
    ARGS *args;
    pthread_t thread;
```

```
    /* start request */
    MPI_Grequest_start(query_fn, free_fn, cancel_fn, NULL, request);

    args = (ARGS*)malloc(sizeof(ARGS));
    args->comm = comm;
    args->tag = tag;
    args->root = root;
    args->valin = valin;
    args->valout = valout;
    args->request = *request;

    /* spawn thread to handle request */
    /* The availability of the pthread_create call is
       system dependent */
    pthread_create(&thread, NULL, reduce_thread, args);

    return MPI_SUCCESS;
}


/* thread code */
void reduce_thread(void *ptr)
{
    int lchild, rchild, parent, lval, rval, val;
    MPI_Request req[2];
    ARGS *args;

    args = (ARGS*)ptr;

    /* compute left,right child and parent in tree; set
       to MPI_PROC_NULL if does not exist  */
    /* code not shown */
    ...

    MPI_Irecv(&lval, 1, MPI_INT, lchild, args->tag, args->comm,
              &req[0]);
    MPI_Irecv(&rval, 1, MPI_INT, rchild, args->tag, args->comm,
              &req[1]);
```

```
    MPI_Waitall(2, req, MPI_STATUSES_IGNORE);
    val = lval + args->valin + rval;
    MPI_Send( &val, 1, MPI_INT, parent, args->tag, args->comm );
    if (parent == MPI_PROC_NULL) *(args->valout) = val;
    MPI_Grequest_complete((args->request));
    free(ptr);
    return;
}


int query_fn(void *extra_state, MPI_Status *status)
{
    /* always send just one int */
    MPI_Status_set_elements(status, MPI_INT, 1);
    /* can never cancel so always true */
    MPI_Status_set_cancelled(status, 0);
    /* choose not to return a value for this */
    status->MPI_SOURCE = MPI_UNDEFINED;
    /* tag has not meaning for this generalized request */
    status->MPI_TAG = MPI_UNDEFINED;
    /* this generalized request never fails */
    return MPI_SUCCESS;
}



int free_fn(void *extra_state)
{
    /* this generalized request does not need to do any freeing */
    /* as a result it never fails here */
    return MPI_SUCCESS;
}



int cancel_fn(void *extra_state, int complete)
{
    /* This generalized request does not support cancelling.
       Abort if not already done.  If done then treat as if
       cancel failed. */
    if (!complete) {
```

```
        fprintf(stderr,
          "Cannot cancel generalized request - aborting program\n");
     MPI_Abort(MPI_COMM_WORLD, 99);
     }
     return MPI_SUCCESS;
}
```

6.3   Associating Information with Status

In MPI-1, requests were associated with point-to-point-operations. In MPI-2, requests may also be associated with I/O or, through the generalized request mechanism, with user-defined operations. All of these requests can be given to MPI_{TEST|WAIT}{ANY|SOME|ALL}, which return a status object with information about the request. A status contains five values, of which three are accessible as fields, and two, "count" and "cancelled", are opaque. MPI-1 provides accessor functions to retrieve these opaque fields. In order for MPI-2 generalized requests to work, the query_fn function introduced in the previous section must be able to set the other two. The two routines in this section provide this functionality. Values not explicitly set are undefined.

MPI_STATUS_SET_ELEMENTS(status, datatype, count)

INOUT	status	status to associate count with (Status)
IN	datatype	datatype associated with count (handle)
IN	count	number of elements to associate with status (integer)

```
int MPI_Status_set_elements(MPI_Status *status, MPI_Datatype
    datatype, int count)
```

```
MPI_STATUS_SET_ELEMENTS(STATUS, DATATYPE, COUNT, IERROR)
    INTEGER STATUS(MPI_STATUS_SIZE), DATATYPE, COUNT, IERROR
```

```
void MPI::Status::Set_elements(const MPI::Datatype& datatype,
    int count)
```

This call modifies the opaque part of status so that a call to MPI_GET_ELEMENTS will return count. MPI_GET_COUNT will return a compatible value.

Rationale.   The number of elements is set instead of the count of datatypes because the former can deal with nonintegral number of datatypes. ☐

A subsequent call to MPI_GET_COUNT(status, datatype, count) or to MPI_GET_-ELEMENTS(status, datatype, count) must use a datatype argument that has the same type signature as the datatype argument that was used in the call to MPI_-STATUS_SET_ELEMENTS.

Rationale.   This is similar to the restriction that holds when when count is set by a receive operation: in that case, the calls to MPI_GET_COUNT and MPI_GET_-ELEMENTS must use a datatype with the same signature as the datatype used in the receive call. ☐

MPI_STATUS_SET_CANCELLED(status, flag)

| INOUT | status | status to associate cancel flag with (Status) |
| IN | flag | if true indicates request was cancelled (logical) |

```
int MPI_Status_set_cancelled(MPI_Status *status, int flag)
```

```
MPI_STATUS_SET_CANCELLED(STATUS, FLAG, IERROR)
    INTEGER STATUS(MPI_STATUS_SIZE), IERROR
    LOGICAL FLAG
```

```
void MPI::Status::Set_cancelled(bool flag)
```

If flag is set to true then a subsequent call to MPI_TEST_CANCELLED(status, flag) will also return flag = true, otherwise it will return false.

Advice to users.   Users are advised not to reuse the status fields for values other than those for which they were intended. Doing so may lead to unexpected results when using the status object. For example, calling MPI_GET_ELEMENTS may cause an error if the value is out of range or it may be impossible to detect such an error. The extra_state argument provided with a generalized request can be used to return information that does not logically belong in status. Furthermore, modifying the values in a status set internally by MPI, for example, by MPI_RECV, may lead to unpredictable results and is strongly discouraged. ☐

6.4   Naming Objects

There are many occasions on which it would be useful to allow a user to associate a printable identifier with an MPI communicator, window, or datatype, for instance when reporting errors, debugging, or profiling. Such names should not propagate when the object is duplicated or copied by MPI routines. For communicators this functionality is provided by the following two functions.

MPI_COMM_SET_NAME(comm, comm_name)

| INOUT | comm | communicator whose identifier is to be set (handle) |
| IN | comm_name | the character string which is remembered as the name (string) |

```
int MPI_Comm_set_name(MPI_Comm comm, char *comm_name)
```

```
MPI_COMM_SET_NAME(COMM, COMM_NAME, IERROR)
    INTEGER COMM, IERROR
    CHARACTER*(*) COMM_NAME
```

```
void MPI::Comm::Set_name(const char* comm_name)
```

MPI_COMM_SET_NAME allows a user to associate a name string with a communicator. The character string which is passed to MPI_COMM_SET_NAME will be saved inside the MPI library (so it can be freed by the caller immediately after the call, or allocated on the stack). Leading spaces in name are significant but trailing ones are not.

MPI_COMM_SET_NAME is a local (noncollective) operation, which only affects the name of the communicator as seen in the process which made the MPI_COMM_-SET_NAME call. There is no requirement that the same (or any) name be assigned to a communicator in every process where it exists.

Advice to users.   Since MPI_COMM_SET_NAME is provided to help debug code, it is sensible to give the same name to a communicator in all of the processes where it exists, to avoid confusion. ☐

The number of characters that can be stored is at least 64 and is limited to the value of MPI_MAX_OBJECT_NAME in Fortran and MPI_MAX_OBJECT_NAME−1 in C and C++ (where the constant is known as MPI::MAX_OBJECT_NAME) to allow for the null terminator (see Section 2.2.8). Attempts to assign names longer than this will result in truncation of the name.

Advice to users. Under circumstances of store exhaustion an attempt to put a name of any length could fail, therefore the value of MPI_MAX_OBJECT_NAME should be viewed only as a strict upper bound on the name length, not a guarantee that setting names of less than this length will always succeed. ▯

Advice to implementors. Implementations which pre-allocate a fixed size space for a name should use the length of that allocation as the value of MPI_MAX_OBJECT_NAME. Implementations which allocate space for the name from the heap should still define MPI_MAX_OBJECT_NAME to be a relatively small value, since the user has to allocate space for a string of up to this size when calling MPI_COMM_GET_NAME. ▯

MPI_COMM_GET_NAME(comm, comm_name, resultlen)

IN	comm	communicator whose name is to be returned (handle)
OUT	comm_name	the name previously stored on the communicator, or an empty string if no such name exists (string)
OUT	resultlen	length of returned name (integer)

```
int MPI_Comm_get_name(MPI_Comm comm, char *comm_name, int *resultlen)
```

```
MPI_COMM_GET_NAME(COMM, COMM_NAME, RESULTLEN, IERROR)
    INTEGER COMM, RESULTLEN, IERROR
    CHARACTER*(*) COMM_NAME
```

```
void MPI::Comm::Get_name(char* comm_name, int& resultlen) const
```

MPI_COMM_GET_NAME returns the last name which has previously been associated with the given communicator. The name may be set and taken from any language. The same name will be returned independent of the language used. name should be allocated so that it can hold a resulting string of length MPI_MAX_OBJECT_NAME characters. MPI_COMM_GET_NAME returns a copy of the set name in name.

If the user has not associated a name with a communicator, or an error occurs, MPI_COMM_GET_NAME will return an empty string (all spaces in Fortran, "" in C and C++). The predefined communicators will have predefined names associated with them. Thus, the names of MPI_COMM_WORLD and MPI_COMM_SELF, and the communicator returned by MPI_COMM_GET_PARENT will be by default MPI_-COMM_WORLD, MPI_COMM_SELF, and MPI_COMM_PARENT, respectively. The fact that the system may have chosen to give a default name to a communicator does not prevent the user from setting a name on the same communicator; doing this removes the old name and assigns the new one.

Rationale. MPI provides separate functions for setting and getting the name of a communicator, rather than simply providing a predefined attribute key for the following reasons:

- It is not, in general, possible to store a string as an attribute from Fortran.

- It is not easy to set up the delete function for a string attribute unless it is known to have been allocated from the heap.

- To make the attribute key useful additional code to call `strdup` is necessary. If this is not standardized then users have to write it. This is extra unneeded work which can be easily eliminated.

- The Fortran binding is not trivial to write (it will depend on details of the Fortran compilation system), and will not be portable. Therefore it should be in the library rather than in user code.

$\Box$

Advice to users. The above definition means that it is safe simply to print the string returned by MPI_COMM_GET_NAME, as it is always a valid string even if there was no name.

Note that associating a name with a communicator has no effect on the semantics of an MPI program, and will (necessarily) increase the store requirement of the program, since the names must be saved. Therefore there is no requirement that users use these functions to associate names with communicators. However, debugging and profiling MPI applications may be made easier if names are associated with communicators, since the debugger or profiler should then be able to present information in a less cryptic manner. $\Box$

The following functions are used for setting and getting names of datatypes.

MPI_TYPE_SET_NAME(type, type_name)

    INOUT type   datatype whose identifier is to be set (handle)

IN	type_name	the character string which is remembered as the name (string)

```
int MPI_Type_set_name(MPI_Datatype type, char *type_name)
```

```
MPI_TYPE_SET_NAME(TYPE, TYPE_NAME, IERROR)
    INTEGER TYPE, IERROR
    CHARACTER*(*) TYPE_NAME
```

```
void MPI::Datatype::Set_name(const char* type_name)
```

MPI_TYPE_GET_NAME(type, type_name, resultlen)

IN	type	datatype whose name is to be returned (handle)
OUT	type_name	the name previously stored on the datatype, or an empty string if no such name exists (string)
OUT	resultlen	length of returned name (integer)

```
int MPI_Type_get_name(MPI_Datatype type, char *type_name, int
    *resultlen)
```

```
MPI_TYPE_GET_NAME(TYPE, TYPE_NAME, RESULTLEN, IERROR)
    INTEGER TYPE, RESULTLEN, IERROR
    CHARACTER*(*) TYPE_NAME
```

```
void MPI::Datatype::Get_name(char* type_name, int& resultlen) const
```

Named predefined datatypes have the default names of the datatype name. For example, MPI_WCHAR has the default name of MPI_WCHAR.

The following functions are used for setting and getting names of windows.

MPI_WIN_SET_NAME(win, win_name)

INOUT	win	window whose identifier is to be set (handle)
IN	win_name	the character string which is remembered as the name (string)

```
int MPI_Win_set_name(MPI_Win win, char *win_name)
```

```
MPI_WIN_SET_NAME(WIN, WIN_NAME, IERROR)
```

```
INTEGER WIN, IERROR
CHARACTER*(*) WIN_NAME
```

```
void MPI::Win::Set_name(const char* win_name)
```

MPI_WIN_GET_NAME(win, win_name, resultlen)

IN	win	window whose name is to be returned (handle)
OUT	win_name	the name previously stored on the window, or an empty string if no such name exists (string)
OUT	resultlen	length of returned name (integer)

```
int MPI_Win_get_name(MPI_Win win, char *win_name, int *resultlen)
```

```
MPI_WIN_GET_NAME(WIN, WIN_NAME, RESULTLEN, IERROR)
    INTEGER WIN, RESULTLEN, IERROR
    CHARACTER*(*) WIN_NAME
```

```
void MPI::Win::Get_name(char* win_name, int& resultlen) const
```

6.5 Error Classes, Error Codes, and Error Handlers

Users may want to write a layered library on top of an existing MPI implementation, and this library may have its own set of error codes and classes. An example of such a library is an I/O library based on the I/O chapter in MPI-2. For this purpose, functions are needed to:

1. Add a new error class to the ones an MPI implementation already knows.

2. Associate error codes with this error class, so that MPI_ERROR_CLASS works.

3. Associate strings with these error codes, so that MPI_ERROR_STRING works.

4. Invoke the error handler associated with a communicator, window, or object.

Several new functions are provided to do this. They are all local. No functions are provided to free error strings or error classes: it is not expected that an application will generate them in significant numbers.

MPI_ADD_ERROR_CLASS(errorclass)

   OUT   errorclass   value for the new error class (integer)

```
int MPI_Add_error_class(int *errorclass)
```

```
MPI_ADD_ERROR_CLASS(ERRORCLASS, IERROR)
    INTEGER ERRORCLASS, IERROR
```

```
int MPI::Add_error_class()
```

MPI_ADD_ERROR_CLASS creates a new error class and returns the value for it.

Rationale. To avoid conflicts with existing error codes and classes, the value is set by the implementation and not by the user. ▯

Advice to implementors. A high-quality implementation will return the value for a new errorclass in the same deterministic way on all processes. ▯

Advice to users. Since a call to MPI_ADD_ERROR_CLASS is local, the same errorclass may not be returned on all processes that make this call. Thus, it is not safe to assume that registering a new error on a set of processes at the same time will yield the same errorclass on all of the processes. However, if an implementation returns the new errorclass in a deterministic way, and they are always generated in the same order on the same set of processes (for example, all processes), then the value will be the same. However, even if a deterministic algorithm is used, the value can vary across processes. This can happen, for example, if different but overlapping groups of processes make a series of calls. As a result of these issues, getting the "same" error on multiple processes may not cause the same value of error code to be generated. This is why displaying an error string can be more useful than an error code. ▯

The value of MPI_ERR_LASTCODE is not affected by new user-defined error codes and classes. As in MPI-1, it is a constant value. Instead, a predefined attribute key MPI_LASTUSEDCODE (MPI::LASTUSEDCODE in C++) is associated with MPI_COMM_WORLD. The attribute value corresponding to this key is the current maximum error class including the user-defined ones. This is a local value and may be different on different processes. The value returned by this key is always greater than or equal to MPI_ERR_LASTCODE.

Advice to users.   The value returned by the key MPI_LASTUSEDCODE will not change unless the user calls a function to explicitly add an error class/code. In a multithreaded environment, the user must take extra care in assuming this value has not changed. Note that error codes and error classes are not necessarily dense. A user may not assume that each error class below MPI_LASTUSEDCODE is valid. □

MPI_ADD_ERROR_CODE(errorclass, errorcode)

IN	errorclass	error class (integer)
OUT	errorcode	new error code to associated with errorclass (integer)

```
int MPI_Add_error_code(int errorclass, int *errorcode)
```

```
MPI_ADD_ERROR_CODE(ERRORCLASS, ERRORCODE, IERROR)
    INTEGER ERRORCLASS, ERRORCODE, IERROR
```

```
int MPI::Add_error_code(int errorclass)
```

MPI_ADD_ERROR_CODE creates a new error code associated with errorclass and returns its value in errorcode.

Rationale.   To avoid conflicts with existing error codes and classes, the value of the new error code is set by the implementation and not by the user. □

Advice to implementors.   A high-quality implementation will return the value for a new errorcode in the same deterministic way on all processes. □

MPI_ADD_ERROR_STRING(errorcode, string)

IN	errorcode	error code or class (integer)
IN	string	text corresponding to errorcode (string)

```
int MPI_Add_error_string(int errorcode, char *string)
```

```
MPI_ADD_ERROR_STRING(ERRORCODE, STRING, IERROR)
    INTEGER ERRORCODE, IERROR
    CHARACTER*(*) STRING
```

```
void MPI::Add_error_string(int errorcode, const char* string)
```

MPI_ADD_ERROR_STRING associates an error string with an error code or class. The string must be no more than MPI_MAX_ERROR_STRING characters long. The length of the string is as defined in the calling language. The length of the string does not include the null terminator in C or C++. Trailing blanks will be stripped in Fortran. Calling MPI_ADD_ERROR_STRING for an errorcode that already has a string will replace the old string with the new string. It is erroneous to call MPI_-ADD_ERROR_STRING for an error code or class with a value less than or equal to MPI_ERR_LASTCODE.

If MPI_ERROR_STRING is called when no string has been set, it will return an empty string (all spaces in Fortran, "" in C and C++).

Section I-7.5.1 describes the methods for creating and associating error handlers with communicators, files, and windows. The calls for invoking an error are described below.

MPI_COMM_CALL_ERRHANDLER(comm, errorcode)

| IN | comm | communicator with error handler (handle) |
| IN | errorcode | error code (integer) |

```
int MPI_Comm_call_errhandler(MPI_Comm comm, int errorcode)
```

```
MPI_COMM_CALL_ERRHANDLER(COMM, ERRORCODE, IERROR)
    INTEGER COMM, ERRORCODE, IERROR
```

```
void MPI::Comm::Call_errhandler(int errorcode) const
```

This function invokes the error handler assigned to the communicator with the error code supplied. This function returns MPI_SUCCESS in C and the same value in IERROR if the error handler was successfully called (assuming the process is not aborted and the error handler returns).

Advice to users. Users should note that the default error handler is MPI_ERRORS_-ARE_FATAL. Thus, calling MPI_COMM_CALL_ERRHANDLER will abort processes in comm if the default error handler has not been changed for this communicator or on the parent before the communicator was created. ☐

MPI_WIN_CALL_ERRHANDLER(win, errorcode)

| IN | win | window with error handler (handle) |
| IN | errorcode | error code (integer) |

```
int MPI_Win_call_errhandler(MPI_Win win, int errorcode)
```

```
MPI_WIN_CALL_ERRHANDLER(WIN, ERRORCODE, IERROR)
    INTEGER WIN, ERRORCODE, IERROR
```

```
void MPI::Win::Call_errhandler(int errorcode) const
```

This function invokes the error handler assigned to the window with the error code supplied. This function returns MPI_SUCCESS in C and the same value in IERROR if the error handler was successfully called (assuming the process is not aborted and the error handler returns).

Advice to users. As with communicators, the default error handler for windows is MPI_ERRORS_ARE_FATAL. □

MPI_FILE_CALL_ERRHANDLER(fh, errorcode)

| IN | fh | file with error handler (handle) |
| IN | errorcode | error code (integer) |

```
int MPI_File_call_errhandler(MPI_File fh, int errorcode)
```

```
MPI_FILE_CALL_ERRHANDLER(FH, ERRORCODE, IERROR)
    INTEGER FH, ERRORCODE, IERROR
```

```
void MPI::File::Call_errhandler(int errorcode) const
```

This function invokes the error handler assigned to the file with the error code supplied. This function returns MPI_SUCCESS in C and the same value in IERROR if the error handler was successfully called (assuming the process is not aborted and the error handler returns).

Advice to users. Unlike errors on communicators and windows, the default behavior for files is to have MPI_ERRORS_RETURN. □

Advice to users. Users are warned that handlers should not be called recursively with MPI_COMM_CALL_ERRHANDLER, MPI_FILE_CALL_ERRHANDLER, or MPI_WIN_CALL_ERRHANDLER. Doing this can create a situation where an infinite recursion is created. This can occur if MPI_COMM_CALL_ERRHANDLER, MPI_FILE_CALL_ERRHANDLER, or MPI_WIN_CALL_ERRHANDLER is called inside an error handler.

Error codes and classes are associated with a process. As a result, they may be used in any error handler. An error handler should be prepared to deal with any error code it is given. Furthermore, it is good practice to only call an error handler with the appropriate error codes. For example, file errors would normally be sent to the file error handler. □

6.6 Decoding a Datatype

MPI-1 provides datatype objects, which allow users to specify an arbitrary layout of data in memory. The layout information, once put in a datatype, cannot be decoded from the datatype using MPI-1 functions. There are several cases, however, where accessing the layout information in opaque datatype objects would be useful.

The two functions in this section are used together to decode datatypes to recreate the calling sequence used in their initial definition. These can be used to allow a user to determine the type map and type signature of a datatype.

MPI_TYPE_GET_ENVELOPE(datatype, num_integers, num_addresses, num_datatypes, combiner)

IN	datatype	datatype to access (handle)
OUT	num_integers	number of input integers used in the call constructing **combiner** (nonnegative integer)
OUT	num_addresses	number of input addresses used in the call constructing **combiner** (nonnegative integer)
OUT	num_datatypes	number of input datatypes used in the call constructing **combiner** (nonnegative integer)
OUT	combiner	combiner (state)

```
int MPI_Type_get_envelope(MPI_Datatype datatype, int *num_integers,
    int *num_addresses, int *num_datatypes, int *combiner)
```

```
MPI_TYPE_GET_ENVELOPE(DATATYPE, NUM_INTEGERS, NUM_ADDRESSES,
    NUM_DATATYPES, COMBINER, IERROR)
```

```
INTEGER DATATYPE, NUM_INTEGERS, NUM_ADDRESSES, NUM_DATATYPES,
COMBINER, IERROR
```

```
void MPI::Datatype::Get_envelope(int& num_integers,
    int& num_addresses, int& num_datatypes, int& combiner) const
```

For the given datatype, MPI_TYPE_GET_ENVELOPE returns information on the number and type of input arguments used in the call that created the datatype. The number-of-arguments values returned can be used to provide sufficiently large arrays in the decoding routine MPI_TYPE_GET_CONTENTS. This call and the meaning of the returned values is described below. The combiner reflects the MPI datatype constructor call that was used in creating datatype.

Rationale.   By requiring that the combiner reflect the constructor used in the creation of the datatype, the decoded information can be used to effectively recreate the calling sequence used in the original creation. The ability to extract the original constructor sequence was deemed useful enough to constrain implementations which optimize the internal representation of datatypes to also remember the original constructor sequence.

The decoded information keeps track of datatype duplications. This is important as one needs to distinguish between a predefined datatype and a dup of a predefined datatype. The former is a constant object that cannot be freed, while the latter is a derived datatype that can be freed. □

Advice to users.   Decoding and re-encoding a datatype will not necessarily give an exact copy. Cached information will not be recreated with this mechanism. This must be copied with other methods (assuming all the keys are known). The datatype duplication function in Section I-3.4.1 can be used to give an exact copy of the original datatype. □

Table 6.1 has the values that can be returned in combiner on the left and the call associated with them on the right.

If combiner is MPI_COMBINER_NAMED then datatype is a named predefined data-type.

For calls with address arguments, one sometimes need to differentiate whether the call used an integer- or an address-sized argument. For example, there are two combiners for hvector: MPI_COMBINER_HVECTOR_INTEGER and MPI_COMBINER_-HVECTOR. The former is used if it was the MPI-1 call from Fortran, and the latter

Table 6.1
Values of combiners and their meanings. Note that in C++ the names of the constants begin MPI::COMBINER rather than MPI_COMBINER.

MPI_COMBINER_NAMED	a named predefined datatype
MPI_COMBINER_DUP	MPI_TYPE_DUP
MPI_COMBINER_CONTIGUOUS	MPI_TYPE_CONTIGUOUS
MPI_COMBINER_VECTOR	MPI_TYPE_VECTOR
MPI_COMBINER_HVECTOR_INTEGER	MPI_TYPE_HVECTOR from Fortran
MPI_COMBINER_HVECTOR	MPI_TYPE_HVECTOR from C or C++ and in some cases Fortran, or MPI_TYPE_CREATE_HVECTOR
MPI_COMBINER_INDEXED	MPI_TYPE_INDEXED
MPI_COMBINER_HINDEXED_INTEGER	MPI_TYPE_HINDEXED from Fortran
MPI_COMBINER_HINDEXED	MPI_TYPE_HINDEXED from C or C++ and in some cases Fortran or MPI_TYPE_CREATE_HINDEXED
MPI_COMBINER_INDEXED_BLOCK	MPI_TYPE_CREATE_INDEXED_BLOCK
MPI_COMBINER_STRUCT_INTEGER	MPI_TYPE_STRUCT from Fortran
MPI_COMBINER_STRUCT	MPI_TYPE_STRUCT from C or C++ and in some cases Fortran or MPI_TYPE_CREATE_STRUCT
MPI_COMBINER_SUBARRAY	MPI_TYPE_CREATE_SUBARRAY
MPI_COMBINER_DARRAY	MPI_TYPE_CREATE_DARRAY
MPI_COMBINER_F90_REAL	MPI_TYPE_CREATE_F90_REAL
MPI_COMBINER_F90_COMPLEX	MPI_TYPE_CREATE_F90_COMPLEX
MPI_COMBINER_F90_INTEGER	MPI_TYPE_CREATE_F90_INTEGER
MPI_COMBINER_RESIZED	MPI_TYPE_CREATE_RESIZED

is used if it was the MPI-1 call from C or C++. However, on systems where MPI-ADDRESS_KIND = MPI_INTEGER_KIND (i.e., where integer arguments and address-sized arguments are the same), the combiner MPI_COMBINER_HVECTOR may be returned for a datatype constructed by a call to MPI_TYPE_HVECTOR from Fortran. Similarly, MPI_COMBINER_HINDEXED may be returned for a datatype constructed by a call to MPI_TYPE_HINDEXED from Fortran, and MPI_COMBINER_STRUCT may be returned for a datatype constructed by a call to MPI_TYPE_STRUCT from Fortran. On such systems, one need not differentiate constructors that take address-sized arguments from constructors that take integer arguments, since these are the same. The new MPI-2 calls all use address-sized arguments.

Rationale.   For recreating the original call, it is important to know if address information may have been truncated. The MPI-1 calls from Fortran for a few routines could be subject to truncation in the case where the default `INTEGER` size is smaller than the size of an address. ☐

The actual arguments used in the creation call for a datatype can be obtained from the call:

MPI_TYPE_GET_CONTENTS(datatype, max_integers, max_addresses,
    max_datatypes, array_of_integers, array_of_addresses, array_of_datatypes)

IN	datatype	datatype to access (handle)
IN	max_integers	number of elements in array_of_integers (nonnegative integer)
IN	max_addresses	number of elements in array_of_addresses (nonnegative integer)
IN	max_datatypes	number of elements in array_of_datatypes (nonnegative integer)
OUT	array_of_integers	contains integer arguments used in constructing datatype (array of integers)
OUT	array_of_addresses	contains address arguments used in constructing datatype (array of integers)
OUT	array_of_datatypes	contains datatype arguments used in constructing datatype (array of handles)

```
int MPI_Type_get_contents(MPI_Datatype datatype, int max_integers,
    int max_addresses, int max_datatypes, int *array_of_integers,
    MPI_Aint *array_of_addresses, MPI_Datatype *array_of_datatypes)
```

```
MPI_TYPE_GET_CONTENTS(DATATYPE, MAX_INTEGERS, MAX_ADDRESSES,
    MAX_DATATYPES, ARRAY_OF_INTEGERS, ARRAY_OF_ADDRESSES,
    ARRAY_OF_DATATYPES, IERROR)
    INTEGER DATATYPE, MAX_INTEGERS, MAX_ADDRESSES, MAX_DATATYPES,
    ARRAY_OF_INTEGERS(*), ARRAY_OF_DATATYPES(*), IERROR
    INTEGER(KIND=MPI_ADDRESS_KIND) ARRAY_OF_ADDRESSES(*)
```

```
void MPI::Datatype::Get_contents(int max_integers,
    int max_addresses, int max_datatypes, int array_of_integers[],
    MPI::Aint array_of_addresses[],
    MPI::Datatype array_of_datatypes[]) const
```

datatype must be a predefined unnamed or a derived datatype; the call is erroneous if datatype is a predefined named datatype.

The values given for max_integers, max_addresses, and max_datatypes must be at least as large as the value returned in num_integers, num_addresses, and num_datatypes, respectively, in the call MPI_TYPE_GET_ENVELOPE for the same datatype argument.

Rationale. The arguments max_integers, max_addresses, and max_datatypes allow for error checking in the call. This is analogous to the arguments in topology routines in MPI-1. □

The datatypes returned in array_of_datatypes are handles to datatype objects that are equivalent to the datatypes used in the original construction call. If these were derived datatypes, then the returned datatypes are new datatype objects, and the user is responsible for freeing these datatypes with MPI_TYPE_FREE. If these were predefined datatypes, then the returned datatype is equal to that (constant) predefined datatype and cannot be freed.

The committed state of returned derived datatypes is undefined; that is, the datatypes may or may not be committed. Furthermore, the content of attributes of returned datatypes is undefined.

Note that MPI_TYPE_GET_CONTENTS can be invoked with a datatype argument that was constructed using MPI_TYPE_CREATE_F90_REAL, MPI_TYPE_CREATE_F90_INTEGER, or MPI_TYPE_CREATE_F90_COMPLEX (an unnamed predefined datatype). In such a case, an empty array_of_datatypes is returned.

Rationale. The definition of datatype equivalence implies that equivalent predefined datatypes are equal. By requiring the same handle for named predefined datatypes, it is possible to use the == or .EQ. comparison operator to determine the datatype involved. ☐

Advice to implementors.   The datatypes returned in array_of_datatypes must appear to the user as if each is an equivalent copy of the datatype used in the type constructor call. Whether this is done by creating a new datatype or via another mechanism such as a reference count mechanism is up to the implementation as long as the semantics are preserved. ☐

Rationale.   The committed state and attributes of the returned datatype are deliberately left vague. The datatype used in the original construction may have been modified since its use in the constructor call. Attributes can be added, removed, or modified as well as having the datatype committed. The semantics given allow for a reference count implementation without having to track these changes. ☐

In the MPI-1 datatype constructor calls, the address arguments in Fortran are of type INTEGER. In the new MPI-2 calls, the address arguments are of type INTEGER(KIND=MPI_ADDRESS_KIND). The call MPI_TYPE_GET_CONTENTS returns all addresses in an argument of type INTEGER(KIND=MPI_ADDRESS_KIND). This is true even if the old MPI-1 calls were used. Thus, the location of values returned can be thought of as being returned by the C bindings. It can also be determined by examining the new MPI-2 calls for datatype constructors for the deprecated MPI-1 calls that involve addresses.

Rationale.   By having all address arguments returned in the array_of_addresses argument, the result from a C and Fortran decoding of a datatype gives the result in the same argument. It is assumed that an integer of type INTEGER(KIND=MPI_-ADDRESS_KIND) will be at least as large as the INTEGER argument used in datatype construction with the old MPI-1 calls so no loss of information will occur. ☐

The following defines what values are placed in each entry of the returned arrays depending on the datatype constructor used for datatype. It also specifies the size of the arrays needed which is the values returned by MPI_TYPE_GET_ENVELOPE. In Fortran, the following calls were made:

```
INTEGER LARGE
PARAMETER (LARGE = 1000)
INTEGER TYPE, NI, NA, ND, COMBINER, I(LARGE), D(LARGE), IERROR
INTEGER(KIND=MPI_ADDRESS_KIND) A(LARGE)
!   CONSTRUCT DATATYPE TYPE (NOT SHOWN)
```

```
      CALL MPI_TYPE_GET_ENVELOPE(TYPE, NI, NA, ND, COMBINER, IERROR)
      IF ((NI .GT. LARGE) .OR. (NA .GT. LARGE) .OR. &
          (ND .GT. LARGE)) THEN
        WRITE (*, *) "NI, NA, OR ND = ", NI, NA, ND, &
    " RETURNED BY MPI_TYPE_GET_ENVELOPE IS LARGER THAN LARGE = ",&
            LARGE
        CALL MPI_ABORT(MPI_COMM_WORLD, 99, IERROR)
      ENDIF
      CALL MPI_TYPE_GET_CONTENTS(TYPE, NI, NA, ND, I, A, D, IERROR)
```

or in C the analogous calls of:

```
#define LARGE 1000
int ni, na, nd, combiner, i[LARGE];
MPI_Aint a[LARGE];
MPI_Datatype type, d[LARGE];
/* construct datatype type (not shown) */
MPI_Type_get_envelope(type, &ni, &na, &nd, &combiner);
if ((ni > LARGE) || (na > LARGE) || (nd > LARGE)) {
    fprintf(stderr, "ni, na, or nd = %d %d %d returned by ",
                    ni, na, nd);
    fprintf(stderr,
            "MPI_Type_get_envelope is larger than LARGE = %d\n",
            LARGE);
    MPI_Abort(MPI_COMM_WORLD, 99);
}
MPI_Type_get_contents(type, ni, na, nd, i, a, d);
```

The C++ code is analogous to the C code above with the same values returned. In the descriptions that follow, the lowercase name of arguments is used.

If combiner is MPI_COMBINER_NAMED then it is erroneous to call MPI_TYPE_-GET_CONTENTS.

If combiner is MPI_COMBINER_DUP then

Constructor argument	C & C++ location	Fortran location
oldtype	d[0]	D(1)

and ni = 0, na = 0, nd = 1.

If combiner is MPI_COMBINER_CONTIGUOUS then

Constructor argument	C & C++ location	Fortran location
count	i[0]	I(1)
oldtype	d[0]	D(1)

and ni = 1, na = 0, nd = 1.

If combiner is MPI_COMBINER_VECTOR then

Constructor argument	C & C++ location	Fortran location
count	i[0]	I(1)
blocklength	i[1]	I(2)
stride	i[2]	I(3)
oldtype	d[0]	D(1)

and ni = 3, na = 0, nd = 1.

If combiner is MPI_COMBINER_HVECTOR_INTEGER or MPI_COMBINER_HVECTOR then

Constructor argument	C & C++ location	Fortran location
count	i[0]	I(1)
blocklength	i[1]	I(2)
stride	a[0]	A(1)
oldtype	d[0]	D(1)

and ni = 2, na = 1, nd = 1.

If combiner is MPI_COMBINER_INDEXED then

Constructor argument	C & C++ location	Fortran location
count	i[0]	I(1)
array_of_blocklengths	i[1] to i[i[0]]	I(2) to I(I(1)+1)
array_of_displacements	i[i[0]+1] to i[2*i[0]]	I(I(1)+2) to I(2*I(1)+1)
oldtype	d[0]	D(1)

and ni = 2*count+1, na = 0, nd = 1.

If combiner is MPI_COMBINER_HINDEXED_INTEGER or MPI_COMBINER_HINDEXED then

Constructor argument	C & C++ location	Fortran location
count	i[0]	I(1)
array_of_blocklengths	i[1] to i[i[0]]	I(2) to I(I(1)+1)
array_of_displacements	a[0] to a[i[0]-1]	A(1) to A(I(1))
oldtype	d[0]	D(1)

and ni = count+1, na = count, nd = 1.

If combiner is MPI_COMBINER_INDEXED_BLOCK then

Constructor argument	C & C++ location	Fortran location
count	i[0]	I(1)
blocklength	i[1]	I(2)
array_of_displacements	i[2] to i[i[0]+1]	I(3) to I(I(1)+2)
oldtype	d[0]	D(1)

and ni = count+2, na = 0, nd = 1.

If the combiner is MPI_COMBINER_STRUCT_INTEGER or MPI_COMBINER_STRUCT then

Constructor argument	C & C++ location	Fortran location
count	i[0]	I(1)
array_of_blocklengths	i[1] to i[i[0]]	I(2) to I(I(1)+1)
array_of_displacements	a[0] to a[i[0]-1]	A(1) to A(I(1))
array_of_types	d[0] to d[i[0]-1]	D(1) to D(I(1))

and ni = count+1, na = count, nd = count.

If combiner is MPI_COMBINER_SUBARRAY then

Constructor argument	C & C++ location	Fortran location
ndims	i[0]	I(1)
array_of_sizes	i[1] to i[i[0]]	I(2) to I(I(1)+1)
array_of_subsizes	i[i[0]+1] to i[2*i[0]]	I(I(1)+2) to I(2*I(1)+1)
array_of_starts	i[2*i[0]+1] to i[3*i[0]]	I(2*I(1)+2) to I(3*I(1)+1)
order	i[3*i[0]+1]	I(3*I(1)+2)
oldtype	d[0]	D(1)

and ni = 3*ndims+2, na = 0, nd = 1.

If combiner is MPI_COMBINER_DARRAY then

Constructor argument	C & C++ location	Fortran location
size	i[0]	I(1)
rank	i[1]	I(2)
ndims	i[2]	I(3)
array_of_gsizes	i[3] to i[i[2]+2]	I(4) to I(I(3)+3)
array_of_distribs	i[i[2]+3] to i[2*i[2]+2]	I(I(3)+4) to I(2*I(3)+3)
array_of_dargs	i[2*i[2]+3] to i[3*i[2]+2]	I(2*I(3)+4) to I(3*I(3)+3)
array_of_psizes	i[3*i[2]+3] to i[4*i[2]+2]	I(3*I(3)+4) to I(4*I(3)+3)
order	i[4*i[2]+3]	I(4*I(3)+4)
oldtype	d[0]	D(1)

and ni = 4*ndims+4, na = 0, nd = 1.

If combiner is MPI_COMBINER_F90_REAL then

Constructor argument	C & C++ location	Fortran location
p	i[0]	I(1)
r	i[1]	I(2)

and ni = 2, na = 0, nd = 0.

  If combiner is MPI_COMBINER_F90_COMPLEX then

Constructor argument	C & C++ location	Fortran location
p	i[0]	I(1)
r	i[1]	I(2)

and ni = 2, na = 0, nd = 0.

  If combiner is MPI_COMBINER_F90_INTEGER then

Constructor argument	C & C++ location	Fortran location
r	i[0]	I(1)

and ni = 1, na = 0, nd = 0.

  If combiner is MPI_COMBINER_RESIZED then

Constructor argument	C & C++ location	Fortran location
lb	a[0]	A(1)
extent	a[1]	A(2)
oldtype	d[0]	D(1)

and ni = 0, na = 2, nd = 1.

Example 6.2   This example shows how a datatype can be decoded. The routine `printdatatype` prints out the elements of the datatype. Note the use of MPI_Type_free for datatypes that are not predefined.

```
/*
  Example of decoding a datatype.
  Returns 0 if the datatype is predefined, 1 otherwise.
 */
#include <stdio.h>
#include <stdlib.h>
#include "mpi.h"
int printdatatype( MPI_Datatype datatype )
{
    int *array_of_ints;
    MPI_Aint *array_of_adds;
    MPI_Datatype *array_of_dtypes;
```

```
int num_ints, num_adds, num_dtypes, combiner;
int i;

MPI_Type_get_envelope( datatype, &num_ints, &num_adds,
                       &num_dtypes, &combiner );
switch (combiner) {
case MPI_COMBINER_NAMED:
    printf( "Datatype is named:" );
    /* To print the specific type, one can match against the
       predefined forms. One can NOT use a switch statement
       here.  One could also use MPI_TYPE_GET_NAME if one
       preferred to use names that the user may have changed.
     */
    if      (datatype == MPI_INT)    printf( "MPI_INT\n" );
    else if (datatype == MPI_DOUBLE) printf( "MPI_DOUBLE\n" );
    ... else test for other types ...
    return 0;
    break;
case MPI_COMBINER_STRUCT:
case MPI_COMBINER_STRUCT_INTEGER:
    printf( "Datatype is struct containing" );
    array_of_ints   = (int *)malloc( num_ints * sizeof(int) );
    array_of_adds   =
            (MPI_Aint *) malloc( num_adds * sizeof(MPI_Aint) );
    array_of_dtypes = (MPI_Datatype *)
        malloc( num_dtypes * sizeof(MPI_Datatype) );
    MPI_Type_get_contents( datatype,
            num_ints, num_adds, num_dtypes,
            array_of_ints, array_of_adds, array_of_dtypes );
    printf( " %d datatypes:\n", array_of_ints[0] );
    for (i=0; i<array_of_ints[0]; i++) {
        printf( "blocklength %d, displacement %ld, type:\n",
                array_of_ints[i+1], array_of_adds[i] );
        if (printdatatype( array_of_dtypes[i] )) {
            /* Note that one frees the type ONLY if it
               is not predefined */
            MPI_Type_free( &array_of_dtypes[i] );
        }
```

```
        }
        free( array_of_ints );
        free( array_of_adds );
        free( array_of_dtypes );
        break;
        ... other combiner values ...
    default:
        printf( "Unrecognized combiner type\n" );
    }
    return 1;
}
```

6.7 Caching on Windows and on Datatypes

Caching on communicators has been a useful feature for library developers. This function has been expanded in MPI-2 to include windows and datatypes.

Rationale. Caching has a cost associated with it and should be provided only when it is clearly needed and the increased cost is modest. Thus, caching has not been expanded to opaque objects that are created frequently, such as requests, so as not to slow down MPI. Also, caching has not been provided for opaque objects for which it seems to make little sense, such as error handlers. □

The attribute manipulation functions for windows and datatypes are presented below. These functions are similar to the attribute caching functions for communicators. The reader is referred to the description of attribute caching for communicators in Section I-5.6 for additional information on the behavior of these functions.

6.7.1 Windows

The functions for caching on windows are:

MPI_WIN_CREATE_KEYVAL(win_copy_attr_fn, win_delete_attr_fn, win_keyval, extra_state)

IN	win_copy_attr_fn	copy callback function for win_keyval (function)
IN	win_delete_attr_fn	delete callback function for win_keyval (function)
OUT	win_keyval	key value for future access (integer)
IN	extra_state	extra state for callback functions

```
int MPI_Win_create_keyval(MPI_Win_copy_attr_function *win_copy_attr_fn,
    MPI_Win_delete_attr_function *win_delete_attr_fn, int *win_keyval,
    void *extra_state)
```

```
MPI_WIN_CREATE_KEYVAL(WIN_COPY_ATTR_FN, WIN_DELETE_ATTR_FN, WIN_KEYVAL,
    EXTRA_STATE, IERROR)
    EXTERNAL WIN_COPY_ATTR_FN, WIN_DELETE_ATTR_FN
    INTEGER WIN_KEYVAL, IERROR
    INTEGER(KIND=MPI_ADDRESS_KIND) EXTRA_STATE
```

```
static int MPI::Win::Create_keyval(MPI::Win::Copy_attr_function*
    win_copy_attr_fn, MPI::Win::Delete_attr_function*
    win_delete_attr_fn, void* extra_state)
```

The argument win_copy_attr_fn may be specified as MPI_WIN_NULL_COPY_FN or MPI_WIN_DUP_FN from either C, C++, or Fortran. MPI_WIN_NULL_COPY_FN is a function that does nothing other than returning flag = 0 and MPI_SUCCESS. MPI_WIN_DUP_FN is a simple-minded copy function that sets flag = 1, returns the value of attribute_val_in in attribute_val_out, and returns MPI_SUCCESS.

The argument win_delete_attr_fn may be specified as MPI_WIN_NULL_DELETE_-FN from either C, C++, or Fortran. MPI_WIN_NULL_DELETE_FN is a function that does nothing, other than returning MPI_SUCCESS.

The C callback functions are:

```
typedef int MPI_Win_copy_attr_function(MPI_Win oldwin, int win_keyval,
    void *extra_state, void *attribute_val_in,
    void *attribute_val_out, int *flag);
```

and

```
typedef int MPI_Win_delete_attr_function(MPI_Win win, int win_keyval,
    void *attribute_val, void *extra_state);
```

The Fortran callback functions are:

```
SUBROUTINE WIN_COPY_ATTR_FN(OLDWIN, WIN_KEYVAL, EXTRA_STATE,
    ATTRIBUTE_VAL_IN, ATTRIBUTE_VAL_OUT, FLAG, IERROR)
    INTEGER OLDWIN, WIN_KEYVAL, IERROR
    INTEGER(KIND=MPI_ADDRESS_KIND) EXTRA_STATE, ATTRIBUTE_VAL_IN,
        ATTRIBUTE_VAL_OUT
    LOGICAL FLAG
```

and

SUBROUTINE WIN_DELETE_ATTR_FN(WIN, WIN_KEYVAL, ATTRIBUTE_VAL,
    EXTRA_STATE, IERROR)
    INTEGER WIN, WIN_KEYVAL, IERROR
    INTEGER(KIND=MPI_ADDRESS_KIND) ATTRIBUTE_VAL, EXTRA_STATE

The C++ callbacks are:
typedef int MPI::Win::Copy_attr_function(const MPI::Win& oldwin,
    int win_keyval, void* extra_state, void* attribute_val_in,
    void* attribute_val_out, bool& flag);

and
typedef int MPI::Win::Delete_attr_function(MPI::Win& win,
    int win_keyval, void* attribute_val, void* extra_state);

MPI_WIN_FREE_KEYVAL(win_keyval)

  INOUT win_keyval   key value (integer)

---

int MPI_Win_free_keyval(int *win_keyval)

MPI_WIN_FREE_KEYVAL(WIN_KEYVAL, IERROR)
    INTEGER WIN_KEYVAL, IERROR

static void MPI::Win::Free_keyval(int& win_keyval)

MPI_WIN_SET_ATTR(win, win_keyval, attribute_val)

  INOUT win   window to which attribute will be attached (handle)
  IN   win_keyval   key value (integer)
  IN   attribute_val   attribute value

---

int MPI_Win_set_attr(MPI_Win win, int win_keyval, void *attribute_val)

MPI_WIN_SET_ATTR(WIN, WIN_KEYVAL, ATTRIBUTE_VAL, IERROR)
    INTEGER WIN, WIN_KEYVAL, IERROR
    INTEGER(KIND=MPI_ADDRESS_KIND) ATTRIBUTE_VAL

void MPI::Win::Set_attr(int win_keyval, const void* attribute_val)

MPI_WIN_GET_ATTR(win, win_keyval, attribute_val, flag)

IN	win	window to which the attribute is attached (handle)
IN	win_keyval	key value (integer)
OUT	attribute_val	attribute value, unless flag = false
OUT	flag	false if no attribute is associated with the key (logical)

```
int MPI_Win_get_attr(MPI_Win win, int win_keyval, void *attribute_val,
    int *flag)
```

```
MPI_WIN_GET_ATTR(WIN, WIN_KEYVAL, ATTRIBUTE_VAL, FLAG, IERROR)
    INTEGER WIN, WIN_KEYVAL, IERROR
    INTEGER(KIND=MPI_ADDRESS_KIND) ATTRIBUTE_VAL
    LOGICAL FLAG
```

```
bool MPI::Win::Get_attr(const MPI::Win& win, int win_keyval,
    void* attribute_val) const
```

MPI_WIN_DELETE_ATTR(win, win_keyval)

| INOUT | win | window from which the attribute is deleted (handle) |
| IN | win_keyval | key value (integer) |

```
int MPI_Win_delete_attr(MPI_Win win, int win_keyval)
```

```
MPI_WIN_DELETE_ATTR(WIN, WIN_KEYVAL, IERROR)
    INTEGER WIN, WIN_KEYVAL, IERROR
```

```
void MPI::Win::Delete_attr(int win_keyval)
```

Rationale. The attribute copy callback function that is associated with window attribute keys is superfluous, since there is no MPI_WIN_DUP function to duplicate windows. This may be an omission of the MPI-2 Forum that will be corrected in the future. □

6.7.2 Datatypes

The functions for caching on datatypes are:

MPI_TYPE_CREATE_KEYVAL(type_copy_attr_fn, type_delete_attr_fn, type_keyval,
   extra_state)

IN	type_copy_attr_fn	copy callback function for type_keyval (function)
IN	type_delete_attr_fn	delete callback function for type_keyval (function)
OUT	type_keyval	key value for future access (integer)
IN	extra_state	extra state for callback functions

```
int MPI_Type_create_keyval(
    MPI_Type_copy_attr_function *type_copy_attr_fn,
    MPI_Type_delete_attr_function *type_delete_attr_fn,
    int *type_keyval, void *extra_state)
```

```
MPI_TYPE_CREATE_KEYVAL(TYPE_COPY_ATTR_FN, TYPE_DELETE_ATTR_FN,
    TYPE_KEYVAL, EXTRA_STATE, IERROR)
    EXTERNAL TYPE_COPY_ATTR_FN, TYPE_DELETE_ATTR_FN
    INTEGER TYPE_KEYVAL, IERROR
    INTEGER(KIND=MPI_ADDRESS_KIND) EXTRA_STATE
```

```
static int MPI::Datatype::Create_keyval(
    MPI::Datatype::Copy_attr_function* type_copy_attr_fn,
    MPI::Datatype::Delete_attr_function* type_delete_attr_fn,
    void* extra_state)
```

The argument type_copy_attr_fn may be specified as MPI_TYPE_NULL_COPY_FN
or MPI_TYPE_DUP_FN from either C, C++, or Fortran. MPI_TYPE_NULL_COPY_-
FN is a function that does nothing other than returning flag = 0 and MPI_SUCCESS.
MPI_TYPE_DUP_FN is a simple-minded copy function that sets flag = 1, returns
the value of attribute_val_in in attribute_val_out, and returns MPI_SUCCESS.

The argument type_delete_attr_fn may be specified as MPI_TYPE_NULL_DELETE_-
FN from either C, C++, or Fortran. MPI_TYPE_NULL_DELETE_FN is a function
that does nothing, other than returning MPI_SUCCESS.

The C callback functions are:

```
typedef int MPI_Type_copy_attr_function(MPI_Datatype oldtype,
    int type_keyval, void *extra_state, void *attribute_val_in,
    void *attribute_val_out, int *flag);
```

and

```
typedef int MPI_Type_delete_attr_function(MPI_Datatype type,
    int type_keyval, void *attribute_val, void *extra_state);
```

The Fortran callback functions are:

```
SUBROUTINE TYPE_COPY_ATTR_FN(OLDTYPE, TYPE_KEYVAL, EXTRA_STATE,
    ATTRIBUTE_VAL_IN, ATTRIBUTE_VAL_OUT, FLAG, IERROR)
    INTEGER OLDTYPE, TYPE_KEYVAL, IERROR
    INTEGER(KIND=MPI_ADDRESS_KIND) EXTRA_STATE,
        ATTRIBUTE_VAL_IN, ATTRIBUTE_VAL_OUT
    LOGICAL FLAG
```

and

```
SUBROUTINE TYPE_DELETE_ATTR_FN(TYPE, TYPE_KEYVAL, ATTRIBUTE_VAL,
    EXTRA_STATE, IERROR)
    INTEGER TYPE, TYPE_KEYVAL, IERROR
    INTEGER(KIND=MPI_ADDRESS_KIND) ATTRIBUTE_VAL, EXTRA_STATE
```

The C++ callbacks are:

```
typedef int MPI::Datatype::Copy_attr_function(
    const MPI::Datatype& oldtype, int type_keyval, void* extra_state,
    const void* attribute_val_in, void* attribute_val_out,
    bool& flag);
```

and

```
typedef int MPI::Datatype::Delete_attr_function(MPI::Datatype& type,
    int type_keyval, void* attribute_val, void* extra_state);
```

MPI_TYPE_FREE_KEYVAL(type_keyval)

INOUT	type_keyval	key value (integer)

```
int MPI_Type_free_keyval(int *type_keyval)

MPI_TYPE_FREE_KEYVAL(TYPE_KEYVAL, IERROR)
    INTEGER TYPE_KEYVAL, IERROR

static void MPI::Datatype::Free_keyval(int& type_keyval)
```

MPI_TYPE_SET_ATTR(type, type_keyval, attribute_val)

INOUT	type	datatype to which attribute will be attached (handle)

IN	type_keyval	key value (integer)
IN	attribute_val	attribute value

```
int MPI_Type_set_attr(MPI_Datatype type, int type_keyval,
    void *attribute_val)
```

```
MPI_TYPE_SET_ATTR(TYPE, TYPE_KEYVAL, ATTRIBUTE_VAL, IERROR)
    INTEGER TYPE, TYPE_KEYVAL, IERROR
    INTEGER(KIND=MPI_ADDRESS_KIND) ATTRIBUTE_VAL
```

```
void MPI::Datatype::Set_attr(int type_keyval, const void*
    attribute_val)
```

MPI_TYPE_GET_ATTR(type, type_keyval, attribute_val, flag)

IN	type	datatype to which the attribute is attached (handle)
IN	type_keyval	key value (integer)
OUT	attribute_val	attribute value, unless flag = false
OUT	flag	false if no attribute is associated with the key (logical)

```
int MPI_Type_get_attr(MPI_Datatype type, int type_keyval, void
    *attribute_val, int *flag)
```

```
MPI_TYPE_GET_ATTR(TYPE, TYPE_KEYVAL, ATTRIBUTE_VAL, FLAG, IERROR)
    INTEGER TYPE, TYPE_KEYVAL, IERROR
    INTEGER(KIND=MPI_ADDRESS_KIND) ATTRIBUTE_VAL
    LOGICAL FLAG
```

```
bool MPI::Datatype::Get_attr(int type_keyval, void* attribute_val)
    const
```

MPI_TYPE_DELETE_ATTR(type, type_keyval)

INOUT	type	datatype from which the attribute is deleted (handle)
IN	type_keyval	key value (integer)

```
int MPI_Type_delete_attr(MPI_Datatype type, int type_keyval)
```

```
MPI_TYPE_DELETE_ATTR(TYPE, TYPE_KEYVAL, IERROR)
    INTEGER TYPE, TYPE_KEYVAL, IERROR
```

```
void MPI::Datatype::Delete_attr(int type_keyval)
```

7 I/O

MPI provides a rich set of routines (point-to-point, collective, and one-sided) for transferring data between MPI processes. Such data transfer is called *communication* in MPI. MPI also provides routines for transferring data into or out of an application, typically (but not necessarily) to or from files on an external storage device. Such data transfer is called *I/O* in MPI. We will use the term *parallel I/O* in its most general sense to mean any I/O done by a parallel (MPI) application, but the area in which MPI adds the most new functionality is in the area of *cooperative I/O*, in which many processes concurrently access a single file.

7.1 Introduction

While POSIX provides a widely-available filesystem interface, this interface is not sufficient for high performance parallel I/O. Many performance optimizations (e.g., grouping [19], collective buffering [2, 3, 20, 22, 24], and disk-directed I/O [17]) cannot be performed unless the I/O interface allows an application to describe how file data is partitioned among processes and unless that interface provides collective data transfer operations. MPI provides additional potential for optimization by providing mechanisms for asynchronous I/O, strided accesses, and control over physical file layout on storage devices (disks). Finally, through its use of MPI datatypes to describe all data, MPI enables greater portability of files and the possibility of seamless operation in heterogeneous environments.

While MPI specifies a programming interface for I/O, it does not specify a filesystem. More specifically, MPI specifies only the library interface needed by an MPI program to access data, and does not specify how file data can be accessed by a non-MPI program, how files are organized in directories, what filenames are allowed, how file protection works, how files are stored, etc. POSIX specifies quite a bit more than MPI in this regard. The MPI-2 I/O interface is designed to be able to interact with a wide range of existing filesystems.

What about traditional "language I/O" (e.g., OPEN, READ, etc. in Fortran and fopen, fread, etc. in C)? While language I/O may be appropriate for some applications, MPI does not require that language I/O be available on all processes, so that portable applications cannot (technically) rely on it. More important, though, is the fact that language I/O interfaces, like the POSIX interface, do not provide the functionality described above. Note that support for "standard I/O" (e.g., I/O to stdout or sterr and from stdin in C, and usually associated with I/O to and from a terminal) is not mandated by MPI, nor is such I/O specifically supported by MPI-2 I/O.

MPI uses derived datatypes to express the partitioning of file data among processes. An alternative approach, used in other parallel I/O interfaces, would be to define a set of I/O access modes to express common patterns for accessing a shared file (broadcast, reduction, scatter, gather). The MPI approach has the advantages of added flexibility and expressiveness.

Since I/O errors are common and often recoverable, they are treated differently from communication errors in MPI. Error handlers for I/O are associated with MPI file handles rather than with communicators, and the default error handler returns an error code to the application, rather than aborting.

7.1.1 Definitions

file: An MPI *file* is an ordered collection of typed data items. MPI supports random or sequential access to a file. A file is opened collectively by a group of processes. All subsequent collective I/O operations on the file are collective over this group.

displacement: A file *displacement* is an absolute byte position relative to the beginning of a file. The displacement defines the location where a *view* begins. Note that a "file displacement" is distinct from a "typemap displacement," which is a relative byte displacement from the beginning of a datatype.

etype: An *etype* (*elementary* datatype) is the unit of data access and positioning within a file. An etype is an MPI datatype, and can be any predefined datatype or any derived datatype in which the typemap displacements are nonnegative and monotonically nondecreasing. MPI I/O routines perform data access in etype units, reading or writing whole data items of type etype. Offsets (see definition below) are expressed as a count of etypes; file pointers (see definition below) point to the beginning of etypes. Depending on context, the term "etype" is used to describe one of three aspects of an elementary datatype: a particular MPI type, a data item of that type, or the extent of that type.

filetype: A *filetype* defines a template for accessing a file and is the basis for partitioning a file among processes. A filetype is either a single etype or a derived MPI datatype constructed from multiple instances of the same etype. A filetype may contain holes, and the extent of any hole in the filetype must be a multiple of the etype's extent. For more information about filetype restrictions, see Section 7.1.2.

view: A *view* defines what file data are accessible by a process. Different processes may have different views of the same file and views can be changed by the user during program execution.

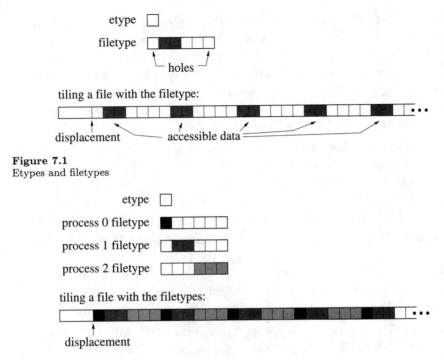

Figure 7.1
Etypes and filetypes

Figure 7.2
Partitioning a file among several processes

A view is specified by a displacement, an etype, and a filetype. These define what data are accessible by a process as illustrated in Figure 7.1. Starting at the byte offset given by the displacement, the filetype is repeated, tiling the file, in the same pattern that MPI_TYPE_CONTIGUOUS would produce if it were passed the filetype and an arbitrarily large count. The file data accessible by a process are the nonempty etype slots in this tiling. In other words, a write to the file will write only the shaded etype slots, "skipping" the holes. Similarly, a read from the file will read only the shaded etype slots. In this way, file data can be partitioned among processes using complementary views to achieve a global data distribution (see Figure 7.2). Note that the filetype in this example must have explicit lower and upper bounds set in order for the initial and final holes to be repeated in the view.

The default view is a linear byte stream (displacement is zero; etype and filetype are equal to MPI_BYTE).

offset: An *offset* is a position in the file relative to the current view, expressed as a count of etypes. This position is calculated skipping holes in the view's filetype. Offset 0 is the location of the first etype visible in the view (after skipping the displacement and any initial holes in the view). For example, offsets 0, 1 and 2 for process 1 in Figure 7.2 are the positions of the of the 2nd, 3rd and 8th etypes in the file after the displacement. An "explicit offset" is an offset that is used as a formal parameter in explicit data access routines.

file size and end of file: The *size* of an MPI file is measured in bytes from the beginning of the file. A newly created file has a size of zero bytes. Using the size as an absolute displacement gives the position of the byte immediately following the last byte in the file. For any given view, the *end of file* is the offset of the first etype accessible in the current view starting after the last byte in the file.

file pointer: A *file pointer* is an implicit offset maintained by MPI. An "Individual file pointer" is a file pointer that is local to the process that opened the file. A "shared file pointer" is a file pointer that is shared by the group of processes that opened the file. For every file handle, MPI maintains an individual file pointer on every process that opened the file, as well as a single shared file pointer.

file handle: A *file handle* is an opaque object created by MPI_FILE_OPEN and freed by MPI_FILE_CLOSE. All operations on an open file reference the file through the file handle. This object is of type MPI_File in C, MPI::File in C++, and INTEGER (as usual) in Fortran.

7.1.2   Constraints on filetypes and etypes

A filetype is either a single etype or a derived MPI datatype constructed from multiple instances of the same etype. In addition, the extent of any hole in the filetype must be a multiple of the etype's extent. These displacements are not required to be distinct, but they cannot be negative, and they must be monotonically nondecreasing.

If the file is opened for writing, neither the etype nor the filetype is permitted to contain overlapping regions. This restriction is equivalent to the "datatype used in a receive cannot specify overlapping regions" restriction for communication (Section I-3.5.4). Note that filetypes from different processes may still overlap each other.

It is erroneous to use absolute addresses in the construction of the etype and filetype.

7.2   File Manipulation

7.2.1   Opening a File

MPI_FILE_OPEN(comm, filename, amode, info, fh)

IN	comm	communicator (handle)
IN	filename	name of file to open (string)
IN	amode	file access mode (integer)
IN	info	info object (handle)
OUT	fh	new file handle (handle)

```
int MPI_File_open(MPI_Comm comm, char *filename, int amode,
    MPI_Info info, MPI_File *fh)
```

```
MPI_FILE_OPEN(COMM, FILENAME, AMODE, INFO, FH, IERROR)
    CHARACTER*(*) FILENAME
    INTEGER COMM, AMODE, INFO, FH, IERROR
```

```
static MPI::File MPI::File::Open(const MPI::Intracomm& comm,
    const char* filename, int amode, const MPI::Info& info)
```

MPI_FILE_OPEN opens the file identified by the file name filename on all processes in the comm communicator group. MPI_FILE_OPEN is collective over this group. All processes must provide the same value for amode, and all processes must provide filenames that reference the same file. The contents of info may be different on different processes. comm must be an intracommunicator; it is erroneous to pass an intercommunicator to MPI_FILE_OPEN. Errors in MPI_FILE_OPEN are raised using the default file error handler (see Section 7.7). A process can open a file independently of other processes by using the MPI_COMM_SELF communicator. The file handle returned, fh, can be subsequently used to access the file until the file is closed using MPI_FILE_CLOSE. Before calling MPI_FINALIZE, the user is required to close (via MPI_FILE_CLOSE) all files that were opened with MPI_FILE_OPEN. Note that the communicator comm is unaffected by MPI_FILE_OPEN and continues to be usable in all MPI routines (e.g., MPI_SEND). Furthermore, the use of comm will not interfere with I/O behavior.

The format for specifying the file name in the filename argument is implementation-dependent and must be documented by the implementation.

Advice to implementors.   An implementation may require that filename include a string or strings specifying additional information about the file. Examples include the type of filesystem (e.g., a prefix of `ufs:`), a remote hostname (e.g., a prefix of `machine.univ.edu:`), or a file password (e.g., a suffix of `/PASSWORD=SECRET`).

Advice to users.   On some implementations of MPI, the file namespace may not be identical for all processes of all applications. For example, `/tmp/foo` may denote different files on different processes, or a single file may have many names, dependent on process location. The user is responsible for ensuring that a single file is referenced by the filename argument, as it may be impossible for an implementation to detect this type of namespace error.

Initially, all processes view the file as a linear byte stream, and each process views data in its own native representation (no data representation conversion is performed). (POSIX files are linear byte streams in the native representation.) The file view can be changed via the MPI_FILE_SET_VIEW routine.

The following access modes are supported (specified in `amode`, a bitwise OR of the following integer constants):

MPI_MODE_RDONLY: read only,

MPI_MODE_RDWR: reading and writing,

MPI_MODE_WRONLY: write only,

MPI_MODE_CREATE: create the file if it does not exist,

MPI_MODE_EXCL: error if creating file that already exists,

MPI_MODE_DELETE_ON_CLOSE: delete file on close,

MPI_MODE_UNIQUE_OPEN: file will not be concurrently opened elsewhere,

MPI_MODE_SEQUENTIAL: file will only be accessed sequentially,

MPI_MODE_APPEND: set initial position of all file pointers to end of file.

In C++ these names begin MPI::MODE instead of MPI_MODE.

Advice to users.   C/C++ users can use bitwise OR (|) to combine these constants; Fortran 90 users can use the bit vector IOR intrinsic. Fortran 77 users can use (nonportably) bit vector IOR on systems that support it. Alternatively, Fortran users can portably use integer addition to OR the constants (each constant should appear at most once in the addition).

Advice to implementors. The values of these constants must be defined such that the bitwise OR and the sum of any distinct set of these constants is equivalent. ⬜

The modes MPI_MODE_RDONLY, MPI_MODE_RDWR, MPI_MODE_WRONLY, MPI_-MODE_CREATE, and MPI_MODE_EXCL have semantics identical to those of their POSIX counterparts [15]. Exactly one of MPI_MODE_RDONLY, MPI_MODE_RDWR, or MPI_MODE_WRONLY, must be specified. It is erroneous to specify MPI_MODE_-CREATE or MPI_MODE_EXCL in conjunction with MPI_MODE_RDONLY; it is erroneous to specify MPI_MODE_SEQUENTIAL together with MPI_MODE_RDWR.

The MPI_MODE_DELETE_ON_CLOSE mode causes the file to be deleted (equivalent to performing an MPI_FILE_DELETE) when the file is closed.

The MPI_MODE_UNIQUE_OPEN mode allows an implementation to optimize access by eliminating the overhead of file locking. It is erroneous to open a file in this mode unless the file will not be concurrently opened elsewhere.

Advice to users. For MPI_MODE_UNIQUE_OPEN, *not opened elsewhere* includes both inside and outside the MPI environment. In particular, one needs to be aware of potential external events which may open files (e.g., automated backup facilities). When MPI_MODE_UNIQUE_OPEN is specified, the user is responsible for ensuring that no such external events take place. ⬜

The MPI_MODE_SEQUENTIAL is required for sequential stream files, such as network streams and tape files that do not allow random access. It is erroneous to attempt nonsequential access to a file that has been opened in this mode. See Section 7.6.2 for more details.

Specifying MPI_MODE_APPEND sets the initial positions of all shared and individual file pointers to the end of the file when MPI_FILE_OPEN returns, but does not prohibit subsequent repositioning of file pointers by the application. If an application repositions these pointers, subsequent writes may not append to the file.

Errors related to the access mode are raised in the class MPI_ERR_AMODE.

The info argument is used to provide information regarding file access patterns and file system specifics (see Section 7.2.8). The constant MPI_INFO_NULL can be used.

Advice to users. Some file attributes are inherently implementation-dependent (e.g., file permissions). These attributes must be set using either the info argument or facilities outside the scope of MPI. ⬜

Files are opened by default using nonatomic mode file consistency semantics (see Section 7.6.1). The more stringent atomic mode consistency semantics, required for atomicity of conflicting accesses, can be set using MPI_FILE_SET_ATOMICITY.

7.2.2   Closing a File

MPI_FILE_CLOSE(fh)
  INOUT fh   file handle (handle)

```
int MPI_File_close(MPI_File *fh)
```

```
MPI_FILE_CLOSE(FH, IERROR)
    INTEGER FH, IERROR
```

```
void MPI::File::Close()
```

MPI_FILE_CLOSE first synchronizes file state (performing the equivalent of MPI_FILE_SYNC), then closes the file associated with fh. The file is deleted if it was opened with access mode MPI_MODE_DELETE_ON_CLOSE (performing the equivalent of MPI_FILE_DELETE). MPI_FILE_CLOSE is a collective routine.

Advice to users.   If the file is deleted on close, and other processes are currently accessing the file, the status of the file and the behavior of future accesses by these processes are implementation-dependent. □

The user is responsible for ensuring that all outstanding nonblocking and split collective operations associated with fh made by a process have completed before that process calls MPI_FILE_CLOSE.

The MPI_FILE_CLOSE routine deallocates the file handle object and sets fh to MPI_FILE_NULL (MPI::FILE_NULL in C++).

7.2.3   Deleting a File

MPI_FILE_DELETE(filename, info)
  IN   filename   name of file to delete (string)
  IN   info   info object (handle)

```
int MPI_File_delete(char *filename, MPI_Info info)
```

```
MPI_FILE_DELETE(FILENAME, INFO, IERROR)
    CHARACTER*(*) FILENAME
    INTEGER INFO, IERROR
```

```
static void MPI::File::Delete(const char* filename,
    const MPI::Info& info)
```

MPI_FILE_DELETE deletes the file identified by the file name filename. If the file does not exist, MPI_FILE_DELETE raises an error in the class MPI_ERR_NO_SUCH_-FILE.

The info argument can be used to provide information regarding file system specifics (see Section 7.2.8). The constant MPI_INFO_NULL can be used.

If a process currently has the file open, the behavior of any access to the file (as well as the behavior of any outstanding accesses) is implementation-dependent. In addition, whether an open file is deleted or not is also implementation-dependent. If the file is not deleted, an error in the class MPI_ERR_FILE_IN_USE or MPI_ERR_ACCESS will be raised. Errors are raised using the default error handler (see Section 7.7).

7.2.4   Resizing a File

MPI_FILE_SET_SIZE(fh, size)
    INOUT fh   file handle (handle)
    IN   size   size to truncate or expand file (integer)

```
int MPI_File_set_size(MPI_File fh, MPI_Offset size)
```

```
MPI_FILE_SET_SIZE(FH, SIZE, IERROR)
    INTEGER FH, IERROR
    INTEGER(KIND=MPI_OFFSET_KIND) SIZE
```

```
void MPI::File::Set_size(MPI::Offset size)
```

MPI_FILE_SET_SIZE resizes the file associated with the file handle fh. size is measured in bytes from the beginning of the file. MPI_FILE_SET_SIZE is collective; all processes in the group must pass identical values for size.

If size is smaller than the current file size, the file is truncated at the position defined by size. The implementation is free to deallocate file blocks located beyond this position.

If size is larger than the current file size, the file size becomes size. Regions of the file that have been previously written are unaffected. The values of data in the new regions in the file (those locations with displacements between old file size and size) are undefined. It is implementation-dependent whether the MPI_FILE_SET_SIZE routine allocates file space—use MPI_FILE_PREALLOCATE to force file space to be reserved.

MPI_FILE_SET_SIZE does not affect the individual file pointers or the shared file pointer. If MPI_MODE_SEQUENTIAL mode was specified when the file was opened, it is erroneous to call this routine.

Advice to users.   It is possible for the file pointers to point beyond the end of file after a MPI_FILE_SET_SIZE operation truncates a file. This is legal, and equivalent to seeking beyond the current end of file. □

All nonblocking and split collective operations on fh must be completed before calling MPI_FILE_SET_SIZE. Otherwise, calling MPI_FILE_SET_SIZE is erroneous. As far as consistency semantics are concerned, MPI_FILE_SET_SIZE is considered to be a write operation that conflicts with operations that access bytes at displacements between the old and new file sizes (see Section 7.6.1).

7.2.5 Preallocating Space for a File

MPI_FILE_PREALLOCATE(fh, size)
    INOUT   fh   file handle (handle)
    IN   size   size to preallocate file (integer)

```
int MPI_File_preallocate(MPI_File fh, MPI_Offset size)
```

```
MPI_FILE_PREALLOCATE(FH, SIZE, IERROR)
    INTEGER FH, IERROR
    INTEGER(KIND=MPI_OFFSET_KIND) SIZE
```

```
void MPI::File::Preallocate(MPI::Offset size)
```

MPI_FILE_PREALLOCATE ensures that storage space is allocated for the first size bytes of the file associated with fh. MPI_FILE_PREALLOCATE is collective; all processes in the group must pass identical values for size. Regions of the file that have previously been written are unaffected. For newly allocated regions of the file, MPI_FILE_PREALLOCATE has the same effect as writing undefined data. If size is larger than the current file size, the file size increases to size. If size is less than or equal to the current file size, the file size is unchanged.

The treatment of file pointers, pending nonblocking accesses, and file consistency is the same as with MPI_FILE_SET_SIZE. If MPI_MODE_SEQUENTIAL mode was specified when the file was opened, it is erroneous to call this routine.

Advice to users. In some implementations, file preallocation may be expensive.⬚

7.2.6 Querying the Size of a File

MPI_FILE_GET_SIZE(fh, size)

IN	fh	file handle (handle)
OUT	size	size of the file in bytes (integer)

```
int MPI_File_get_size(MPI_File fh, MPI_Offset *size)
```

```
MPI_FILE_GET_SIZE(FH, SIZE, IERROR)
    INTEGER FH, IERROR
    INTEGER(KIND=MPI_OFFSET_KIND) SIZE
```

```
MPI::Offset MPI::File::Get_size() const
```

MPI_FILE_GET_SIZE returns, in size, the current size in bytes of the file associated with the file handle fh. As far as consistency semantics are concerned, MPI_FILE_GET_SIZE is a data access operation (see Section 7.6.1).

7.2.7 Querying File Parameters

MPI_FILE_GET_GROUP(fh, group)

IN	fh	file handle (handle)
OUT	group	group which opened the file (handle)

```
int MPI_File_get_group(MPI_File fh, MPI_Group *group)
```

```
MPI_FILE_GET_GROUP(FH, GROUP, IERROR)
    INTEGER FH, GROUP, IERROR
```

```
MPI::Group MPI::File::Get_group() const
```

MPI_FILE_GET_GROUP returns a duplicate of the group of the communicator used to open the file associated with fh. The group is returned in group. The user is responsible for freeing group.

MPI_FILE_GET_AMODE(fh, amode)

IN	fh	file handle (handle)
OUT	amode	file access mode used to open the file (integer)

```
int MPI_File_get_amode(MPI_File fh, int *amode)
```

```
MPI_FILE_GET_AMODE(FH, AMODE, IERROR)
    INTEGER FH, AMODE, IERROR
```

```
int MPI::File::Get_amode() const
```

MPI_FILE_GET_AMODE returns, in amode, the access mode of the file associated with fh. To determine whether certain bits are set, an application can use IOR in Fortran or the bitwise OR operator (|) in C or C++.

7.2.8   File Info

Hints specified via info (see Section 2.3) allow a user to provide information such as file access patterns and file system specifics to direct optimization. Providing hints may enable an implementation to deliver increased I/O performance or minimize the use of system resources. However, hints do not change the semantics of any of the I/O interfaces. In other words, an implementation is free to ignore all hints. Hints are specified on a per file basis, in MPI_FILE_OPEN, MPI_FILE_DELETE, MPI_-FILE_SET_VIEW, and MPI_FILE_SET_INFO, via the opaque info object.

Advice to users.   info is treated differently by I/O operations and operations related to process management (Chapter 3). For I/O operations, info contains hints that can be used by MPI but don't change the behavior of the operations. For instance, a hint cannot cause an operation to fail that would succeed if the hint were not given. On the other hand, info arguments in Chapter 3 can change the semantics of the operations. □

Advice to implementors.   It may happen that a program is coded with hints for one system, and later executes on another system that does not support these hints. In general, unsupported hints should simply be ignored. Needless to say, no hint can be mandatory. However, for each hint used by a specific implementation, a default value must be provided when the user does not specify a value for this hint. ⬜

MPI_FILE_SET_INFO(fh, info)

INOUT	fh	file handle (handle)
IN	info	info object (handle)

```
int MPI_File_set_info(MPI_File fh, MPI_Info info)
```

```
MPI_FILE_SET_INFO(FH, INFO, IERROR)
    INTEGER FH, INFO, IERROR
```

```
void MPI::File::Set_info(const MPI::Info& info)
```

MPI_FILE_SET_INFO sets new values for the hints of the file associated with fh. MPI_FILE_SET_INFO is a collective routine. The info object may be different on each process, but any info entries that an implementation requires to be the same on all processes must appear with the same value in each process's info object.

Advice to users. Many info items that an implementation can use when it creates or opens a file cannot easily be changed once the file has been created or opened. Thus, an implementation may ignore hints issued in this call that it would have accepted in an open call. ⬜

MPI_FILE_GET_INFO(fh, info_used)

IN	fh	file handle (handle)
OUT	info_used	new info object (handle)

```
int MPI_File_get_info(MPI_File fh, MPI_Info *info_used)
```

```
MPI_FILE_GET_INFO(FH, INFO_USED, IERROR)
    INTEGER FH, INFO_USED, IERROR
```

```
MPI::Info MPI::File::Get_info() const
```

MPI_FILE_GET_INFO returns a new info object containing the hints of the file associated with fh. The current setting of all hints actually used by the system related to this open file is returned in info_used. The user is responsible for freeing info_used via MPI_INFO_FREE.

Advice to users. The info object returned in info_used will contain all hints currently active for this file. This set of hints may be greater or smaller than the set of hints passed in to MPI_FILE_OPEN, MPI_FILE_SET_VIEW, and MPI_FILE_SET_INFO, as the system may not recognize some hints set by the user, and may recognize other hints that the user has not set. □

Reserved File Hints. Some potentially useful hints (info keys) are outlined below. The following keys are reserved. An implementation is not required to interpret these keys, but if it does interpret the key, it must provide the functionality described. (For more details on info, see Section 2.3.)

These hints mainly affect access patterns and the layout of data on parallel I/O devices. For each hint name introduced, we describe the purpose of the hint, and the type of the hint value. The "[**SAME**]" annotation specifies that the hint values provided by all participating processes must be identical; otherwise the program is erroneous. In addition, some hints are context dependent, and are only used by an implementation at specific times (e.g., file_perm is only useful during file creation).

access_style (**comma separated list of strings**): This hint specifies the manner in which the file will be accessed until the file is closed or until the access_style key value is altered. The hint value is a comma separated list of the following: read_once, write_once, read_mostly, write_mostly, sequential, reverse_sequential, and random.

collective_buffering (**boolean**) [**SAME**]: This hint specifies whether the application may benefit from collective buffering. Collective buffering is an optimization performed on collective accesses. Accesses to the file are performed on behalf of all processes in the group by a number of target nodes. These target nodes coalesce small requests into large disk accesses. Legal values for this key are true and false. Collective buffering parameters are further directed via additional hints: cb_block_size, cb_buffer_size, and cb_nodes.

cb_block_size (**integer**) [**SAME**]: This hint specifies the block size to be used for collective buffering file access. *Target nodes* access data in chunks of this size. The chunks are distributed among target nodes in a round-robin (CYCLIC) pattern.

cb_buffer_size (**integer**) [**SAME**]: This hint specifies the total buffer space that can be used for collective buffering on each target node, usually a multiple of cb_block_size.

cb_nodes **(integer)** **[SAME]**: This hint specifies the number of target nodes to be used for collective buffering.

chunked **(comma separated list of integers)** **[SAME]**: This hint specifies that the file consists of a multidimensional array that is often accessed by subarrays. The value for this hint is a comma-separated list of array dimensions, starting from the most significant one (for an array stored in row-major order, as in C, the most significant dimension is the first one; for an array stored in column-major order, as in Fortran, the most significant dimension is the last one, and array dimensions should be reversed).

chunked_item **(comma separated list of integers)** **[SAME]**: This hint specifies the size of each array entry, in bytes.

chunked_size **(comma separated list of integers)** **[SAME]**: This hint specifies the dimensions of the subarrays. This is a comma-separated list of array dimensions, starting from the most significant one.

filename **(string)**: This hint specifies the file name used when the file was opened. If the implementation is capable of returning the file name of an open file, it will be returned using this key by MPI_FILE_GET_INFO. This key is ignored when passed to MPI_FILE_OPEN, MPI_FILE_SET_VIEW, MPI_FILE_SET_INFO, and MPI_FILE_-DELETE.

file_perm **(string)** **[SAME]**: This hint specifies the file permissions to use for file creation. Setting this hint is only useful when passed to MPI_FILE_OPEN with an amode that includes MPI_MODE_CREATE. The set of legal values for this key is implementation-dependent.

io_node_list **(comma separated list of strings)** **[SAME]**: This hint specifies the list of I/O devices that should be used to store the file. This hint is most relevant when the file is created.

nb_proc **(integer)** **[SAME]**: This hint specifies the number of parallel processes that will typically be assigned to run programs that access this file. This hint is most relevant when the file is created.

num_io_nodes **(integer)** **[SAME]**: This hint specifies the number of I/O devices in the system.

striping_factor **(integer)** **[SAME]**: This hint specifies the number of I/O devices that the file should be striped across, and is relevant only when the file is created.

striping_unit **(integer)** **[SAME]**: This hint specifies the suggested striping unit to be used for this file. The striping unit is the amount of consecutive data assigned to one I/O device before progressing to the next device, when striping across a number of devices. It is expressed in bytes. This hint is relevant only when the file is created.

7.3   File Views

MPI_FILE_SET_VIEW(fh, disp, etype, filetype, datarep, info)

INOUT	fh	file handle (handle)
IN	disp	displacement (integer)
IN	etype	elementary datatype (handle)
IN	filetype	filetype (handle)
IN	datarep	data representation (string)
IN	info	info object (handle)

```
int MPI_File_set_view(MPI_File fh, MPI_Offset disp,
    MPI_Datatype etype, MPI_Datatype filetype, char *datarep,
    MPI_Info info)
```

```
MPI_FILE_SET_VIEW(FH, DISP, ETYPE, FILETYPE, DATAREP, INFO, IERROR)
    INTEGER FH, ETYPE, FILETYPE, INFO, IERROR
    CHARACTER*(*) DATAREP
    INTEGER(KIND=MPI_OFFSET_KIND) DISP
```

```
void MPI::File::Set_view(MPI::Offset disp,
    const MPI::Datatype& etype, const MPI::Datatype& filetype,
    const char* datarep, const MPI::Info& info)
```

The MPI_FILE_SET_VIEW routine changes the process's view of the data in the file. The start of the view is set to disp; the type of data is set to etype; the distribution of data to processes is set to filetype; and the representation of data in the file is set to datarep. In addition, MPI_FILE_SET_VIEW resets the individual file pointers and the shared file pointer to zero. MPI_FILE_SET_VIEW is collective; the values for datarep and the extents of etype in the file data representation must be identical on all processes in the group; values for disp, filetype, and info may vary. The datatypes passed in etype and filetype must be committed.

The etype always specifies the data layout in the file. If etype is a portable datatype (see Section 1.4), the extent of etype is computed by scaling any displacements in the datatype to match the file data representation. If etype is not a portable datatype, no scaling is done when computing the extent of etype. The user must

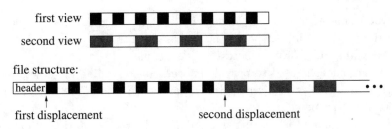

Figure 7.3
Displacements

be careful when using nonportable etypes in heterogeneous environments; see Section 7.5.1 for further details.

If MPI_MODE_SEQUENTIAL mode was specified when the file was opened, the special displacement MPI_DISPLACEMENT_CURRENT (MPI::DISPLACEMENT_CURRENT in C++) must be passed in disp. This sets the displacement to the current position of the shared file pointer.

Rationale. For some sequential files, such as those corresponding to magnetic tapes or streaming network connections, the *displacement* may not be meaningful. MPI_DISPLACEMENT_CURRENT allows the view to be changed for these types of files. □

Advice to implementors. It is expected that a call to MPI_FILE_SET_VIEW will immediately follow MPI_FILE_OPEN in numerous instances. A high-quality implementation will ensure that this behavior is efficient. □

The disp displacement argument specifies the position (absolute offset in bytes from the beginning of the file) where the view begins.

Advice to users. disp can be used to skip headers or when the file includes a sequence of data segments that are to be accessed in different patterns (see Figure 7.3). Separate views, each using a different displacement and filetype, can be used to access each segment. □

Advice to users. In order to ensure interoperability in a heterogeneous environment, additional restrictions must be observed when constructing the etype (see Section 7.5). □

If filetype has holes in it, then the data in the holes is inaccessible to the calling process. However, the disp, etype and filetype arguments can be changed via future calls to MPI_FILE_SET_VIEW to access a different part of the file.

The info argument is used to provide information regarding file access patterns and file system specifics to direct optimization (see Section 7.2.8). The constant MPI_INFO_NULL can be used.

The datarep argument is a string that specifies the representation of data in the file. See Section 7.5 on file interoperability for details and a discussion of valid values.

The user is responsible for ensuring that all nonblocking and split collective operations on fh have been completed before calling MPI_FILE_SET_VIEW—otherwise, the call to MPI_FILE_SET_VIEW is erroneous.

MPI_FILE_GET_VIEW(fh, disp, etype, filetype, datarep)

IN	fh	file handle (handle)
OUT	disp	displacement (integer)
OUT	etype	elementary datatype (handle)
OUT	filetype	filetype (handle)
OUT	datarep	data representation (string)

```
int MPI_File_get_view(MPI_File fh, MPI_Offset *disp,
    MPI_Datatype *etype, MPI_Datatype *filetype, char *datarep)
```

```
MPI_FILE_GET_VIEW(FH, DISP, ETYPE, FILETYPE, DATAREP, IERROR)
    INTEGER FH, ETYPE, FILETYPE, IERROR
    CHARACTER*(*) DATAREP, INTEGER(KIND=MPI_OFFSET_KIND) DISP
```

```
void MPI::File::Get_view(MPI::Offset& disp, MPI::Datatype& etype,
    MPI::Datatype& filetype, char* datarep) const
```

MPI_FILE_GET_VIEW returns the process's view of the data in the file. The current value of the displacement is returned in disp. The etype and filetype are new datatypes with typemaps equal to the typemaps of the current etype and filetype, respectively.

The data representation is returned in datarep. The user is responsible for ensuring that datarep is large enough to hold the returned data representation string. The length of a data representation string is limited to the value of MPI_MAX_DATAREP_STRING (MPI::MAX_DATAREP_STRING in C++).

In addition, if a portable datatype was used to set the current view, then the corresponding datatype returned by MPI_FILE_GET_VIEW is also a portable datatype. If etype or filetype are derived datatypes, the user is responsible for freeing them. The etype and filetype returned are both in a committed state.

7.4 Data Access

7.4.1 Data Access Routines

An application moves data between files and processes by issuing read and write calls. There are three orthogonal aspects to data access: positioning (explicit offset versus implicit file pointer), synchronism (blocking versus nonblocking and split collective), and coordination (noncollective versus collective). Furthermore, implicit file pointers are of two types: individual and shared. Table 7.1 lists the data access routines provided by MPI. These routines are described in detail in subsequent sections.

POSIX read()/fread() and write()/fwrite() are blocking, noncollective operations and use individual file pointers. The MPI equivalents are MPI_FILE_READ and MPI_FILE_WRITE.

Implementations of data access routines may buffer data to improve performance. This does not affect reads, since the data is always available in the user's buffer after a read operation completes. For writes, however, the MPI_FILE_SYNC routine provides the only guarantee that data has been transferred to the storage device.

Positioning. MPI provides three types of positioning for data access routines: explicit offsets, individual file pointers, and shared file pointers. The different positioning methods may be mixed within the same program and do not affect each other.

The data access routines that accept explicit offsets contain _AT in their name (e.g., MPI_FILE_WRITE_AT). Explicit offset operations perform data access at the file position given directly as an argument—no file pointer is used nor updated. Note that this is not equivalent to an atomic seek-and-read or seek-and-write operation, as no "seek" is issued. Operations with explicit offsets are described in Section 7.4.2.

The names of the individual file pointer routines contain no positional qualifier (e.g., MPI_FILE_WRITE). Operations with individual file pointers are described in Section 7.4.3. The data access routines that use shared file pointers contain _SHARED or _ORDERED in their name (e.g., MPI_FILE_WRITE_SHARED). Operations with shared file pointers are described in Section 7.4.4.

Table 7.1
Quick guide to data access routines. All routine names are shown without the MPI_FILE_ prefix
in the interest of space

positioning	synchronism	coordination	
		noncollective	*collective*
explicit offsets	*blocking*	READ_AT WRITE_AT	READ_AT_ALL WRITE_AT_ALL
	nonblocking & split collective	IREAD_AT IWRITE_AT	READ_AT_ALL_BEGIN READ_AT_ALL_END WRITE_AT_ALL_BEGIN WRITE_AT_ALL_END
individual file pointers	*blocking*	READ WRITE	READ_ALL WRITE_ALL
	nonblocking & split collective	IREAD IWRITE	READ_ALL_BEGIN READ_ALL_END WRITE_ALL_BEGIN WRITE_ALL_END
shared file pointer	*blocking*	READ_SHARED WRITE_SHARED	READ_ORDERED WRITE_ORDERED
	nonblocking & split collective	IREAD_SHARED IWRITE_SHARED	READ_ORDERED_BEGIN READ_ORDERED_END WRITE_ORDERED_BEGIN WRITE_ORDERED_END

The main semantic issues related to MPI-maintained file pointers are how and
when they are updated by I/O operations. In general, each I/O operation leaves
the file pointer pointing to the next data item after the last one that is accessed by
the operation. In a nonblocking or split collective operation, the pointer is updated
by the call that initiates the I/O, possibly before the access completes.

More formally,

$$new\_file\_offset = old\_file\_offset + \frac{elements(datatype)}{elements(etype)} \times count$$

where *count* is the number of *datatype* items to be accessed, $elements(X)$ is the
number of predefined datatypes in the typemap of X, and *old_file_offset* is the value
of the implicit offset before the call. The file position, *new_file_offset*, is in terms
of a count of etypes relative to the current view.

Synchronism. MPI supports blocking and nonblocking I/O routines. A *block-ing* I/O call will not return until the I/O request is completed. A *nonblocking*

I/O call initiates an I/O operation, but does not wait for it to complete. Given suitable hardware, this allows the transfer of data out/in the user's buffer to proceed concurrently with computation. A separate *request complete* call (MPI_WAIT, MPI_TEST, or any of their variants) is needed to complete the I/O request, that is, to confirm that the data has been read or written and that it is safe for the user to reuse the buffer. The nonblocking versions of the routines are named MPI_FILE_-I{READ|WRITE|...}, where the I stands for immediate.

It is erroneous to access the local buffer of a nonblocking data access operation, or to use that buffer as the source or target of other communications, between the initiation and completion of the operation.

The split collective routines support a restricted form of "nonblocking" operations for collective data access (see Section 7.4.5).

Coordination. Every noncollective data access routine MPI_FILE_-{READ|WRITE|...} has a collective counterpart. For most routines, this counterpart is MPI_FILE_{READ|WRITE|...}_ALL or a pair of MPI_FILE_{READ_-ALL|WRITE_ALL|...}_BEGIN and MPI_FILE_{READ_ALL|WRITE_ALL|...}_END. The counterparts to the MPI_FILE_{READ|WRITE}_SHARED routines are MPI_FILE_{READ|WRITE}_ORDERED.

The completion of a noncollective call only depends on the activity of the calling process. However, the completion of a collective call (which must be called by all members of the process group) may depend on the activity of the other processes participating in the collective call. See Section 7.6.4 for rules on semantics of collective calls.

Collective operations may perform much better than their noncollective counterparts, since global data accesses have significant potential for automatic optimization.

Data Access Conventions. Data is moved between files and processes by calling read and write routines. Read routines move data from a file into memory. Write routines move data from memory into a file. The file is designated by a file handle, fh. The location of the file data is specified by an offset into the current view. The data in memory is specified by a triple: buf, count, and datatype. Upon completion, the amount of data accessed by the calling process is returned in a status.

An offset designates the starting position in the file for an access. The offset is always in etype units relative to the current view. Explicit offset routines pass offset as an argument (negative values are erroneous). The file pointer routines use implicit offsets maintained by MPI.

A data access routine attempts to transfer (read or write) count data items of type datatype between the user's buffer buf and the file. The datatype passed to the routine must be a committed datatype. The layout of data in memory corresponding to buf, count, datatype is interpreted the same way as in MPI-1 communication functions; see Section I-3.5.3. The data is accessed from those parts of the file specified by the current view (Section 7.3). The type signature of datatype must match the type signature of some number of contiguous copies of the etype of the current view. As in a receive, it is erroneous to specify a datatype for reading that contains overlapping regions (areas of memory which would be stored into more than once).

The nonblocking data access routines indicate that MPI can start a data access and associate a request handle, request, with the I/O operation. Nonblocking operations are completed via MPI_TEST, MPI_WAIT, or any of their variants.

Data access operations, when completed, return the amount of data accessed in status. For blocking routines, status is returned directly. For nonblocking routines and split collective routines, status is returned when the operation is completed. The number of datatype entries and predefined elements accessed by the calling process can be extracted from status by using MPI_GET_COUNT and MPI_GET_ELEMENTS, respectively. The interpretation of the MPI_ERROR field is the same as for other operations—normally undefined, but meaningful if an MPI routine returns MPI_ERR_IN_STATUS. The user can pass (in C and Fortran) MPI_STATUS_IGNORE in the status argument if the return value of this argument is not needed. In C++, the status argument is optional. The status can be passed to MPI_TEST_CANCELLED to determine whether the operation was cancelled. All other fields of status are undefined.

When reading, a program can detect the end of file by noting that the amount of data read is less than the amount requested. Writing past the end of file increases the file size. The amount of data accessed will be the amount requested, unless an error is raised (or a read reaches the end of file).

7.4.2 Data Access with Explicit Offsets

If MPI_MODE_SEQUENTIAL mode was specified when the file was opened, it is erroneous to call the routines in this section.

MPI_FILE_READ_AT(fh, offset, buf, count, datatype, status)

IN	fh	file handle (handle)
IN	offset	file offset (integer)
OUT	buf	initial address of buffer (choice)
IN	count	number of elements in buffer (integer)
IN	datatype	datatype of each buffer element (handle)
OUT	status	status object (Status)

```
int MPI_File_read_at(MPI_File fh, MPI_Offset offset, void *buf,
    int count, MPI_Datatype datatype, MPI_Status *status)
```

```
MPI_FILE_READ_AT(FH, OFFSET, BUF, COUNT, DATATYPE, STATUS, IERROR)
    <type> BUF(*)
    INTEGER FH, COUNT, DATATYPE, STATUS(MPI_STATUS_SIZE), IERROR
    INTEGER(KIND=MPI_OFFSET_KIND) OFFSET
```

```
void MPI::File::Read_at(MPI::Offset offset, void* buf, int count,
    const MPI::Datatype& datatype, MPI::Status& status)
```

```
void MPI::File::Read_at(MPI::Offset offset, void* buf, int count,
    const MPI::Datatype& datatype)
```

MPI_FILE_READ_AT reads a file beginning at the position specified by offset.

MPI_FILE_READ_AT_ALL(fh, offset, buf, count, datatype, status)

IN	fh	file handle (handle)
IN	offset	file offset (integer)
OUT	buf	initial address of buffer (choice)
IN	count	number of elements in buffer (integer)
IN	datatype	datatype of each buffer element (handle)
OUT	status	status object (Status)

```
int MPI_File_read_at_all(MPI_File fh, MPI_Offset offset, void *buf,
    int count, MPI_Datatype datatype, MPI_Status *status)
```

```
MPI_FILE_READ_AT_ALL(FH, OFFSET, BUF, COUNT, DATATYPE, STATUS,
    IERROR)
    <type> BUF(*)
    INTEGER FH, COUNT, DATATYPE, STATUS(MPI_STATUS_SIZE), IERROR
    INTEGER(KIND=MPI_OFFSET_KIND) OFFSET
```

```
void MPI::File::Read_at_all(MPI::Offset offset, void* buf,
    int count, const MPI::Datatype& datatype, MPI::Status& status)

void MPI::File::Read_at_all(MPI::Offset offset, void* buf,
    int count, const MPI::Datatype& datatype)
```

MPI_FILE_READ_AT_ALL is a collective version of the blocking MPI_FILE_READ_-AT interface.

MPI_FILE_WRITE_AT(fh, offset, buf, count, datatype, status)

INOUT	fh	file handle (handle)
IN	offset	file offset (integer)
IN	buf	initial address of buffer (choice)
IN	count	number of elements in buffer (integer)
IN	datatype	datatype of each buffer element (handle)
OUT	status	status object (Status)

```
int MPI_File_write_at(MPI_File fh, MPI_Offset offset, void *buf,
    int count, MPI_Datatype datatype, MPI_Status *status)

MPI_FILE_WRITE_AT(FH, OFFSET, BUF, COUNT, DATATYPE, STATUS, IERROR)
    <type> BUF(*)
    INTEGER FH, COUNT, DATATYPE, STATUS(MPI_STATUS_SIZE), IERROR
    INTEGER(KIND=MPI_OFFSET_KIND) OFFSET

void MPI::File::Write_at(MPI::Offset offset, const void* buf,
    int count, const MPI::Datatype& datatype, MPI::Status& status)

void MPI::File::Write_at(MPI::Offset offset, const void* buf,
    int count, const MPI::Datatype& datatype)
```

MPI_FILE_WRITE_AT writes a file beginning at the position specified by offset.

MPI_FILE_WRITE_AT_ALL(fh, offset, buf, count, datatype, status)

INOUT	fh	file handle (handle)
IN	offset	file offset (integer)
IN	buf	initial address of buffer (choice)
IN	count	number of elements in buffer (integer)
IN	datatype	datatype of each buffer element (handle)
OUT	status	status object (Status)

```
int MPI_File_write_at_all(MPI_File fh, MPI_Offset offset, void *buf,
    int count, MPI_Datatype datatype, MPI_Status *status)
```

```
MPI_FILE_WRITE_AT_ALL(FH, OFFSET, BUF, COUNT, DATATYPE, STATUS,
    IERROR)
    <type> BUF(*)
    INTEGER FH, COUNT, DATATYPE, STATUS(MPI_STATUS_SIZE), IERROR
    INTEGER(KIND=MPI_OFFSET_KIND) OFFSET
```

```
void MPI::File::Write_at_all(MPI::Offset offset, const void* buf,
    int count, const MPI::Datatype& datatype, MPI::Status& status)
```

```
void MPI::File::Write_at_all(MPI::Offset offset, const void* buf,
    int count, const MPI::Datatype& datatype)
```

MPI_FILE_WRITE_AT_ALL is a collective version of the blocking MPI_FILE_WRITE_AT interface.

MPI_FILE_IREAD_AT(fh, offset, buf, count, datatype, request)

IN	fh	file handle (handle)
IN	offset	file offset (integer)
OUT	buf	initial address of buffer (choice)
IN	count	number of elements in buffer (integer)
IN	datatype	datatype of each buffer element (handle)
OUT	request	request object (handle)

```
int MPI_File_iread_at(MPI_File fh, MPI_Offset offset, void *buf,
    int count, MPI_Datatype datatype, MPI_Request *request)
```

```
MPI_FILE_IREAD_AT(FH, OFFSET, BUF, COUNT, DATATYPE, REQUEST, IERROR)
    <type> BUF(*)
    INTEGER FH, COUNT, DATATYPE, REQUEST, IERROR
    INTEGER(KIND=MPI_OFFSET_KIND) OFFSET
```

```
MPI::Request MPI::File::Iread_at(MPI::Offset offset, void* buf,
    int count, const MPI::Datatype& datatype)
```

MPI_FILE_IREAD_AT is a nonblocking version of the MPI_FILE_READ_AT interface.

MPI_FILE_IWRITE_AT(fh, offset, buf, count, datatype, request)

INOUT	fh	file handle (handle)
IN	offset	file offset (integer)
IN	buf	initial address of buffer (choice)
IN	count	number of elements in buffer (integer)
IN	datatype	datatype of each buffer element (handle)
OUT	request	request object (handle)

```
int MPI_File_iwrite_at(MPI_File fh, MPI_Offset offset, void *buf,
    int count, MPI_Datatype datatype, MPI_Request *request)
```

```
MPI_FILE_IWRITE_AT(FH, OFFSET, BUF, COUNT, DATATYPE, REQUEST, IERROR)
    <type> BUF(*)
    INTEGER FH, COUNT, DATATYPE, REQUEST, IERROR
    INTEGER(KIND=MPI_OFFSET_KIND) OFFSET
```

```
MPI::Request MPI::File::Iwrite_at(MPI::Offset offset,
    const void* buf, int count, const MPI::Datatype& datatype)
```

MPI_FILE_IWRITE_AT is a nonblocking version of the MPI_FILE_WRITE_AT interface.

7.4.3   Data Access with Individual File Pointers

MPI maintains one individual file pointer per process per file handle. The current value of this pointer implicitly specifies the offset for the data access routines described in this section. These routines only use and update the individual file pointers maintained by MPI. The shared file pointer is neither used nor updated.

The individual file pointer routines have the same semantics as the explicit offset data access routines described in Section 7.4.2, with the following modifications:

• The offset is defined to be the current value of the MPI-maintained individual file pointer.

• After an individual file pointer operation is initiated, the individual file pointer is updated to point to the next etype after the last one that will be accessed. The file pointer is updated relative to the current view of the file.

If MPI_MODE_SEQUENTIAL mode was specified when the file was opened, it is erroneous to call the routines in this section.

MPI_FILE_READ(fh, buf, count, datatype, status)

INOUT	fh	file handle (handle)
OUT	buf	initial address of buffer (choice)
IN	count	number of elements in buffer (integer)
IN	datatype	datatype of each buffer element (handle)
OUT	status	status object (Status)

```
int MPI_File_read(MPI_File fh, void *buf, int count,
    MPI_Datatype datatype, MPI_Status *status)
```

```
MPI_FILE_READ(FH, BUF, COUNT, DATATYPE, STATUS, IERROR)
    <type> BUF(*)
    INTEGER FH, COUNT, DATATYPE, STATUS(MPI_STATUS_SIZE), IERROR
```

```
void MPI::File::Read(void* buf, int count,
    const MPI::Datatype& datatype, MPI::Status& status)
```

```
void MPI::File::Read(void* buf, int count,
    const MPI::Datatype& datatype)
```

MPI_FILE_READ reads a file using the individual file pointer.

Example 7.1 The following Fortran code fragment is an example of reading a file until the end of file is reached:

```
!   Read a preexisting input file until all data has been read.
!   Call routine "process_input" if all requested data is read.
!   The Fortran 90 "exit" statement exits the loop.

    integer    bufsize, numread, totprocessed
    integer    myfh, ierr, status(MPI_STATUS_SIZE)
    parameter (bufsize=100)
    real       localbuffer(bufsize)

    call MPI_FILE_OPEN( MPI_COMM_WORLD, 'myoldfile', &
                        MPI_MODE_RDONLY, MPI_INFO_NULL, myfh, &
                        ierr )
    call MPI_FILE_SET_VIEW( myfh, 0, MPI_REAL, MPI_REAL, &
                        'native', MPI_INFO_NULL, ierr )
```

```
          totprocessed = 0
          do
              call MPI_FILE_READ( myfh, localbuffer, bufsize, MPI_REAL, &
                                   status, ierr )
              call MPI_GET_COUNT( status, MPI_REAL, numread, ierr )
              call process_input( localbuffer, numread )
              totprocessed = totprocessed + numread
              if ( numread < bufsize ) exit
          enddo

          write(6,1001) numread, bufsize, totprocessed
1001      format( "No more data:  read", I3, "and expected", I3, &
                  "Processed total of", I6, "before terminating job." )

          call MPI_FILE_CLOSE( myfh, ierr )
```

MPI_FILE_READ_ALL(fh, buf, count, datatype, status)

INOUT	fh	file handle (handle)
OUT	buf	initial address of buffer (choice)
IN	count	number of elements in buffer (integer)
IN	datatype	datatype of each buffer element (handle)
OUT	status	status object (Status)

```
int MPI_File_read_all(MPI_File fh, void *buf, int count,
    MPI_Datatype datatype, MPI_Status *status)
```

```
MPI_FILE_READ_ALL(FH, BUF, COUNT, DATATYPE, STATUS, IERROR)
    <type> BUF(*)
    INTEGER FH, COUNT, DATATYPE, STATUS(MPI_STATUS_SIZE), IERROR
```

```
void MPI::File::Read_all(void* buf, int count,
    const MPI::Datatype& datatype, MPI::Status& status)
```

```
void MPI::File::Read_all(void* buf, int count,
    const MPI::Datatype& datatype)
```

MPI_FILE_READ_ALL is a collective version of the blocking MPI_FILE_READ interface.

MPI_FILE_WRITE(fh, buf, count, datatype, status)

INOUT	fh	file handle (handle)
IN	buf	initial address of buffer (choice)
IN	count	number of elements in buffer (integer)
IN	datatype	datatype of each buffer element (handle)
OUT	status	status object (Status)

```
int MPI_File_write(MPI_File fh, void *buf, int count,
    MPI_Datatype datatype, MPI_Status *status)
```

```
MPI_FILE_WRITE(FH, BUF, COUNT, DATATYPE, STATUS, IERROR)
    <type> BUF(*)
    INTEGER FH, COUNT, DATATYPE, STATUS(MPI_STATUS_SIZE), IERROR
```

```
void MPI::File::Write(const void* buf, int count,
    const MPI::Datatype& datatype, MPI::Status& status)
```

```
void MPI::File::Write(const void* buf, int count,
    const MPI::Datatype& datatype)
```

MPI_FILE_WRITE writes a file using the individual file pointer.

MPI_FILE_WRITE_ALL(fh, buf, count, datatype, status)

INOUT	fh	file handle (handle)
IN	buf	initial address of buffer (choice)
IN	count	number of elements in buffer (integer)
IN	datatype	datatype of each buffer element (handle)
OUT	status	status object (Status)

```
int MPI_File_write_all(MPI_File fh, void *buf, int count,
    MPI_Datatype datatype, MPI_Status *status)
```

```
MPI_FILE_WRITE_ALL(FH, BUF, COUNT, DATATYPE, STATUS, IERROR)
    <type> BUF(*)
    INTEGER FH, COUNT, DATATYPE, STATUS(MPI_STATUS_SIZE), IERROR
```

```
void MPI::File::Write_all(const void* buf, int count,
    const MPI::Datatype& datatype, MPI::Status& status)
```

```
void MPI::File::Write_all(const void* buf, int count,
    const MPI::Datatype& datatype)
```

MPI_FILE_WRITE_ALL is a collective version of the blocking MPI_FILE_WRITE interface.

MPI_FILE_IREAD(fh, buf, count, datatype, request)

INOUT	fh	file handle (handle)
OUT	buf	initial address of buffer (choice)
IN	count	number of elements in buffer (integer)
IN	datatype	datatype of each buffer element (handle)
OUT	request	request object (handle)

```
int MPI_File_iread(MPI_File fh, void *buf, int count,
    MPI_Datatype datatype, MPI_Request *request)
```

```
MPI_FILE_IREAD(FH, BUF, COUNT, DATATYPE, REQUEST, IERROR)
    <type> BUF(*)
    INTEGER FH, COUNT, DATATYPE, REQUEST, IERROR
```

```
MPI::Request MPI::File::Iread(void* buf, int count,
    const MPI::Datatype& datatype)
```

MPI_FILE_IREAD is a nonblocking version of the MPI_FILE_READ interface.

Example 7.2   The following Fortran code fragment illustrates file pointer update semantics:

```
!   Read the first twenty real words in a file into two local
!   buffers.  Note that when the first MPI_FILE_IREAD returns,
!   the file pointer has been updated to point to the
!   eleventh real word in the file.

    integer    bufsize, req1, req2, myfh, ierr
    integer, dimension(MPI_STATUS_SIZE) :: status1, status2
    parameter (bufsize=10)
    real       buf1(bufsize), buf2(bufsize)

    call MPI_FILE_OPEN( MPI_COMM_SELF, 'myoldfile', &
                        MPI_MODE_RDONLY, MPI_INFO_NULL, myfh, &
                        ierr )
    call MPI_FILE_SET_VIEW( myfh, 0, MPI_REAL, MPI_REAL, &
                            'native', MPI_INFO_NULL, ierr )
```

```
call MPI_FILE_IREAD( myfh, buf1, bufsize, MPI_REAL, &
                     req1, ierr )
call MPI_FILE_IREAD( myfh, buf2, bufsize, MPI_REAL, &
                     req2, ierr )

call MPI_WAIT( req1, status1, ierr )
call MPI_WAIT( req2, status2, ierr )

call MPI_FILE_CLOSE( myfh, ierr )
```

MPI_FILE_IWRITE(fh, buf, count, datatype, request)

INOUT	fh	file handle (handle)
IN	buf	initial address of buffer (choice)
IN	count	number of elements in buffer (integer)
IN	datatype	datatype of each buffer element (handle)
OUT	request	request object (handle)

```
int MPI_File_iwrite(MPI_File fh, void *buf, int count,
    MPI_Datatype datatype, MPI_Request *request)
```

```
MPI_FILE_IWRITE(FH, BUF, COUNT, DATATYPE, REQUEST, IERROR)
    <type> BUF(*)
    INTEGER FH, COUNT, DATATYPE, REQUEST, IERROR
```

```
MPI::Request MPI::File::Iwrite(const void* buf, int count,
    const MPI::Datatype& datatype)
```

MPI_FILE_IWRITE is a nonblocking version of the MPI_FILE_WRITE interface.

MPI_FILE_SEEK(fh, offset, whence)

INOUT	fh	file handle (handle)
IN	offset	file offset (integer)
IN	whence	update mode (state)

```
int MPI_File_seek(MPI_File fh, MPI_Offset offset, int whence)
```

```
MPI_FILE_SEEK(FH, OFFSET, WHENCE, IERROR)
    INTEGER FH, WHENCE, IERROR
    INTEGER(KIND=MPI_OFFSET_KIND) OFFSET
```

```
void MPI::File::Seek(MPI::Offset offset, int whence)
```

MPI_FILE_SEEK updates the individual file pointer according to whence, which has the following possible values:

MPI_SEEK_SET: the pointer is set to offset

MPI_SEEK_CUR: the pointer is set to the current pointer position plus offset

MPI_SEEK_END: the pointer is set to the end of file plus offset

In C++, the names of the above constants begin MPI::SEEK instead of MPI_SEEK.

The offset can be negative, which allows seeking backwards. It is erroneous to seek to a negative position in the view.

MPI_FILE_GET_POSITION(fh, offset)

IN	fh	file handle (handle)
OUT	offset	offset of individual pointer (integer)

```
int MPI_File_get_position(MPI_File fh, MPI_Offset *offset)
```

```
MPI_FILE_GET_POSITION(FH, OFFSET, IERROR)
    INTEGER FH, IERROR
    INTEGER(KIND=MPI_OFFSET_KIND) OFFSET
```

```
MPI::Offset MPI::File::Get_position() const
```

MPI_FILE_GET_POSITION returns, in offset, the current position of the individual file pointer in etype units relative to the current view.

Advice to users. The offset can be used in a future call to MPI_FILE_SEEK using whence = MPI_SEEK_SET to return to the current position. To set the displacement to the current file pointer position, first convert offset into an absolute byte position using MPI_FILE_GET_BYTE_OFFSET, then call MPI_FILE_SET_VIEW with the resulting displacement. □

MPI_FILE_GET_BYTE_OFFSET(fh, offset, disp)

IN	fh	file handle (handle)
IN	offset	offset (integer)
OUT	disp	absolute byte position of offset (integer)

```
int MPI_File_get_byte_offset(MPI_File fh, MPI_Offset offset,
    MPI_Offset *disp)
```

```
MPI_FILE_GET_BYTE_OFFSET(FH, OFFSET, DISP, IERROR)
    INTEGER FH, IERROR
    INTEGER(KIND=MPI_OFFSET_KIND) OFFSET, DISP
```

```
MPI::Offset MPI::File::Get_byte_offset(const MPI::Offset disp) const
```

MPI_FILE_GET_BYTE_OFFSET converts a view-relative offset into an absolute byte position. The absolute byte position (from the beginning of the file) of offset relative to the current view of fh is returned in disp.

7.4.4 Data Access with Shared File Pointers

MPI maintains exactly one shared file pointer per collective MPI_FILE_OPEN (shared among processes in the communicator's group). The current value of this pointer implicitly specifies the offset in the data access routines described in this section. These routines only use and update the shared file pointer maintained by MPI. The individual file pointers are neither used nor updated.

The shared file pointer routines have the same semantics as the data access with explicit offset routines described in Section 7.4.2 with the following modifications:

- The offset is defined to be the current value of the MPI-maintained shared file pointer,
- The effect of multiple calls to shared file pointer routines is defined to behave as if the calls were serialized, and
- The use of shared file pointer routines is erroneous unless all processes use the same file view.

For the noncollective shared file pointer routines, the serialization ordering is not deterministic. The user needs to use other synchronization means to enforce a specific order.

After a shared file pointer operation is initiated, the shared file pointer is updated to point to the next etype after the last one that will be accessed. The file pointer is updated relative to the current view of the file.

Noncollective Operations.

MPI_FILE_READ_SHARED(fh, buf, count, datatype, status)

INOUT	fh	file handle (handle)
OUT	buf	initial address of buffer (choice)
IN	count	number of elements in buffer (integer)
IN	datatype	datatype of each buffer element (handle)
OUT	status	status object (Status)

```
int MPI_File_read_shared(MPI_File fh, void *buf, int count,
    MPI_Datatype datatype, MPI_Status *status)
```

```
MPI_FILE_READ_SHARED(FH, BUF, COUNT, DATATYPE, STATUS, IERROR)
    <type> BUF(*)
    INTEGER FH, COUNT, DATATYPE, STATUS(MPI_STATUS_SIZE), IERROR
```

```
void MPI::File::Read_shared(void* buf, int count,
    const MPI::Datatype& datatype, MPI::Status& status)
```

```
void MPI::File::Read_shared(void* buf, int count,
    const MPI::Datatype& datatype)
```

MPI_FILE_READ_SHARED reads a file using the shared file pointer.

MPI_FILE_WRITE_SHARED(fh, buf, count, datatype, status)

INOUT	fh	file handle (handle)
IN	buf	initial address of buffer (choice)
IN	count	number of elements in buffer (integer)
IN	datatype	datatype of each buffer element (handle)
OUT	status	status object (Status)

```
int MPI_File_write_shared(MPI_File fh, void *buf, int count,
    MPI_Datatype datatype, MPI_Status *status)
```

```
MPI_FILE_WRITE_SHARED(FH, BUF, COUNT, DATATYPE, STATUS, IERROR)
    <type> BUF(*)
```

```
      INTEGER FH, COUNT, DATATYPE, STATUS(MPI_STATUS_SIZE), IERROR
```

void MPI::File::Write_shared(const void* buf, int count,
    const MPI::Datatype& datatype, MPI::Status& status)

void MPI::File::Write_shared(const void* buf, int count,
    const MPI::Datatype& datatype)

MPI_FILE_WRITE_SHARED writes a file using the shared file pointer.

MPI_FILE_IREAD_SHARED(fh, buf, count, datatype, request)

INOUT	fh	file handle (handle)
OUT	buf	initial address of buffer (choice)
IN	count	number of elements in buffer (integer)
IN	datatype	datatype of each buffer element (handle)
OUT	request	request object (handle)

---

int MPI_File_iread_shared(MPI_File fh, void *buf, int count,
    MPI_Datatype datatype, MPI_Request *request)

MPI_FILE_IREAD_SHARED(FH, BUF, COUNT, DATATYPE, REQUEST, IERROR)
    <type> BUF(*)
    INTEGER FH, COUNT, DATATYPE, REQUEST, IERROR

MPI::Request MPI::File::Iread_shared(void* buf, int count,
    const MPI::Datatype& datatype)

MPI_FILE_IREAD_SHARED is a nonblocking version of the MPI_FILE_READ_-
SHARED interface.

MPI_FILE_IWRITE_SHARED(fh, buf, count, datatype, request)

INOUT	fh	file handle (handle)
IN	buf	initial address of buffer (choice)
IN	count	number of elements in buffer (integer)
IN	datatype	datatype of each buffer element (handle)
OUT	request	request object (handle)

---

int MPI_File_iwrite_shared(MPI_File fh, void *buf, int count,
    MPI_Datatype datatype, MPI_Request *request)

MPI_FILE_IWRITE_SHARED(FH, BUF, COUNT, DATATYPE, REQUEST, IERROR)

```
<type> BUF(*)
INTEGER FH, COUNT, DATATYPE, REQUEST, IERROR
```

MPI::Request MPI::File::Iwrite_shared(const void* buf, int count,
    const MPI::Datatype& datatype)

MPI_FILE_IWRITE_SHARED is a nonblocking version of the MPI_FILE_WRITE_-
SHARED interface.

Collective Operations.   The semantics of a collective access using a shared file
pointer is that the accesses to the file will be in the order determined by the ranks
of the processes within the group. For each process, the location in the file at which
data is accessed is the position at which the shared file pointer would be after all
processes whose ranks within the group less than that of this process had accessed
their data. In addition, in order to prevent subsequent shared offset accesses by
the same processes from interfering with this collective access, the call might return
only after all the processes within the group have initiated their accesses. When the
call returns, the shared file pointer points to the next etype accessible, according
to the file view used by all processes, after the last etype requested.

Advice to users.   There may be some programs in which all processes in the
group need to access the file using the shared file pointer, but the program may not
require that data be accessed in order of process rank. In such programs, using the
shared ordered routines (e.g., MPI_FILE_WRITE_ORDERED rather than MPI_FILE_-
WRITE_SHARED) may enable an implementation to optimize access, improving
performance. □

Advice to implementors.   Accesses to the data requested by all processes do not
have to be serialized. Once all processes have issued their requests, locations within
the file for all accesses can be computed, and accesses can proceed independently
from each other, possibly in parallel. □

MPI_FILE_READ_ORDERED(fh, buf, count, datatype, status)

INOUT	fh	file handle (handle)
OUT	buf	initial address of buffer (choice)
IN	count	number of elements in buffer (integer)
IN	datatype	datatype of each buffer element (handle)
OUT	status	status object (Status)

```
int MPI_File_read_ordered(MPI_File fh, void *buf, int count,
    MPI_Datatype datatype, MPI_Status *status)
```

```
MPI_FILE_READ_ORDERED(FH, BUF, COUNT, DATATYPE, STATUS, IERROR)
    <type> BUF(*)
    INTEGER FH, COUNT, DATATYPE, STATUS(MPI_STATUS_SIZE), IERROR
```

```
void MPI::File::Read_ordered(void* buf, int count,
    const MPI::Datatype& datatype, MPI::Status& status)
```

```
void MPI::File::Read_ordered(void* buf, int count,
    const MPI::Datatype& datatype)
```

MPI_FILE_READ_ORDERED is a collective version of the MPI_FILE_READ_-SHARED interface.

MPI_FILE_WRITE_ORDERED(fh, buf, count, datatype, status)

INOUT	fh	file handle (handle)
IN	buf	initial address of buffer (choice)
IN	count	number of elements in buffer (integer)
IN	datatype	datatype of each buffer element (handle)
OUT	status	status object (Status)

```
int MPI_File_write_ordered(MPI_File fh, void *buf, int count,
    MPI_Datatype datatype, MPI_Status *status)
```

```
MPI_FILE_WRITE_ORDERED(FH, BUF, COUNT, DATATYPE, STATUS, IERROR)
    <type> BUF(*)
    INTEGER FH, COUNT, DATATYPE, STATUS(MPI_STATUS_SIZE), IERROR
```

```
void MPI::File::Write_ordered(const void* buf, int count,
    const MPI::Datatype& datatype, MPI::Status& status)
```

```
void MPI::File::Write_ordered(const void* buf, int count,
    const MPI::Datatype& datatype)
```

MPI_FILE_WRITE_ORDERED is a collective version of the MPI_FILE_WRITE_-SHARED interface.

Seek. If MPI_MODE_SEQUENTIAL mode was specified when the file was opened, it is erroneous to call the following two routines (MPI_FILE_SEEK_SHARED and MPI_FILE_GET_POSITION_SHARED).

MPI_FILE_SEEK_SHARED(fh, offset, whence)

INOUT	fh	file handle (handle)
IN	offset	file offset (integer)
IN	whence	update mode (state)

```
int MPI_File_seek_shared(MPI_File fh, MPI_Offset offset, int whence)
```

```
MPI_FILE_SEEK_SHARED(FH, OFFSET, WHENCE, IERROR)
    INTEGER FH, WHENCE, IERROR
    INTEGER(KIND=MPI_OFFSET_KIND) OFFSET
```

```
void MPI::File::Seek_shared(MPI::Offset offset, int whence)
```

MPI_FILE_SEEK_SHARED updates the shared file pointer according to whence, which has the following possible values:

MPI_SEEK_SET: the pointer is set to offset

MPI_SEEK_CUR: the pointer is set to the current pointer position plus offset

MPI_SEEK_END: the pointer is set to the end of file plus offset

MPI_FILE_SEEK_SHARED is collective; all the processes in the communicator group associated with the file handle fh must call MPI_FILE_SEEK_SHARED with the same values for offset and whence.

The offset can be negative, which allows seeking backwards. It is erroneous to seek to a negative position in the view.

MPI_FILE_GET_POSITION_SHARED(fh, offset)

| IN | fh | file handle (handle) |
| OUT | offset | offset of shared pointer (integer) |

```
int MPI_File_get_position_shared(MPI_File fh, MPI_Offset *offset)
```

```
MPI_FILE_GET_POSITION_SHARED(FH, OFFSET, IERROR)
    INTEGER FH, IERROR
    INTEGER(KIND=MPI_OFFSET_KIND) OFFSET
```

```
MPI::Offset MPI::File::Get_position_shared() const
```

MPI_FILE_GET_POSITION_SHARED returns, in offset, the current position of the shared file pointer in etype units relative to the current view.

Advice to users.   The offset can be used in a future call to MPI_FILE_SEEK_-
SHARED using whence = MPI_SEEK_SET to return to the current position. To set
the displacement to the current file pointer position, first convert offset into an
absolute byte position using MPI_FILE_GET_BYTE_OFFSET, then call MPI_FILE_-
SET_VIEW with the resulting displacement. ⬜

7.4.5   Split Collective Data Access Routines

MPI provides a restricted form of "nonblocking collective" I/O operations for all
data accesses using *split collective* data access routines.   These routines are referred
to as "split" collective routines because a single collective operation is split in two:
a begin routine and an end routine. The begin routine begins the operation, much
like a nonblocking data access (e.g., MPI_FILE_IREAD). The end routine completes
the operation, much like the matching test or wait (e.g., MPI_WAIT). As with
nonblocking data access operations, the user must not use the buffer passed to a
begin routine while the routine is outstanding; the operation must be completed
with an end routine before it is safe to free buffers, etc.

   Split collective data access operations on a file handle fh are subject to the rules
given below.

• On any MPI process, each file handle may have at most one active split collective
operation at any time.

• Begin calls are collective over the group of processes that participated in the
collective open and follow the ordering rules for collective calls.

• End calls are collective over the group of processes that participated in the
collective open and follow the ordering rules for collective calls. Each end call
matches the preceding begin call for the same collective operation. When an end
call is made, exactly one unmatched begin call for the same operation must precede
it.

• An implementation is free to implement any split collective data access routine
using the corresponding blocking collective routine when either the begin call (e.g.,
MPI_FILE_READ_ALL_BEGIN) or the end call (e.g., MPI_FILE_READ_ALL_END) is
issued. The begin and end calls are provided to allow the user and MPI implementation to optimize the collective operation.

• Split collective operations do not match the corresponding regular collective
operations. For example, in a single collective read operation, an MPI_FILE_READ_-
ALL on one process does not match an MPI_FILE_READ_ALL_BEGIN/MPI_FILE_-
READ_ALL_END pair on another process.

• Split collective routines must specify the same buffer in both the begin and end routines. By specifying the buffer that receives data in the end routine, we can avoid many (though not all) of the problems described in "A Problem with Register Optimization," Section 8.2.2.

• No collective I/O operations are permitted on a file handle concurrently with a split collective access on that file handle (i.e., between the begin and end of the access). That is,

```
MPI_File_read_all_begin(fh, ...);
...
MPI_File_read_all(fh, ...);
...
MPI_File_read_all_end(fh, ...);
```

is erroneous.

• In a multithreaded implementation, any split collective begin and end operation called by a process must be called from the same thread. This restriction is made to simplify the implementation in the multithreaded case. (Note that we have already disallowed having two threads begin a split collective operation on the same file handle since only one split collective operation can be active on a file handle at any time.)

The arguments for these routines have the same meanings as for the equivalent collective versions (e.g., the argument definitions for MPI_FILE_READ_ALL_BEGIN and MPI_FILE_READ_ALL_END are equivalent to the arguments for MPI_FILE_READ_ALL). The begin routine (e.g., MPI_FILE_READ_ALL_BEGIN) begins a split collective operation that, when completed with the matching end routine (i.e., MPI_FILE_READ_ALL_END) produces the result as defined for the equivalent collective routine (i.e., MPI_FILE_READ_ALL).

For the purpose of consistency semantics (Section 7.6.1), a matched pair of split collective data access operations (e.g., MPI_FILE_READ_ALL_BEGIN and MPI_FILE_READ_ALL_END) compose a single data access.

MPI_FILE_READ_AT_ALL_BEGIN(fh, offset, buf, count, datatype)

IN	fh	file handle (handle)
IN	offset	file offset (integer)
OUT	buf	initial address of buffer (choice)
IN	count	number of elements in buffer (integer)
IN	datatype	datatype of each buffer element (handle)

```
int MPI_File_read_at_all_begin(MPI_File fh, MPI_Offset offset,
    void *buf, int count, MPI_Datatype datatype)
```

```
MPI_FILE_READ_AT_ALL_BEGIN(FH, OFFSET, BUF, COUNT, DATATYPE, IERROR)
    <type> BUF(*)
    INTEGER FH, COUNT, DATATYPE, IERROR
    INTEGER(KIND=MPI_OFFSET_KIND) OFFSET
```

```
void MPI::File::Read_at_all_begin(MPI::Offset offset, void* buf,
    int count, const MPI::Datatype& datatype)
```

MPI_FILE_READ_AT_ALL_END(fh, buf, status)

IN	fh	file handle (handle)
OUT	buf	initial address of buffer (choice)
OUT	status	status object (Status)

```
int MPI_File_read_at_all_end(MPI_File fh, void *buf,
    MPI_Status *status)
```

```
MPI_FILE_READ_AT_ALL_END(FH, BUF, STATUS, IERROR)
    <type> BUF(*)
    INTEGER FH, STATUS(MPI_STATUS_SIZE), IERROR
```

```
void MPI::File::Read_at_all_end(void* buf, MPI::Status& status)
```

```
void MPI::File::Read_at_all_end(void* buf)
```

MPI_FILE_WRITE_AT_ALL_BEGIN(fh, offset, buf, count, datatype)

INOUT	fh	file handle (handle)
IN	offset	file offset (integer)
IN	buf	initial address of buffer (choice)
IN	count	number of elements in buffer (integer)
IN	datatype	datatype of each buffer element (handle)

```
int MPI_File_write_at_all_begin(MPI_File fh, MPI_Offset offset,
    void *buf, int count, MPI_Datatype datatype)
```

```
MPI_FILE_WRITE_AT_ALL_BEGIN(FH, OFFSET, BUF, COUNT, DATATYPE, IERROR)
    <type> BUF(*)
```

```
    INTEGER FH, COUNT, DATATYPE, IERROR
    INTEGER(KIND=MPI_OFFSET_KIND) OFFSET

void MPI::File::Write_at_all_begin(MPI::Offset offset,
    const void* buf, int count, const MPI::Datatype& datatype)
```

MPI_FILE_WRITE_AT_ALL_END(fh, buf, status)

INOUT	fh	file handle (handle)
IN	buf	initial address of buffer (choice)
OUT	status	status object (Status)

```
int MPI_File_write_at_all_end(MPI_File fh, void *buf,
    MPI_Status *status)

MPI_FILE_WRITE_AT_ALL_END(FH, BUF, STATUS, IERROR)
    <type> BUF(*)
    INTEGER FH, STATUS(MPI_STATUS_SIZE), IERROR

void MPI::File::Write_at_all_end(const void* buf,
    MPI::Status& status)

void MPI::File::Write_at_all_end(const void* buf)
```

MPI_FILE_READ_ALL_BEGIN(fh, buf, count, datatype)

INOUT	fh	file handle (handle)
OUT	buf	initial address of buffer (choice)
IN	count	number of elements in buffer (integer)
IN	datatype	datatype of each buffer element (handle)

```
int MPI_File_read_all_begin(MPI_File fh, void *buf, int count,
    MPI_Datatype datatype)

MPI_FILE_READ_ALL_BEGIN(FH, BUF, COUNT, DATATYPE, IERROR)
    <type> BUF(*)
    INTEGER FH, COUNT, DATATYPE, IERROR

void MPI::File::Read_all_begin(void* buf, int count,
    const MPI::Datatype& datatype)
```

MPI_FILE_READ_ALL_END(fh, buf, status)

INOUT	fh	file handle (handle)
OUT	buf	initial address of buffer (choice)
OUT	status	status object (Status)

---

int MPI_File_read_all_end(MPI_File fh, void *buf, MPI_Status *status)

MPI_FILE_READ_ALL_END(FH, BUF, STATUS, IERROR)
    <type> BUF(*)
    INTEGER FH, STATUS(MPI_STATUS_SIZE), IERROR

void MPI::File::Read_all_end(void* buf, MPI::Status& status)

void MPI::File::Read_all_end(void* buf)

MPI_FILE_WRITE_ALL_BEGIN(fh, buf, count, datatype)

INOUT	fh	file handle (handle)
IN	buf	initial address of buffer (choice)
IN	count	number of elements in buffer (integer)
IN	datatype	datatype of each buffer element (handle)

---

int MPI_File_write_all_begin(MPI_File fh, void *buf, int count,
    MPI_Datatype datatype)

MPI_FILE_WRITE_ALL_BEGIN(FH, BUF, COUNT, DATATYPE, IERROR)
    <type> BUF(*)
    INTEGER FH, COUNT, DATATYPE, IERROR

void MPI::File::Write_all_begin(const void* buf, int count,
    const MPI::Datatype& datatype)

MPI_FILE_WRITE_ALL_END(fh, buf, status)

INOUT	fh	file handle (handle)
IN	buf	initial address of buffer (choice)
OUT	status	status object (Status)

```
int MPI_File_write_all_end(MPI_File fh, void *buf, MPI_Status *status)
```

```
MPI_FILE_WRITE_ALL_END(FH, BUF, STATUS, IERROR)
    <type> BUF(*)
    INTEGER FH, STATUS(MPI_STATUS_SIZE), IERROR
```

```
void MPI::File::Write_all_end(const void* buf, MPI::Status& status)
```

```
void MPI::File::Write_all_end(const void* buf)
```

MPI_FILE_READ_ORDERED_BEGIN(fh, buf, count, datatype)

INOUT	fh	file handle (handle)
OUT	buf	initial address of buffer (choice)
IN	count	number of elements in buffer (integer)
IN	datatype	datatype of each buffer element (handle)

```
int MPI_File_read_ordered_begin(MPI_File fh, void *buf, int count,
    MPI_Datatype datatype)
```

```
MPI_FILE_READ_ORDERED_BEGIN(FH, BUF, COUNT, DATATYPE, IERROR)
    <type> BUF(*)
    INTEGER FH, COUNT, DATATYPE, IERROR
```

```
void MPI::File::Read_ordered_begin(void* buf, int count,
    const MPI::Datatype& datatype)
```

MPI_FILE_READ_ORDERED_END(fh, buf, status)

INOUT	fh	file handle (handle)
OUT	buf	initial address of buffer (choice)
OUT	status	status object (Status)

```
int MPI_File_read_ordered_end(MPI_File fh, void *buf,
    MPI_Status *status)
```

```
MPI_FILE_READ_ORDERED_END(FH, BUF, STATUS, IERROR)
    <type> BUF(*)
    INTEGER FH, STATUS(MPI_STATUS_SIZE), IERROR
```

```
void MPI::File::Read_ordered_end(void* buf, MPI::Status& status)
```

```
void MPI::File::Read_ordered_end(void* buf)
```

MPI_FILE_WRITE_ORDERED_BEGIN(fh, buf, count, datatype)

INOUT	fh	file handle (handle)
IN	buf	initial address of buffer (choice)
IN	count	number of elements in buffer (integer)
IN	datatype	datatype of each buffer element (handle)

```
int MPI_File_write_ordered_begin(MPI_File fh, void *buf, int count,
    MPI_Datatype datatype)
```

```
MPI_FILE_WRITE_ORDERED_BEGIN(FH, BUF, COUNT, DATATYPE, IERROR)
    <type> BUF(*)
    INTEGER FH, COUNT, DATATYPE, IERROR
```

```
void MPI::File::Write_ordered_begin(const void* buf, int count,
    const MPI::Datatype& datatype)
```

MPI_FILE_WRITE_ORDERED_END(fh, buf, status)

INOUT	fh	file handle (handle)
IN	buf	initial address of buffer (choice)
OUT	status	status object (Status)

```
int MPI_File_write_ordered_end(MPI_File fh, void *buf,
    MPI_Status *status)
```

```
MPI_FILE_WRITE_ORDERED_END(FH, BUF, STATUS, IERROR)
    <type> BUF(*)
    INTEGER FH, STATUS(MPI_STATUS_SIZE), IERROR
```

```
void MPI::File::Write_ordered_end(const void* buf,
    MPI::Status& status)
```

```
void MPI::File::Write_ordered_end(const void* buf)
```

7.5   File Interoperability

At the most basic level, file interoperability is the ability to read the information previously written to a file—not just the bits of data, but the actual information the bits represent. MPI guarantees full interoperability within a single MPI environment, and supports increased interoperability outside that environment through the external data representation (Section 7.5.2) as well as the data conversion functions (Section 7.5.3).

Interoperability within a single MPI environment (which could be considered "operability") ensures that file data written by one MPI process can be read by any other MPI process, subject to the consistency constraints (see Section 7.6.1), provided that it would have been possible to start the two processes simultaneously and have them reside in a single MPI_COMM_WORLD. Furthermore, both processes must see the same data values at every absolute byte offset in the file for which data was written.

This single environment file interoperability implies that file data is accessible regardless of the number of processes.

There are three aspects to file interoperability:

- transferring the bits,
- converting between different file structures, and
- converting between different machine representations.

The first two aspects of file interoperability are beyond the scope of this standard, as both are highly machine-dependent. However, transferring the bits of a file into and out of the MPI environment (e.g., by writing a file to tape) is required to be supported by all MPI implementations. In particular, an implementation must specify how familiar operations similar to POSIX cp, rm, and mv can be performed on the file. Furthermore, it is expected that the facility provided maintains the correspondence between absolute byte offsets (e.g., after possible file structure conversion, the data bits at byte offset 102 in the MPI environment are at byte offset 102 outside the MPI environment). As an example, a simple off-line conversion utility that transfers and converts files between the native file system and the MPI environment would suffice, provided it maintained the offset coherence mentioned above. In a high-quality implementation of MPI, users will be able to manipulate MPI files using the same or similar tools that the native file system offers for manipulating its files.

The remaining aspect of file interoperability, converting between different machine representations, is supported by the typing information specified in the etype and filetype. This facility allows the information in files to be shared between any two applications, regardless of whether they use MPI, and regardless of the machine architectures on which they run.

MPI supports multiple data representations: native, internal, and external32. An implementation may support additional data representations. MPI also supports user-defined data representations (see Section 7.5.3). The native and internal data representations are implementation-dependent, while the external32 representation is common to all MPI implementations and facilitates file interoperability. The data representation is specified in the *datarep* argument to MPI_FILE_SET_VIEW.

Advice to users.   MPI is not guaranteed to retain knowledge of what data representation was used when a file is written. Therefore, to correctly retrieve file data, an MPI application is responsible for specifying the same data representation as was used to create the file. ▯

native: Data in this representation is stored in a file exactly as it is in memory. The advantage of this data representation is that data precision and I/O performance are not lost in type conversions with a purely homogeneous environment. The disadvantage is the loss of transparent interoperability within a heterogeneous MPI environment.

Advice to users.   This data representation should only be used in a homogeneous MPI environment, or when the MPI application is capable of performing the data type conversions itself. ▯

Advice to implementors.   When implementing read and write operations on top of MPI message passing, the message data should be typed as MPI_BYTE to ensure that the message routines do not perform any type conversions on the data. ▯

internal: This data representation can be used for I/O operations in a homogeneous or heterogeneous environment; the implementation will perform type conversions if necessary. The implementation is free to store data in any format of its choice, with the restriction that it will maintain constant extents for all predefined datatypes in any one file. The environment in which the resulting file can be reused is implementation defined and must be documented by the implementation.

Rationale.   This data representation allows the implementation to perform I/O efficiently in a heterogeneous environment, though with implementation-defined restrictions on how the file can be reused. ▯

Advice to implementors. Since external32 is a superset of the functionality provided by internal, an implementation may choose to implement internal as external32. ⬜

external32: This data representation states that read and write operations convert all data from and to the external32 representation defined in Section 7.5.2. The data conversion rules for communication also apply to these conversions (see Section 3.3.2, page 25–27, of the MPI-1 document). The data on the storage medium is always in this canonical representation, and the data in memory is always in the local process's native representation.

This data representation has several advantages. First, all processes reading the file in a heterogeneous MPI environment will automatically have the data converted to their respective native representations. Second, the file can be exported from one MPI environment and imported into any other MPI environment with the guarantee that the second environment will be able to read all the data in the file.

The disadvantage of this data representation is that data precision and I/O performance may be lost in data type conversions.

Advice to implementors. When implementing read and write operations on top of MPI message passing, the message data should be converted to and from the external32 representation in the client, and sent as type MPI_BYTE. This will avoid possible double data type conversions and the associated further loss of precision and performance. ⬜

7.5.1 Datatypes for File Interoperability

If the file data representation is other than native, care must be taken in constructing etypes and filetypes. Any of the datatype constructor functions may be used; however, for those functions that accept displacements in bytes, the displacements must be specified in terms of their values in the file for the file data representation being used. MPI will interpret these byte displacements as is; no scaling will be done. The function MPI_FILE_GET_TYPE_EXTENT can be used to calculate the extents of datatypes in the file. For etypes and filetypes that are portable datatypes (see Section 1.4), MPI will scale any displacements in the datatypes to match the file data representation. Datatypes passed as arguments to read/write routines specify the data layout in memory; therefore, they must always be constructed using displacements corresponding to displacements in memory.

Advice to users. One can logically think of the file as if it were stored in the memory of a file server. The etype and filetype are interpreted as if they were defined at this file server, by the same sequence of calls used to define them at the calling process. If the data representation is native, then this logical file server runs on the same architecture as the calling process, so that these types define the same data layout on the file as they would define in the memory of the calling process. If the etype and filetype are portable datatypes, then the data layout defined in the file is the same as would be defined in the calling process memory, up to a scaling factor. The routine MPI_FILE_GET_FILE_EXTENT can be used to calculate this scaling factor. Thus, two equivalent portable datatypes define the same data layout in the file, even in a heterogeneous environment with internal, external32, or user-defined data representations. If they are not portable and equivalent, the etype and filetype must be constructed so that their typemap and extent are the same on any architecture. This can be achieved if they have an explicit upper bound and lower bound (defined using MPI_TYPE_CREATE_RESIZED). This condition must also be fulfilled by any datatype that is used in the construction of the etype and filetype, if this datatype is replicated contiguously, either explicitly, by a call to MPI_TYPE_CONTIGUOUS, or implicitly, by a blocklength argument that is greater than one. If an etype or filetype is not portable, and has a typemap or extent that is architecture-dependent, then the data layout specified by it on a file is implementation-dependent.

File data representations other than native may be different from corresponding data representations in memory. Therefore, for these file data representations, it is important not to use hardwired byte offsets for file positioning, including the initial displacement that specifies the view. When a portable datatype (see Section 1.4) is used in a data access operation, any holes in the datatype are scaled to match the data representation. However, note that this technique only works when all the processes that created the file view build their etypes from the same predefined datatypes. For example, if one process uses an etype built from MPI_INT and another uses an etype built from MPI_FLOAT, the resulting views may be nonportable because the relative sizes of these types may differ from one data representation to another. ☐

MPI_FILE_GET_TYPE_EXTENT(fh, datatype, extent)

IN	fh	file handle (handle)
IN	datatype	datatype (handle)
OUT	extent	datatype extent (integer)

```
int MPI_File_get_type_extent(MPI_File fh, MPI_Datatype datatype,
    MPI_Aint *extent)
```

```
MPI_FILE_GET_TYPE_EXTENT(FH, DATATYPE, EXTENT, IERROR)
    INTEGER FH, DATATYPE, IERROR
    INTEGER(KIND=MPI_ADDRESS_KIND) EXTENT
```

```
MPI::Aint MPI::File::Get_type_extent(const MPI::Datatype& datatype)
    const
```

MPI_FILE_GET_TYPE_EXTENT returns the extent of datatype in the file fh. This extent will be the same for all processes accessing the file fh. If the current view uses a user-defined data representation (see Section 7.5.3), MPI uses the dtype_file_-extent_fn callback to calculate the extent.

Advice to implementors.   In the case of user-defined data representations, the extent of a derived datatype can be calculated by first determining the extents of the predefined datatypes in this derived datatype using dtype_file_extent_fn (see Section 7.5.3). □

7.5.2   External Data Representation: external32

All MPI implementations are required to support the data representation defined in this section. Datatypes listed in this section need not be supported if they are not required to be supported by other parts of MPI (e.g., MPI_INTEGER2 on a machine that does not support 2-byte integers).

All floating point values are in big-endian IEEE format [13] of the appropriate size. Floating point values are represented by one of three IEEE formats. These are the IEEE "Single," "Double," and "Double Extended" formats, requiring 4, 8 and 16 bytes of storage, respectively. For the IEEE "Double Extended" formats, MPI specifies a Format Width of 16 bytes, with 15 exponent bits, bias = +10383, 112 fraction bits, and an encoding analogous to the "Double" format. All integral values are in two's complement big-endian format. Big-endian means that the most significant byte is the one with the lowest address. For Fortran LOGICAL and C++ bool, zero implies false and nonzero implies true. Fortran COMPLEX and DOUBLE COMPLEX are represented by a pair of floating point format values for the real and imaginary components. Characters are in ISO 8859-1 format [14]. Wide characters (of type MPI_WCHAR) are in Unicode format [26].

All signed numerals (e.g., MPI_INT, MPI_REAL) have the sign bit at the most significant bit. MPI_COMPLEX and MPI_DOUBLE_COMPLEX have the sign bit of the real and imaginary parts at the most significant bit of each part. The size of each MPI datatype is shown in Table 7.2.

According to IEEE specifications [13], the "NaN" (not a number) is system-dependent. It should not be interpreted within MPI as anything other than "NaN."

Advice to implementors. The MPI treatment of "NaN" is similar to the approach used in XDR (see `ftp://ds.internic.net/rfc/rfc1832.txt`). □

All data is byte aligned, regardless of type. All data items are stored contiguously in the file.

Advice to implementors. All bytes of LOGICAL and bool must be checked to determine the value. □

Advice to users. The type MPI_PACKED is treated as bytes and is not converted. The user should be aware that MPI_PACK has the option of placing a header in the beginning of the pack buffer. □

The size of the predefined datatypes returned from MPI_TYPE_CREATE_-F90_REAL, MPI_TYPE_CREATE_F90_COMPLEX, and MPI_TYPE_CREATE_F90_-INTEGER are defined in Section 8.2.5.

Advice to implementors. When converting a larger-sized integer to a smaller-sized integer, only the less significant bytes are moved. Care must be taken to preserve the sign bit value. This prevents conversion errors if the data range is within the range of the smaller size integer. □

7.5.3 User-Defined Data Representations

There are two situations that cannot be handled by the required representations:

1. A user wants to write a file in a representation unknown to the implementation, and

2. A user wants to read a file written in a representation unknown to the implementation.

User-defined data representations allow the user to insert a third-party converter into the I/O stream to do the data representation conversion.

Table 7.2
Datatypes defined for external32

Type	Length
MPI_PACKED	1
MPI_BYTE	1
MPI_CHAR	1
MPI_UNSIGNED_CHAR	1
MPI_SIGNED_CHAR	1
MPI_WCHAR	2
MPI_SHORT	2
MPI_UNSIGNED_SHORT	2
MPI_INT	4
MPI_UNSIGNED	4
MPI_LONG	4
MPI_UNSIGNED_LONG	4
MPI_FLOAT	4
MPI_DOUBLE	8
MPI_LONG_DOUBLE	16
MPI_CHARACTER	1
MPI_LOGICAL	4
MPI_INTEGER	4
MPI_REAL	4
MPI_DOUBLE_PRECISION	8
MPI_COMPLEX	2*4
MPI_DOUBLE_COMPLEX	2*8

Optional Type	Length
MPI_INTEGER1	1
MPI_INTEGER2	2
MPI_INTEGER4	4
MPI_INTEGER8	8
MPI_LONG_LONG	8
MPI_UNSIGNED_LONG_LONG	8
MPI_REAL4	4
MPI_REAL8	8
MPI_REAL16	16

MPI_REGISTER_DATAREP(datarep, read_conversion_fn, write_conversion_fn,
   dtype_file_extent_fn, extra_state)

IN	datarep	data representation identifier (string)
IN	read_conversion_fn	function invoked to convert from file representation to native representation (function)
IN	write_conversion_fn	function invoked to convert from native representation to file representation (function)
IN	dtype_file_extent_fn	function invoked to get the extent of a datatype as represented in the file (function)
IN	extra_state	extra state

```
int MPI_Register_datarep(char *datarep,
    MPI_Datarep_conversion_function *read_conversion_fn,
    MPI_Datarep_conversion_function *write_conversion_fn,
    MPI_Datarep_extent_function *dtype_file_extent_fn,
    void *extra_state)
```

```
MPI_REGISTER_DATAREP(DATAREP, READ_CONVERSION_FN, WRITE_CONVERSION_FN,
    DTYPE_FILE_EXTENT_FN, EXTRA_STATE, IERROR)
    CHARACTER*(*) DATAREP
    EXTERNAL READ_CONVERSION_FN, WRITE_CONVERSION_FN,
    DTYPE_FILE_EXTENT_FN
    INTEGER(KIND=MPI_ADDRESS_KIND) EXTRA_STATE
    INTEGER IERROR
```

```
void MPI::Register_datarep(const char* datarep,
    MPI::Datarep_conversion_function* read_conversion_fn,
    MPI::Datarep_conversion_function* write_conversion_fn,
    MPI::Datarep_extent_function* dtype_file_extent_fn,
    void* extra_state)
```

The call associates read_conversion_fn, write_conversion_fn, and dtype_file_extent_fn with the data representation identifier datarep. datarep can then be used as an argument to MPI_FILE_SET_VIEW, causing subsequent data access operations to call the conversion functions to convert all data items accessed between file data representation and native representation. MPI_REGISTER_DATAREP is a local operation and only registers the data representation for the calling MPI process. If datarep is already defined, an error in the error class MPI_ERR_DUP_DATAREP is raised using the default file error handler (see Section 7.7). The length of a data representation string is limited to the value of MPI_MAX_DATAREP_STRING (MPI::MAX_DATAREP_STRING in C++). MPI_MAX_DATAREP_STRING must be large enough to represent 64 characters (see Section 2.2.8). No routines are provided to delete data representations and free the associated resources; it is not expected that an application will generate them in significant numbers.

Extent Callback. The following defines the interface for the function that must be provided to provide the extent of a datatype in the file representation.

```
typedef int MPI_Datarep_extent_function(MPI_Datatype datatype,
    MPI_Aint *file_extent, void *extra_state);
```

```
SUBROUTINE DATAREP_EXTENT_FUNCTION(DATATYPE, EXTENT, EXTRA_STATE,
    IERROR)
    INTEGER DATATYPE, IERROR
    INTEGER(KIND=MPI_ADDRESS_KIND) EXTENT, EXTRA_STATE
```

```
typedef MPI::Datarep_extent_function(const MPI::Datatype& datatype,
    MPI::Aint& file_extent, void* extra_state);
```

The function dtype_file_extent_fn must return, in file_extent, the number of bytes required to store datatype in the file representation. The function is passed, in extra_state, the argument that was passed to the MPI_REGISTER_DATAREP call. MPI will only call this routine with predefined datatypes employed by the user.

Datarep Conversion Functions. typedef int

```
    MPI_Datarep_conversion_function(void *userbuf,
    MPI_Datatype datatype, int count, void *filebuf,
    MPI_Offset position, void *extra_state);
```

```
SUBROUTINE DATAREP_CONVERSION_FUNCTION(USERBUF, DATATYPE, COUNT,
    FILEBUF, POSITION, EXTRA_STATE, IERROR)
    <TYPE> USERBUF(*), FILEBUF(*)
    INTEGER COUNT, DATATYPE, IERROR
    INTEGER(KIND=MPI_OFFSET_KIND) POSITION
    INTEGER(KIND=MPI_ADDRESS_KIND) EXTRA_STATE
```

```
typedef MPI::Datarep_conversion_function(void* userbuf,
    MPI::Datatype& datatype, int count, void* filebuf,
    MPI::Offset position, void* extra_state);
```

The function read_conversion_fn must convert from file data representation to native representation. Before calling this routine, MPI allocates and fills filebuf with count contiguous data items. The type of each data item matches the corresponding entry for the predefined datatype in the type signature of datatype. The function is passed, in extra_state, the argument that was passed to the MPI_REGISTER_DATAREP call. The function must copy all count data items from filebuf to userbuf in the distribution described by datatype, converting each data item from file representation to native representation. datatype will be equivalent to the datatype that the user passed to the read or write function. If the size of datatype is less than the size of the count data items, the conversion function must treat datatype as being contiguously tiled over the userbuf. The conversion function must begin storing converted data at the location in userbuf specified by position into the (tiled) datatype.

Advice to users. Although the conversion functions have similarities to MPI_PACK and MPI_UNPACK, one should note the differences in the use of the arguments count and position. In the conversion functions, count is a count of data items (i.e., count of typemap entries of datatype), and position is an index into this typemap. In MPI_PACK, incount refers to the number of whole datatypes, and position is a number of bytes. ☐

Advice to implementors. A converted read operation could be implemented as follows:

1. Get file extent of all data items.
2. Allocate a filebuf large enough to hold all count data items.
3. Read data from file into filebuf.
4. Call read_conversion_fn to convert data and place it into userbuf.
5. Deallocate filebuf.

☐

If MPI cannot allocate a buffer large enough to hold all the data to be converted from a read operation, it may call the conversion function repeatedly using the same datatype and userbuf, and reading successive chunks of data to be converted in filebuf. For the first call (and in the case when all the data to be converted fits into filebuf), MPI will call the function with position set to zero. Data converted during this call will be stored in the userbuf according to the first count data items in datatype. Then in subsequent calls to the conversion function, MPI will increment the value in position by the count of items converted in the previous call.

Rationale.   Passing the conversion function a position and one datatype for the transfer allows the conversion function to decode the datatype only once and cache an internal representation of it on the datatype. On subsequent calls, the conversion function can use the position to quickly find its place in the datatype and continue storing converted data where it left off at the end of the previous call. □

Advice to users.   Although the conversion function may usefully cache an internal representation on the datatype, it should not cache any state information specific to an ongoing conversion operation, since it is possible for the same datatype to be used concurrently in multiple conversion operations. □

   The function write_conversion_fn must convert from native representation to file data representation. Before calling this routine, MPI allocates filebuf of a size large enough to hold count contiguous data items. The type of each data item matches the corresponding entry for the predefined datatype in the type signature of datatype. The function must copy count data items from userbuf in the distribution described by datatype, to a contiguous distribution in filebuf, converting each data item from native representation to file representation. If the size of datatype is less than the size of count data items, the conversion function must treat datatype as being contiguously tiled over the userbuf.

   The function must begin copying at the location in userbuf specified by position into the (tiled) datatype. datatype will be equivalent to the datatype that the user passed to the read or write function. The function is passed, in extra_state, the argument that was passed to the MPI_REGISTER_DATAREP call.

   The predefined constant MPI_CONVERSION_FN_NULL (MPI::CONVERSION_FN_-NULL in C++) may be used as either write_conversion_fn or read_conversion_fn. In that case, MPI will not attempt to invoke write_conversion_fn or read_conversion_-fn, respectively, but will perform the requested data access using the native data representation.

   An MPI implementation must ensure that all data accessed is converted, either by using a filebuf large enough to hold all the requested data items or else by making repeated calls to the conversion function with the same datatype argument and appropriate values for position.

   An implementation will only invoke the callback routines in this section (read_-conversion_fn, write_conversion_fn, and dtype_file_extent_fn) when one of the read or write routines in Section 7.4 or MPI_FILE_GET_TYPE_EXTENT is called by the user. dtype_file_extent_fn will only be passed predefined datatypes employed by the user.

The conversion functions will only be passed datatypes equivalent to those that the user has passed to one of the routines noted above.

The conversion functions must be reentrant. User-defined data representations are restricted to use byte alignment for all types. Furthermore, it is erroneous for the conversion functions to call any collective routines or to free datatype.

The conversion functions should return an error code. If the returned error code has a value other than MPI_SUCCESS, the implementation will raise an error in the class MPI_ERR_CONVERSION.

7.5.4 Matching Data Representations

It is the user's responsibility to ensure that the data representation used to read data from a file is *compatible* with the data representation that was used to write that data to the file.

In general, using the same data representation name when writing and reading a file does not guarantee that the representation is compatible. Similarly, using different representation names on two different implementations may yield compatible representations.

Compatibility can be obtained when external32 representation is used, although precision may be lost and the performance may be less than when native representation is used. Compatibility is guaranteed using external32 provided at least one of the following conditions is met.

- The data access routines directly use types enumerated in Section 7.5.2 that are supported by all implementations participating in the I/O. The predefined type used to write a data item must also be used to read a data item.
- In the case of Fortran 90 programs, the programs participating in the data accesses obtain compatible datatypes using MPI routines that specify precision and/or range (Section 8.2.5).
- For any given data item, the programs participating in the data accesses use compatible predefined types to write and read the data item.

User-defined data representations may be used to provide an implementation compatibility with another implementation's native or internal representation.

Advice to users.   Section 8.2.5 defines routines that support the use of matching datatypes in heterogeneous environments and contains examples illustrating their use. □

7.6   Consistency and Semantics

7.6.1   File Consistency

Consistency semantics define the outcome of multiple accesses to a single file. All file accesses in MPI are relative to a specific file handle created from a collective open. MPI provides three levels of consistency: sequential consistency among all accesses using a single file handle, sequential consistency among all accesses using file handles created from a single collective open with atomic mode enabled, and user-imposed consistency among accesses other than the above.

We say that a set of data access operations $A_1 \ldots A_n$ is sequentially consistent if they behave as if they were performed sequentially in an order consistent with program order—each access appears atomic, although the exact ordering of accesses is unspecified. All data access operations are considered separate operations. In particular, a collective operation on N processes is considered N separate operations for the purposes of this section, except for MPI_FILE_SET_SIZE and MPI_FILE_PREALLOCATE. User-imposed consistency may be obtained using program order and calls to MPI_FILE_SYNC.

Advice to users.   Consider, for example, a write operation A_1 and a read operation A_2 that access the same data, possibly from separate processes. If A_1 and A_2 are sequentially consistent, then either the read gets old data (before the write), or new data (after the write), but never a mixture. Note however that the definition of sequential consistency says nothing about whether A_1 and A_2 access the same data or are on the same process.

A standard counterexample to expectations about sequential consistency is I/O operations on an NFS filesystem accessed from processes on different hosts. Such I/O operations are not necessarily sequentially consistent even if they access different data. For instance two write operations to different areas of the same filesystem block may interfere with one another, as data is written in blocks at a time. Indeed, lack of such sequential consistency in the filesystem is an important reason to use MPI I/O. ▢

Let FH_1 be the set of file handles created from one particular collective open of the file foo and FH_2 be the set of file handles created from a different collective open of foo. Note that nothing restrictive is said about FH_1 and FH_2: the sizes of FH_1 and FH_2 may be different, the groups of processes used for each open may or may not intersect, the file handles in FH_1 may be destroyed before those in FH_2 are created, etc. We will consider the following three cases: a single file handle (e.g.,

$\mathrm{fh}_1 \in \mathrm{FH}_1$), two file handles created from a single collective open (e.g., $\mathrm{fh}_{1a} \in \mathrm{FH}_1$ and $\mathrm{fh}_{1b} \in \mathrm{FH}_1$), and two file handles from different collective opens (e.g., $\mathrm{fh}_1 \in \mathrm{FH}_1$ and $\mathrm{fh}_2 \in \mathrm{FH}_2$).

For the purpose of consistency semantics, a matched pair (Section 7.4.5) of split collective data access operations (e.g., MPI_FILE_READ_ALL_BEGIN and MPI_FILE_READ_ALL_END) compose a single data access operation. Similarly, a nonblocking data access routine (e.g., MPI_FILE_IREAD) and the routine which completes the request (e.g., MPI_WAIT) also compose a single data access operation. For all cases below, these data access operations are subject to the same constraints as blocking data access operations.

Advice to users.   For an MPI_FILE_IREAD and MPI_WAIT pair, the operation begins when MPI_FILE_IREAD is called and ends when MPI_WAIT returns. □

Let A_1 and A_2 be data access operations. Let D_1 (D_2) be the set of absolute byte displacements of every byte accessed in A_1 (A_2). The two data accesses *overlap* if $D_1 \cap D_2 \neq \emptyset$. The two data accesses *conflict* if they overlap and at least one is a write access.

Let SEQ_{fh} be a sequence of file operations on a single file handle, bracketed by MPI_FILE_SYNCs on that file handle. (Both opening and closing a file implicitly perform an MPI_FILE_SYNC.) SEQ_{fh} is a "write sequence" if any of the data access operations in the sequence are writes or if any of the file manipulation operations in the sequence change the state of the file (e.g., MPI_FILE_SET_SIZE or MPI_FILE_PREALLOCATE). Two sequences SEQ_1 and SEQ_2 or two operations A_1 and A_2 are *concurrent* if one may begin before the other is complete.

The requirements for guaranteeing sequential consistency among all accesses to a particular file are divided into the three cases given below. If any of these requirements are not met, then the value of all data in that file is implementation-dependent.

Case 1: $\mathbf{fh}_1 \in \mathbf{FH}_1$:   All operations on fh_1 are sequentially consistent if atomic mode is set. If nonatomic mode is set, then all operations on fh_1 are sequentially consistent if they are either not concurrent, not conflicting, or both.

Case 2: $\mathbf{fh}_{1a} \in \mathbf{FH}_1$ and $\mathbf{fh}_{1b} \in \mathbf{FH}_1$:   Let A_1 be a data access operation using fh_{1a}, and let A_2 be a data access operation using fh_{1b}. If A_1 does not conflict with A_2, MPI guarantees that the operations are sequentially consistent.

However, unlike POSIX semantics, the default MPI semantics for conflicting accesses do not guarantee sequential consistency. If A_1 and A_2 conflict, sequential consistency can be guaranteed by either enabling atomic mode via the MPI_FILE_-SET_ATOMICITY routine, or meeting the condition described in Case 3.

Case 3: $fh_1 \in FH_1$ and $fh_2 \in FH_2$: A write sequence SEQ_1 on fh_1 and another sequence SEQ_2 on fh_2. are guaranteed to be sequentially consistent if they are not concurrent or if fh_1 and fh_2 refer to different files. In other words, MPI_FILE_SYNC must be used together with a mechanism that guarantees nonconcurrency of the sequences.

See the examples in Section 7.6.10 for further clarification of some of these consistency semantics.

MPI_FILE_SET_ATOMICITY(fh, flag)

INOUT	fh	file handle (handle)
IN	flag	true to set atomic mode, false to set nonatomic mode (logical)

```
int MPI_File_set_atomicity(MPI_File fh, int flag)
```

```
MPI_FILE_SET_ATOMICITY(FH, FLAG, IERROR)
    INTEGER FH, IERROR
    LOGICAL FLAG
```

```
void MPI::File::Set_atomicity(bool flag)
```

Let FH be the set of file handles created by one collective open. The consistency semantics for data access operations using FH is set by collectively calling MPI_FILE_SET_ATOMICITY on FH. MPI_FILE_SET_ATOMICITY is collective; all processes in the group must pass identical values for fh and flag. If flag is true, atomic mode is set; if flag is false, nonatomic mode is set.

Changing the consistency semantics for an open file only affects new data accesses. All completed data accesses are guaranteed to abide by the consistency semantics in effect during their execution. Nonblocking data accesses and split collective operations that have not completed (e.g., via MPI_WAIT) are only guaranteed to abide by nonatomic mode consistency semantics.

Advice to implementors.   Since the semantics guaranteed by atomic mode are stronger than those guaranteed by nonatomic mode, an implementation is free to adhere to the more stringent atomic mode semantics for outstanding requests. ☐

MPI_FILE_GET_ATOMICITY(fh, flag)

IN	fh	file handle (handle)
OUT	flag	true if atomic mode, false if nonatomic mode (logical)

```
int MPI_File_get_atomicity(MPI_File fh, int *flag)
```

```
MPI_FILE_GET_ATOMICITY(FH, FLAG, IERROR)
    INTEGER FH, IERROR
    LOGICAL FLAG
```

```
bool MPI::File::Get_atomicity() const
```

MPI_FILE_GET_ATOMICITY returns the current consistency semantics for data access operations on the set of file handles created by one collective open. If flag is true, atomic mode is enabled; if flag is false, nonatomic mode is enabled.

MPI_FILE_SYNC(fh)

INOUT	fh	file handle (handle)

```
int MPI_File_sync(MPI_File fh)
```

```
MPI_FILE_SYNC(FH, IERROR)
    INTEGER FH, IERROR
```

```
void MPI::File::Sync()
```

Calling MPI_FILE_SYNC with fh causes all previous writes to fh by the calling process to be transferred to the storage device. If other processes have made updates to the storage device, then all such updates become visible to subsequent reads of fh by the calling process. MPI_FILE_SYNC may be necessary to ensure sequential consistency in certain cases (see above). MPI_FILE_SYNC is a collective operation.

The user is responsible for ensuring that all nonblocking and split collective operations on fh have been completed before calling MPI_FILE_SYNC—otherwise, the call to MPI_FILE_SYNC is erroneous.

Advice to users.   MPI does not define precisely a "storage device" and it may be unwise to make assumptions here (e.g., if the power goes off the data will be available when it comes back on). The storage device is a convenient abstraction that makes it possible to guarantee that file updates will be visible in other processes. A "sync" behaves like an I/O flush after a write, and like an I/O cache flush before a read. □

7.6.2   Random Access versus Sequential Files

MPI distinguishes ordinary random access files from sequential stream files, such as pipes and tape files. Sequential stream files must be opened with the MPI_MODE_SEQUENTIAL flag set in the amode. For these files, the only permitted data access operations are shared file pointer reads and writes. Filetypes and etypes with holes are erroneous. In addition, the notion of a repositionable file pointer is not meaningful; therefore, calls to MPI_FILE_SEEK_SHARED and MPI_FILE_GET_POSITION_SHARED are erroneous, and the pointer update rules specified for the data access routines do not apply. The amount of data accessed by a data access operation will be the amount requested unless the end of file is reached or an error is raised.

Rationale.   This implies that reading on a pipe will always wait until the requested amount of data is available or until the process writing to the pipe has issued an end of file. □

Finally, for some sequential files, such as those corresponding to magnetic tapes or streaming network connections, writes to the file may be destructive. In other words, a write may act as a truncate (an MPI_FILE_SET_SIZE with size set to the current position) followed by the write.

7.6.3   Progress

The progress rules of MPI are both a promise to users and a set of constraints on implementors. In cases where the progress rules restrict possible implementation choices more than the interface specification alone, the progress rules take precedence.

All blocking routines must complete in finite time unless an exceptional condition (such as resource exhaustion) causes an error.

Nonblocking data access routines inherit the following progress rule from non-blocking point-to-point communication: a nonblocking write is equivalent to a nonblocking send for which a receive is eventually posted, and a nonblocking read is equivalent to a nonblocking receive for which a send is eventually posted.

Finally, an implementation is free to delay progress of collective routines until all processes in the group associated with the collective call have invoked the routine. Once all processes in the group have invoked the routine, the progress rule of the equivalent noncollective routine must be followed.

7.6.4 Collective File Operations

Collective file operations are subject to the same restrictions as collective communication operations. For a complete discussion, please refer to the semantics set forth in Section I-4.14.

Collective file operations are collective over a dup of the communicator used to open the file—this duplicate communicator is implicitly specified via the file handle argument. Different processes can pass different values for other arguments of a collective routine unless specified otherwise.

7.6.5 Type Matching

The type matching rules for I/O mimic the type matching rules for communication with one exception: if etype is MPI_BYTE, then this matches any datatype in a data access operation. In general, the etype of data items written must match the etype used to read the items, and for each data access operation, the current etype must also match the type declaration of the data access buffer.

Advice to users.   In most cases, use of MPI_BYTE as a wild card will defeat the file interoperability features of MPI. File interoperability can only perform automatic conversion between heterogeneous data representations when the exact datatypes accessed are explicitly specified. □

7.6.6 Miscellaneous Clarifications

Once an I/O routine completes, it is safe to free any opaque objects passed as arguments to that routine. For example, the comm and info used in an MPI_FILE_OPEN, or the etype and filetype used in an MPI_FILE_SET_VIEW, can be freed without affecting access to the file. Note that for nonblocking routines and split collective operations, the operation must be completed before it is safe to reuse data buffers passed as arguments.

As in communication, datatypes must be committed before they can be used in file manipulation or data access operations. For example, the etype and filetype must be committed before calling MPI_FILE_SET_VIEW, and the datatype must be committed before calling MPI_FILE_READ or MPI_FILE_WRITE.

7.6.7   MPI_Offset **Type**

MPI_Offset is a C integer type of size sufficient to represent the size (in bytes) of the largest file supported by MPI. Displacements and offsets are always specified as values of type MPI_Offset. The corresponding type in C++ is MPI::Offset.

In Fortran, the corresponding integer is an integer of kind MPI_OFFSET_KIND (MPI::OFFSET_KIND in C++), defined in mpif.h and the mpi module.

In Fortran 77 environments that do not support KIND parameters, MPI_Offset arguments should be declared as an INTEGER of suitable size. The language interoperability implications for MPI_Offset are similar to those for addresses (see Section 2.2).

7.6.8   **Logical versus Physical File Layout**

MPI specifies how the data should be laid out in a virtual file structure (the view), not how that file structure is to be stored on one or more disks. Specification of the physical file structure was avoided because it is expected that the mapping of files to disks will be system specific, and any specific control over file layout would therefore restrict program portability. However, there are still cases where some information may be necessary to optimize file layout. This information can be provided as *hints* specified via *info* when a file is created (see Section 7.2.8).

7.6.9   **File Size**

The size of a file may be increased by writing to the file after the current end of file. The size may also be changed by calling MPI *size changing* routines, such as MPI_FILE_SET_SIZE. A call to a size changing routine does not necessarily change the file size. For example, calling MPI_FILE_PREALLOCATE with a size less than the current size does not change the size.

Consider a set of bytes that has been written to a file since the most recent call to a size changing routine, or since MPI_FILE_OPEN if no such routine has been called. Let the *high byte* be the byte in that set with the largest displacement. The file size is the larger of

- one plus the displacement of the high byte or

- the size immediately after the size changing routine or MPI_FILE_OPEN has returned.

When applying consistency semantics, calls to MPI_FILE_SET_SIZE and MPI_FILE_PREALLOCATE are considered writes to the file (which conflict with operations that access bytes at displacements between the old and new file sizes), and MPI_FILE_GET_SIZE is considered a read of the file (which overlaps with all accesses to the file).

Advice to users. Any sequence of operations containing the collective routines MPI_FILE_SET_SIZE and MPI_FILE_PREALLOCATE is a write sequence. As such, sequential consistency in nonatomic mode is not guaranteed unless the conditions in Section 7.6.1 are satisfied. ☐

File pointer update semantics (i.e., file pointers are updated by the amount accessed) are only guaranteed if file size changes are sequentially consistent.

Advice to users. Consider the following example. Given two operations made by separate processes to a file containing 100 bytes: an MPI_FILE_READ of 10 bytes and an MPI_FILE_SET_SIZE to 0 bytes. If the user does not enforce sequential consistency between these two operations, the file pointer may be updated by the amount requested (10 bytes) even if the amount accessed is zero bytes. ☐

7.6.10 Consistency and Semantics Examples

The examples in this section illustrate the application of the MPI consistency and semantics guarantees. These address

- conflicting accesses on file handles obtained from a single collective open, and
- all accesses on file handles obtained from two separate collective opens.

The simplest way to achieve consistency for conflicting accesses is to obtain sequential consistency by setting atomic mode. For the code below, process 1 will read either 0 or 10 integers. If the latter, every element of b will be 5. If nonatomic mode is set, the results of the read are undefined.

```
/* Process 0 */
int  i, a[10] ;
int  TRUE = 1;

for ( i=0;i<10;i++)
```

```
   a[i] = 5 ;

MPI_File_open( MPI_COMM_WORLD, "workfile",
               MPI_MODE_RDWR | MPI_MODE_CREATE,
               MPI_INFO_NULL, &fh0 ) ;
MPI_File_set_view( fh0, 0, MPI_INT, MPI_INT, "native",
                   MPI_INFO_NULL ) ;
MPI_File_set_atomicity( fh0, TRUE ) ;
MPI_File_write_at(fh0, 0, a, 10, MPI_INT, &status) ;
/* MPI_Barrier( MPI_COMM_WORLD ) ; */

/* Process 1 */
int   b[10] ;
int   TRUE = 1;
MPI_File_open( MPI_COMM_WORLD, "workfile",
               MPI_MODE_RDWR | MPI_MODE_CREATE,
               MPI_INFO_NULL, &fh1 ) ;
MPI_File_set_view( fh1, 0, MPI_INT, MPI_INT, "native",
                   MPI_INFO_NULL ) ;
MPI_File_set_atomicity( fh1, TRUE ) ;
/* MPI_Barrier( MPI_COMM_WORLD ) ; */
MPI_File_read_at(fh1, 0, b, 10, MPI_INT, &status) ;
```

A user may guarantee that the write on process 0 precedes the read on process 1 by imposing temporal order with, for example, calls to MPI_BARRIER (which are commented out in the code above).

Advice to users.   Routines other than MPI_BARRIER may be used to impose temporal order. In the example above, process 0 could use MPI_SEND to send a 0 byte message, received by process 1 using MPI_RECV. □

Alternatively, a user can impose consistency with nonatomic mode set:

```
/* Process 0 */
int  i, a[10] ;
for ( i=0;i<10;i++)
   a[i] = 5 ;

MPI_File_open( MPI_COMM_WORLD, "workfile",
               MPI_MODE_RDWR | MPI_MODE_CREATE,
```

```
                     MPI_INFO_NULL, &fh0 ) ;
MPI_File_set_view( fh0, 0, MPI_INT, MPI_INT,
                   "native", MPI_INFO_NULL ) ;
MPI_File_write_at(fh0, 0, a, 10, MPI_INT, &status) ;
MPI_File_sync( fh0 ) ;
MPI_Barrier( MPI_COMM_WORLD ) ;
MPI_File_sync( fh0 ) ;

/* Process 1 */
int   b[10] ;
MPI_File_open( MPI_COMM_WORLD, "workfile",
               MPI_MODE_RDWR | MPI_MODE_CREATE,
               MPI_INFO_NULL, &fh1 ) ;
MPI_File_set_view( fh1, 0, MPI_INT, MPI_INT,
                   "native", MPI_INFO_NULL ) ;
MPI_File_sync( fh1 ) ;
MPI_Barrier( MPI_COMM_WORLD ) ;
MPI_File_sync( fh1 ) ;
MPI_File_read_at(fh1, 0, b, 10, MPI_INT, &status) ;
```

The "sync-barrier-sync" construct is required because:

• The barrier ensures that the write on process 0 occurs before the read on process 1.

• The first sync guarantees that the data written by all processes is transferred to the storage device.

• The second sync guarantees that all data which has been transferred to the storage device is visible to all processes. (This does not affect process 0 in this example.)

The following program represents an erroneous attempt to achieve consistency by eliminating the apparently superfluous second "sync" call for each process.

```
/* ---------------- THIS EXAMPLE IS ERRONEOUS --------------- */
/* Process 0 */
int  i, a[10] ;
for ( i=0;i<10;i++)
    a[i] = 5 ;

MPI_File_open( MPI_COMM_WORLD, "workfile",
```

```
                        MPI_MODE_RDWR | MPI_MODE_CREATE,
                        MPI_INFO_NULL, &fh0 ) ;
MPI_File_set_view( fh0, 0, MPI_INT, MPI_INT,
                        "native", MPI_INFO_NULL ) ;
MPI_File_write_at(fh0, 0, a, 10, MPI_INT, &status) ;
MPI_File_sync( fh0 ) ;
MPI_Barrier( MPI_COMM_WORLD ) ;

/* Process 1 */
int   b[10] ;
MPI_File_open( MPI_COMM_WORLD, "workfile",
                        MPI_MODE_RDWR | MPI_MODE_CREATE,
                        MPI_INFO_NULL, &fh1 ) ;
MPI_File_set_view( fh1, 0, MPI_INT, MPI_INT,
                        "native", MPI_INFO_NULL ) ;
MPI_Barrier( MPI_COMM_WORLD ) ;
MPI_File_sync( fh1 ) ;
MPI_File_read_at(fh1, 0, b, 10, MPI_INT, &status) ;

/* --------------- THIS EXAMPLE IS ERRONEOUS --------------- */
```

The above program also violates the MPI rule against out-of-order collective operations and will deadlock for implementations in which MPI_FILE_SYNC blocks.

Advice to users.   Some implementations may choose to implement MPI_FILE_-
SYNC as a temporally synchronizing function. In this case, the "sync-barrier-sync"
construct above could be replaced by a single "sync." However, such code is not
portable. ▯

Asynchronous I/O.   The behavior of asynchronous I/O operations is determined
by applying the rules specified above for synchronous I/O operations.

The following examples all access a preexisting file "myfile." Word 10 in myfile
initially contains the integer 2. Each example writes and reads word 10.

First consider the following code fragment:

```
int a = 4, b, TRUE=1;
MPI_File_open( MPI_COMM_WORLD, "myfile",
                        MPI_MODE_RDWR, MPI_INFO_NULL, &fh ) ;
MPI_File_set_view( fh, 0, MPI_INT, MPI_INT, "native",
                        MPI_INFO_NULL );
```

```
/* MPI_File_set_atomicity( fh, TRUE ) ;
   Use this to set atomic mode. */
MPI_File_iwrite_at(fh, 10, &a, 1, MPI_INT, &reqs[0]) ;
MPI_File_iread_at(fh,  10, &b, 1, MPI_INT, &reqs[1]) ;
MPI_Waitall(2, reqs, statuses) ;
```

For asynchronous data access operations, MPI specifies that the access occurs at any time between the call to the asynchronous data access routine and the return from the corresponding request complete routine. Thus, executing either the read before the write, or the write before the read is consistent with program order. If atomic mode is set, then MPI guarantees sequential consistency, and the program will read either 2 or 4 into b. If atomic mode is not set, then sequential consistency is not guaranteed and the program may read something other than 2 or 4 due to the conflicting data access.

Similarly, the following code fragment does not order file accesses:

```
int a = 4, b;
MPI_File_open( MPI_COMM_WORLD, "myfile",
                MPI_MODE_RDWR, MPI_INFO_NULL, &fh ) ;
MPI_File_set_view( fh, 0, MPI_INT, MPI_INT, "native",
                MPI_INFO_NULL ) ;
/* MPI_File_set_atomicity( fh, TRUE ) ;
   Use this to set atomic mode. */
MPI_File_iwrite_at(fh, 10, &a, 1, MPI_INT, &reqs[0]) ;
MPI_File_iread_at(fh,  10, &b, 1, MPI_INT, &reqs[1]) ;
MPI_Wait(&reqs[0], &status) ;
MPI_Wait(&reqs[1], &status) ;
```

If atomic mode is set, either 2 or 4 will be read into b. Again, MPI does not guarantee sequential consistency in nonatomic mode.

On the other hand, the following code fragment:

```
int a = 4;
int b;
MPI_File_open( MPI_COMM_WORLD, "myfile",
                MPI_MODE_RDWR, MPI_INFO_NULL, &fh ) ;
MPI_File_set_view( fh, 0, MPI_INT, MPI_INT, "native",
                MPI_INFO_NULL ) ;
MPI_File_iwrite_at(fh, 10, &a, 1, MPI_INT, &reqs[0]) ;
MPI_Wait(&reqs[0], &status) ;
```

```
MPI_File_iread_at(fh,  10, &b, 1, MPI_INT, &reqs[1]) ;
MPI_Wait(&reqs[1], &status) ;
```

defines the same ordering as:

```
int a = 4, b;
MPI_File_open( MPI_COMM_WORLD, "myfile",
                  MPI_MODE_RDWR, MPI_INFO_NULL, &fh ) ;
MPI_File_set_view( fh, 0, MPI_INT, MPI_INT, "native",
                  MPI_INFO_NULL ) ;
MPI_File_write_at(fh, 10, &a, 1, MPI_INT, &status) ;
MPI_File_read_at(fh,  10, &b, 1, MPI_INT, &status) ;
```

Since

- nonconcurrent operations on a single file handle are sequentially consistent, and
- the program fragments specify an order for the operations,

MPI guarantees that both program fragments will read the value 4 into b. There is no need to set atomic mode for this example.

Similar considerations apply to conflicting accesses of the form:

```
MPI_File_write_all_begin(fh,...) ;
MPI_File_iread(fh,...) ;
MPI_Wait(fh,...) ;
MPI_File_write_all_end(fh,...) ;
```

Recall that constraints governing consistency and semantics are not relevant to the following:

```
MPI_File_write_all_begin(fh,...) ;
MPI_File_read_all_begin(fh,...) ;
MPI_File_read_all_end(fh,...) ;
MPI_File_write_all_end(fh,...) ;
```

since split collective operations on the same file handle may not overlap (see Section 7.4.5).

7.7 I/O Error Handling

By default, communication errors are fatal—MPI_ERRORS_ARE_FATAL is the default error handler associated with MPI_COMM_WORLD. I/O errors are usually less catastrophic (e.g., "file not found") than communication errors, and common practice is to catch these errors and continue executing. For this reason, MPI provides additional error facilities for I/O.

Advice to users. MPI does not specify the state of a computation after an erroneous MPI call has occurred. A high-quality implementation will support the I/O error handling facilities, allowing users to write programs using common practice for I/O. ⬚

Like communicators, each file handle has an error handler associated with it. The MPI I/O error handling routines are defined in Section I-7.5.1.

When MPI calls a user-defined error handler resulting from an error on a particular file handle, the first two arguments passed to the file error handler are the file handle and the error code. For I/O errors that are not associated with a valid file handle (e.g., in MPI_FILE_OPEN or MPI_FILE_DELETE), the first argument passed to the error handler is MPI_FILE_NULL.

I/O error handling differs from communication error handling in another important aspect. By default, the predefined error handler for file handles is MPI_ERRORS_RETURN. The default file error handler has two purposes: when a new file handle is created (by MPI_FILE_OPEN), the error handler for the new file handle is initially set to the default error handler, and I/O routines that have no valid file handle on which to raise an error (e.g., MPI_FILE_OPEN or MPI_FILE_DELETE) use the default file error handler. The default file error handler can be changed by specifying MPI_FILE_NULL as the fh argument to MPI_FILE_SET_ERRHANDLER. The current value of the default file error handler can be determined by passing MPI_FILE_NULL as the fh argument to MPI_FILE_GET_ERRHANDLER.

Rationale. For communication, the default error handler is inherited from MPI_COMM_WORLD. In I/O, there is no analogous "root" file handle from which default properties can be inherited. Rather than invent a new global file handle, the default file error handler is manipulated as if it were attached to MPI_FILE_NULL. ⬚

7.8 I/O Error Classes

The implementation-dependent error codes returned by the I/O routines can be converted into the error classes in Table 7.3. In addition, calls to routines in this chapter may raise errors in other MPI classes, such as MPI_ERR_TYPE.

Table 7.3
Error classes for I/O

MPI_ERR_ACCESS	Permission denied
MPI_ERR_AMODE	Error related to the amode passed to MPI_FILE_OPEN
MPI_ERR_BAD_FILE	Invalid file name (e.g., path name too long)
MPI_ERR_CONVERSION	An error occurred in a user supplied data conversion function.
MPI_ERR_DUP_DATAREP	Conversion functions could not be registered because a data representation identifier that was already defined was passed to MPI_REGISTER_DATAREP
MPI_ERR_FILE	Invalid file handle
MPI_ERR_FILE_EXISTS	File exists
MPI_ERR_FILE_IN_USE	File operation could not be completed, as the file is currently open by some process
MPI_ERR_IO	Other I/O error
MPI_ERR_NO_SPACE	Not enough space
MPI_ERR_NO_SUCH_FILE	File does not exist
MPI_ERR_NOT_SAME	Collective argument not identical on all processes, or collective routines called in a different order by different processes
MPI_ERR_QUOTA	Quota exceeded
MPI_ERR_READ_ONLY	Read-only file or file system
MPI_ERR_UNSUPPORTED_DATAREP	Unsupported datarep passed to MPI_FILE_SET_VIEW
MPI_ERR_UNSUPPORTED_OPERATION	Unsupported operation, such as seeking on a file which supports sequential access only

7.9   Examples

MPI-2 I/O is flexible and comprehensive, but for that reason it may not be immediately obvious to the casual reader how its various features can be used together
to obtain a desired outcome. Etype, filetype, view, independent or shared pointer,
collective or noncollective: all must be chosen correctly. There are sometimes several ways to accomplish the same goal, and there are combinations that do not
make sense.

In the next several subsections, we illustrate the use of MPI-2 I/O routines with
a number of examples. We start with some general guidelines that are appropriate
for many, but not all, cases.

- Chose the filetype either to tile the file (no two processes view the same data)
or equal to etype (all processes view the same data).
- Use the displacement to skip over information of a type different from what is
currently being written (e.g., a header). Normally the displacement is the same on
all processes.
- When a file is tiled, use independent pointers or explicit offsets—shared pointers
are not allowed. When a file is not tiled, use shared pointers or explicit offsets.
- Use collective operations when possible, especially on tiled files.

7.9.1   Example: I/O to Separate Files

The simplest form of I/O is when every process opens its own "private" file. Similar
functionality can be obtained using language I/O, but MPI provides additional
opportunity for interoperability, improved performance, and in some cases access
to special filesystems.

In this example, each process computes an array of double precision numbers
and writes that array to a file. The number of elements is not known a priori,
but depends on runtime data. The files are self-describing, containing an integer
specifying the number of double precision elements, followed by the double precision
data (followed by another integer, double, etc.).

```
int me, ndata;
MPI_Offset pos;
char filename[100];
double *data;
MPI_File fh;
```

```
        MPI_Comm_rank(MPI_COMM_WORLD, &me);
        sprintf(filename, "me.%d", me);
        /* open with MPI_COMM_SELF to make it private */
        MPI_File_open(MPI_COMM_SELF, filename, MPI_MODE_RDWR,
                      MPI_INFO_NULL, &fh);

        /* data items are computed and stored in the dynamically
           allocated array "data". The number of items is "ndata" */

        MPI_File_set_view(fh, 0, MPI_INT, MPI_INT,
                          "native", MPI_INFO_NULL);
        /* note that since the file is opened by a single process,
           semantics of shared and individual pointers are equivalent,
           as are collective and noncollective operations. Use
           the individual file pointer and noncollective
           operations in case the implementation does not
           optimize the special case of one process */
        MPI_File_write(fh, &ndata, 1, MPI_INT, MPI_STATUS_IGNORE);

        /* Compute where to set the displacement for the start
           of the double array. We know we are at offset 1 w.r.t.
           the current view. Note that we could actually calculate
           this using sizeof() since we are in native mode */
        MPI_File_get_byte_offset(fh, (MPI_Offset)1, &pos);

        /* now reset the view so we can start writing doubles
           after the integer we just wrote */
        MPI_File_set_view(fh, pos, MPI_DOUBLE, MPI_DOUBLE,
                          "native", MPI_INFO_NULL);
        MPI_File_write(fh, data, ndata, MPI_DOUBLE, MPI_STATUS_IGNORE);
```

7.9.2 Example: Log File

The following example shows one way of implementing a log file. Processes write independently to the log file, appending a line of information with each write operation. A write from one process should not be interleaved with a write from another.

To implement a log file, the processes collectively open the file for writing. In this example, they use an etype of MPI_CHAR since they will be writing character data.

The filetype is the same as the etype because no tiling will be needed — the file is always accessed using the shared file pointer, which is automatically incremented with each write. The write operations are noncollective, because the processes do not write at the same time. Consistency is not an issue when using a shared file pointer, as file accesses are nonconflicting.

```
MPI_File log_file;
int result, me, i;
char log_str[200];

MPI_Comm_rank(MPI_COMM_WORLD, &me);
MPI_File_open(MPI_COMM_WORLD, "/logs/mylog",
         MPI_MODE_WRONLY | MPI_MODE_CREATE | MPI_MODE_APPEND,
         MPI_INFO_NULL, &log_file);
MPI_File_set_view(log_file, MPI_DISPLACEMENT_CURRENT, MPI_CHAR,
              MPI_CHAR, "external32", MPI_INFO_NULL);

for (i = 0; i < 100; i++) {
    result = process_next_item(me, i);
    if (result != SUCCESS) {
        sprintf(log_str, "ERROR on process %d: %s\n", result,
               errstrings[result]);
        MPI_File_write_shared(log_file, log_str, strlen(log_str),
                           MPI_CHAR, MPI_STATUS_IGNORE);
    }
}
```

7.9.3   Example: Writing a Large Matrix to a Single File

In this example, we assume that we have a large (100×100) double precision array that we want to write to a single file. This array is distributed among four processes as shown in Figure 7.4, such that each process has a block of 25 columns (e.g., process 0 has columns 0–24, process 1 has columns 25–49, etc.

We want to write this array to a single file in the same order it would be if it were in the memory of a single process. This makes it easy to read the array back in on a single process and is also a useful format if we want to read it in on any other number of processors.

We take the convention that the first dimension of the array labels the vertical dimension (from top to bottom) and that the second dimension of the array labels

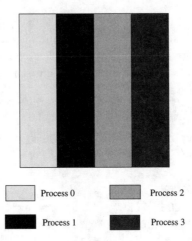

Figure 7.4
Example array file layout

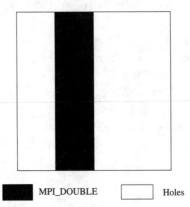

Figure 7.5
Example local array filetype for process 1

the horizontal dimension. If the array is a Fortran array (Fortran has column-major array ordering), each process writes a large contiguous block of $100 \times 25 = 2500$ double precision numbers to the file. If the array is a C array, each process writes 100 blocks of 25 double precision numbers each at 100 different offsets within the file, so that rows are stored contiguously.

In either case, the file is tiled by data from the four processes, and we will use a filetype to express this tiling. Each process will use a filetype containing double precision datatypes where it will write data and "holes" where other processes will write data, as shown in Figure 7.5.

We show how to construct the filetype in two ways. The first uses MPI-1 constructors. The second uses the MPI-2 constructor MPI_Type_create_subarray. In practice one would always use this constructor, but we show both for illustration.

The local subarray and filetype are declared as:

```
double subarray[100][25];
MPI_Datatype filetype;
```

There are several ways to do the first construction. In our example, we note that the filetype can be constructed recursively. The basic element of the filetype is a "row" which has 3 blocks of 25 "holes" and 1 block of 25 doubles, where the position of the doubles depends on the processor number. The full file type is just 100 contiguous copies of this row datatype. We create the row datatype by creating a struct datatype with the appropriate number of holes at the beginning, followed by the 25 contiguous doubles. Finally, we pad the row datatype with the right number of holes at the end. We assume we're using native representation so that we can compute file displacements using sizeof().

```
MPI_Datatype filetype, type, rowtype, padded_rowtype;
int blocklength, me;
MPI_Aint displacement;

MPI_Comm_rank(MPI_COMM_WORLD, &me);
blocklength = 25;
displacement = me*25*sizeof(double);
type = MPI_DOUBLE;
MPI_Type_create_struct(1, &blocklength, &displacement,
                       &type, &rowtype);
MPI_Type_create_resized(rowtype, (MPI_Aint)0,
                        (MPI_Aint)100*sizeof(double),
                        &padded_rowtype);
MPI_Type_contiguous(100, padded_rowtype, &filetype);
MPI_Type_commit(&filetype);
MPI_Type_free(&rowtype);
MPI_Type_free(&padded_rowtype);
```

A better way to create a filetype with the same typemap is to use the subarray constructor, as shown below.

```
MPI_Datatype filetype;
int sizes[2], subsizes[2], starts[2];
int rank;

MPI_Comm_rank(MPI_COMM_WORLD, &rank);
sizes[0]=100; sizes[1]=100;
subsizes[0]=100; subsizes[1]=25;
starts[0]=0; starts[1]=rank*subsizes[1];

MPI_Type_create_subarray(2, sizes, subsizes, starts, MPI_ORDER_C,
                         MPI_DOUBLE, &filetype);
```

In Fortran, the corresponding code looks nearly identical, though of course it creates a filetype appropriate for Fortran's column-major ordering.

```
double precision subarray(100,25)
integer filetype, rank, ierror
integer sizes(2), subsizes(2), starts(2)

call MPI_COMM_RANK(MPI_COMM_WORLD, rank, ierror)
sizes(1)=100
sizes(2)=100
subsizes(1)=100
subsizes(2)=25
starts(1)=0
starts(2)=rank*subsizes(2)

call MPI_TYPE_CREATE_SUBARRAY(2, sizes, subsizes, starts, &
        MPI_ORDER_FORTRAN, MPI_DOUBLE_PRECISION,        &
        filetype, ierror)
```

Now that we have shown how to create the filetype, here is how to use it in a program. Since we know that this example will benefit from collective buffering, we specify a "hint" through the info argument that lets MPI know this. We don't change the behavior of the program by giving the hint, but we may change the performance.

```
MPI_File fh;
MPI_Info myinfo;
```

```
double subarray[100][25];
MPI_Datatype filetype;

/* assume that subarray is filled with data and filetype is
   created as above */

MPI_Info_create(&myinfo);
MPI_Info_set(myinfo, "collective_buffering", "true");

MPI_Comm_rank(MPI_COMM_WORLD, &me);
MPI_File_open(MPI_COMM_WORLD, "matrixfile",
              MPI_MODE_WRONLY | MPI_MODE_CREATE,
              myinfo, &fh);
MPI_File_set_view(fh, 0, MPI_DOUBLE, filetype, "native",
              MPI_INFO_NULL);

/* process data will be automatically tiles in the
   file, even though it looks like we're writing
   2500 contiguous doubles */
MPI_File_write_all(fh, subarray, 100*25, MPI_DOUBLE,
                         MPI_STATUS_IGNORE);
```

7.9.4 Example: NAS BT Benchmark

This final example is similar to the previous one, but the array decomposition is much more complicated. We include it to show that a filetype for a complex distribution can be created fairly easily with the subarray constructor.

The example in this section is based on the BT (Block Tridiagonal) benchmark from the NAS Parallel Benchmark II suite [1]. BT contains the essential elements of a flow solver heavily used at NASA Ames Research Center, and solves the Navier-Stokes equations using an Alternating Direction Implicit (ADI) scheme. The core of the solver calculates the solutions to a large number of independent block-tridiagonal linear systems with 5×5 blocks. Each system of equations corresponds to a grid-line in a three-dimensional Cartesian grid.

In order to obtain good load-balance and coarse-grained communication, the code uses a complex decomposition of the grid. The resulting parallel algorithm is known as the multipartition method [16].

In the BT code, the data on a cubic three-dimensional grid (Figure 7.6) is divided into N^3 subcubes, called *cells* (Figure 7.7), where $N \geq 1$. In the example figures

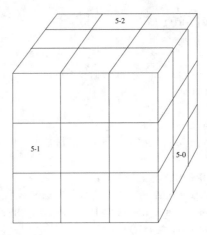

Figure 7.6
Global data structure for the nine process version of the BT solver. The labeled cells are owned by process five.

N is equal to three. The code must be run on N^2 processes, where each process is assigned N disjoint cells. With each grid point are associated five double precision numbers that correspond to the five physical variables at each point in space. This data is contained in the variable U.

The cells are distributed among processes so that for any slice through the cube in the x, y or z directions, each process owns exactly one of the N^2 cells in that slice. During the solution of the block-tridiagonal systems, computations are performed in parallel on a single slice of the cube at a time, each process working on its own cell within the particular slice. The problem is advanced in time by repeated calls to subroutines that sweep back and forth across the cube (corresponding to forward elimination and backsubstitution) once for each spatial dimension. The example below writes U periodically as the calculation proceeds.

MPI datatypes representing the grid points in each cell are combined to form the process's filetype. The grid point (five words of data) is also an MPI datatype.

To further understand the details of the data distribution in the file and in memory, consider the following. The components of U owned by a single process are contained in the array:

```
double precision u(5,-2:cellmax+1,-2:cellmax+1,-2:cellmax+1,ncells)
```

The first dimension represents the five physical variables at each grid point. The next three dimensions are spatial grid dimensions containing the cell's sizes in each of the three coordinate direction, including two elements on either side of each

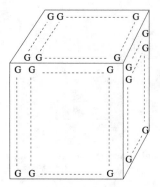

Figure 7.7
Cell used by BT solver. The data at each grid point is represented by G.

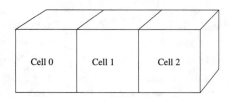

Figure 7.8
Buffer datatype used by single process in BT solver. Cell sizes are allowed to differ, although
they are the same in this example.

dimension for boundary data from neighboring cells (see below). The last dimension
is an index that determines the cell number.

The MPI write routines use buffer datatypes to map data from their locations
in a single MPI process's memory to the file view. This datatype (Figure 7.8) is
composed of three MPI datatypes, each of which represents a cell's buffer. The cell's
datatype (Figure 7.9) must exclude the boundary conditions from neighboring cells
(two grid points on either side in all dimensions) that are stored in the cell's buffers.
A process only writes data that it owns. (Note that an interesting optimization
when reading the solution in from the MPI file is to create filetypes and buffer
datatypes which include the boundary conditions so that no additional message
passing is required after the read completes.)

```
!-------------------------------------------------------------------
! - This program fragment highlights those pieces of the code
!    relevant to MPI-2 parallel I/O.
```

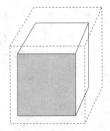

Figure 7.9
A cell buffer datatype (solid-line cube) and the actual cell buffer (dashed-line cube).

```
! -- btio declarations
      integer ncells, ndims, num_procs, cellmax, PROBLEM_SIZE

      parameter (ndims= 3)                 ! 3 spatial dimensions
      parameter (num_procs = 9)            ! no. of processes
      parameter (ncells = 3)               ! sqrt(num_procs)
      parameter (numgridptvars = 5)        ! 5 variables per grid pt.
      parameter (PROBLEM_SIZE = 102)       ! (102)^3 grid points
      parameter (cellmax = (PROBLEM_SIZE/ncells)+1) ! maximum cell
                                                    ! dimension
! -- the solution array
      double precision  u( numgridptvars, -2:cellmax+1, &
                           -2:cellmax+1, -2:cellmax+1, ncells )


! -- MPI type declarations
      integer cell_size( ndims, ncells )   ! size of each cell,
                                           ! exclusive of boundary
                                           ! condition data
      integer cell_low( ndims, ncells )    ! starting (zero-based)
                                           ! index for each cell
! -- MPI I/O-specific declarations
      integer btio_fh, writesize, status(MPI_STATUS_SIZE)
      integer(kind=MPI_OFFSET_KIND) wr_offset, view_displacement
      integer gridpt, gridpt_size, combined_buftype
      integer combined_filetype


! -- build the gridpt type
```

```
        call build_gridpt( gridpt, gridpt_size )

! -- build the buftype, which describes the layout in memory of
! -- the data owned by the process.
        call build_buftype( gridpt, ndims, ncells, cell_size, &
                            cellmax, combined_buftype )
        call MPI_TYPE_SIZE( combined_buftype, writesize, ierr )

! -- build the filetype, which defines the storage order of data
! -- in the file
        call build_filetype( gridpt, ndims, ncells, &
                             cell_size, cell_low, &
                             PROBLEM_SIZE, combined_filetype )

! -- Open with the default view, and immediately reset to
! -- the ``btio'' view.
        call MPI_FILE_OPEN( comm_solve, &
                           'ufs:/scratch1/example/out.mpiio-example', &
                            MPI_MODE_WRONLY + MPI_MODE_CREATE, &
                            MPI_INFO_NULL, btio_fh, ierr )
        view_displacement = 0
        call MPI_FILE_SET_VIEW( btio_fh, view_displacement, gridpt, &
                                combined_filetype, "native", &
                                MPI_INFO_NULL, ierr )

! -- Compute, writing the data every wr_interval steps as we go:

        do iter=1,numiters
          call adi    ! do all the computational work here
          if ( mod( iter, wr_interval ) .eq. 0 ) then
            call MPI_FILE_WRITE_AT_ALL( btio_fh, wr_offset, u, 1, &
                                        combined_buftype, status, ierr )

! -- Advance the offset by the size of the buftype, i.e., the amount
!    of data written.  The next call to MPI_FILE_WRITE_AT_ALL will
!    write at this offset in the current view.  The data from the
!    next collective write will immediately follow what was just
!    written.
```

```
              wr_offset = wr_offset + writesize/gridpt_size
                    ! note that wr_offset is expressed in
                    ! units of etype = gridpt
            endif
          enddo
!   --
        call MPI_FILE_CLOSE( btio_fh, ierr )
      end


!--------------- Begin btio type constructor routines --------------
      subroutine build_gridpt( gridpt, gridpt_size )
      use MPI
      integer gridpt, ierr
      integer(kind=mpi_address_kind) gridpt_size

!  "gridpt" is the solution vector at a single point in a cell,
!  and contains five words of data.
      call MPI_TYPE_CONTIGUOUS( 5, MPI_DOUBLE_PRECISION, gridpt, &
                               ierr )
      call MPI_TYPE_COMMIT( gridpt, ierr )
      call MPI_TYPE_SIZE( gridpt, gridpt_size, ierr )
      return
      end


!------------------------------------------------------------------
      subroutine build_filetype( gridpt, ndims, ncells, cell_size, &
                                cell_low, &
                                problem_size, combined_filetype )
      use MPI
      integer gridpt, ndims, ncells
      integer cell_size( ndims, ncells), cell_low( ndims, ncells)
      integer problem_size
      integer combined_filetype

      integer cell_blklengths( ncells )
      integer(kind=MPI_ADDRESS_KIND) cell_displacements( ncells )
      integer sizes(ndims), starts(ndims), subsizes(ndims)
      integer cell_filetypes( ncells )
```

```
        integer cell, ierr

! - Build the filetype.  The filetype describes where data is stored
!     in the file.  The data is broken up into cells, which are
!     subsets of the overall cubic data structure.  Cells may vary
!     in size and are not necessarily cubes.  The
!     MPI_TYPE_CREATE_SUBARRAY calls in the DO loop describe the
!     cells that are accessed by this process.  No other process
!     will access these cells.  "sizes" contains the total problem
!     size,  and "starts" contains the starting point for each cell
!     in the total array.

!     Build an array of MPI types, with one type for each cell:
      sizes(1) = problem_size
      sizes(2) = problem_size
      sizes(3) = problem_size
      do cell = 1, ncells
        subsizes(1) = cell_size( 1, cell )
        subsizes(2) = cell_size( 2, cell )
        subsizes(3) = cell_size( 3, cell )

        starts(1) = cell_low( 1, cell ) !  cell_low gives the
        starts(2) = cell_low( 2, cell ) !  starting point for a
        starts(3) = cell_low( 3, cell ) !  cell in the total array

        call MPI_TYPE_CREATE_SUBARRAY( &
                ndims, sizes, subsizes, starts,  &
                MPI_ORDER_FORTRAN, gridpt,       &
                cell_filetypes(cell), ierr )
        cell_blklengths(cell)     = 1  ! tells MPI_TYPE_CREATE_STRUCT
                                       ! that we are passing in a
                                       ! single block of type
                                       ! cell_filetypes(cell)
        cell_displacements(cell) = 0  ! all displacements are
                                       ! w.r.t. the origin of the
                                       ! global data structure u
      enddo
```

```
!     Create the "combined_filetype" from the array of newly-created
!     MPI types:
      call MPI_TYPE_CREATE_STRUCT( ncells, cell_blklengths, &
                          cell_displacements, cell_filetypes, &
                          combined_filetype, ierr )
      call MPI_TYPE_COMMIT( combined_filetype, ierr )
      return
!
      end

!-----------------------------------------------------------------
      subroutine build_buftype( gridpt, ndims, ncells, cell_size, &
                          cellmax, combined_buftype )
      use MPI
      integer gridpt, ndims, ncells, cellmax
      integer cell_size( ndims, ncells), combined_buftype

      integer sizes(ndims+1), starts(ndims+1), subsizes(ndims+1)
      integer cell_blklengths( ncells )
      integer(kind=MPI_ADDRESS_KIND) cell_displacements( ncells )
      integer cell_buftypes( ncells )
      integer cell, ierr

! -- build the buffer datatype (buftype).  The buftype describes the
!     location in memory of the data owned by this process.
!     For reference, remember that u is dimensioned in each process:
!          u( 5, -2:cellmax+1, -2:cellmax+1, -2:cellmax+1, ncells )
!     (u may be declared to be larger than is needed for a
!     particular program invocation, and must be large enough to
!     accommodate the largest cell.)

!     The data is broken up into cells, which are subsets of the
!     overall cubic data structure.  Cells may vary in size and are
!     not necessarily cubes.  The fifth (ncells) dimension of u
!     provides a convenient mechanism for referencing cells.  The
!     MPI_TYPE_CREATE_SUBARRAY calls in the DO loop describe the
!     cells that are accessed by this process, picking out the part
!     of memory containing data belonging to the cell proper.  (A
```

```
!     cell's boundary condition data is owned by other processes,
!     and is not part of the cell.)

!  First build an array of MPI types, with one type for each cell.
        sizes(1) = cellmax + 4    ! "sizes" spans the whole cell,
        sizes(2) = cellmax + 4    ! plus boundary values
        sizes(3) = cellmax + 4
        sizes(4) = ncells

        starts(1) = 2    ! "starts" is the zero-based starting point
        starts(2) = 2    ! of the subarrray
        starts(3) = 2

        subsizes(4) = 1
        do cell = 1, ncells
          subsizes(1) = cell_size( 1, cell )  ! "subsizes" excludes
          subsizes(2) = cell_size( 2, cell )  ! the boundary
          subsizes(3) = cell_size( 3, cell )  ! condition data

          starts(4) = cell - 1

          call MPI_TYPE_CREATE_SUBARRAY( ndims+1, sizes, subsizes, &
                                         starts, MPI_ORDER_FORTRAN, &
                                         gridpt,                 &
                                         cell_buftypes(cell), ierr )
          cell_blklengths(cell)    = 1 ! tells
                                       ! MPI_TYPE_CREATE_STRUCT
                                       ! that we are passing in a
                                       ! single block of type
                                       ! cell_buftypes(cell)
          cell_displacements(cell) = 0 ! all displacements are
                                       ! w.r.t. the origin of the
        enddo                          ! local data structure u

!  Create the "combined_buftype".
        call MPI_TYPE_CREATE_STRUCT( ncells, cell_blklengths, &
                        cell_displacements, &
                        cell_buftypes, combined_buftype, &
```

```
                              ierr )
              call MPI_TYPE_COMMIT( combined_buftype, ierr )

! Most of the complexity in this routine is due to the fact that
! cell sizes may vary.  If cell sizes were fixed, then all array
! element initialization except for starts(4) could be pulled out
! of the DO loop.  If array u were also recast to use offsets
! instead of a special (''ncells'') index for the different
! cells, the buftype could be built using a single call to
! MPI_TYPE_CREATE_SUBARRAY followed by a call to
! MPI_TYPE_CONTIGUOUS.


              return
              end
```

7.9.5   Example: Double Buffering with Split Collective I/O

This final example shows how to overlap computation and output. The computation
is performed by the function compute_buffer().

```
/*=====================================================================
 *
 * Function:              double_buffer
 *
 * Synopsis:
 *     void double_buffer(
 *             MPI_File fh,                        ** IN
 *             MPI_Datatype buftype,               ** IN
 *             int bufcount                        ** IN
 *     )
 *
 * Description:
 *     Performs the steps to overlap computation with a collective
 *     write by using a double-buffering technique.
 *
 * Parameters:
 *     fh                    previously opened MPI file handle
 *     buftype               MPI datatype for memory layout (Assumes a
```

```
 *                         compatible view has been set on fh)
 *      bufcount             # buftype elements to transfer
 *--------------------------------------------------------------*/

/* this macro switches which buffer "x" is pointing to */
#define TOGGLE_PTR(x) (((x)==(buffer1)) ? (x=buffer2) : (x=buffer1))

void double_buffer(MPI_File fh, MPI_Datatype buftype, int bufcount)
{

   MPI_Status status;        /* status for MPI calls */
   float *buffer1, *buffer2; /* buffers to hold results */
   float *compute_buf_ptr;   /* destination  buffer */
                             /*   for computing */
   float *write_buf_ptr;     /* source for writing */
   int done;                 /* determines when to quit */

   /* buffer initialization */
   buffer1 = (float *)
                    malloc(bufcount*sizeof(float)) ;
   buffer2 = (float *)
                    malloc(bufcount*sizeof(float)) ;
   compute_buf_ptr = buffer1 ;   /* initially point to buffer1 */
   write_buf_ptr   = buffer1 ;   /* initially point to buffer1 */


   /* DOUBLE-BUFFER prolog:
    *   compute buffer1; then initiate writing buffer1 to disk
    */
   compute_buffer(compute_buf_ptr, bufcount, &done);
   MPI_File_write_all_begin(fh, write_buf_ptr, bufcount, buftype);

   /* DOUBLE-BUFFER steady state:
    * Overlap writing old results from buffer pointed to by
    * write_buf_ptr with computing new results into buffer pointed
    * to by compute_buf_ptr.
    *
    * There is always one write-buffer and one compute-buffer in use
```

```
 *   during steady state.
 */
while (!done) {
   TOGGLE_PTR(compute_buf_ptr);
   compute_buffer(compute_buf_ptr, bufcount, &done);
   MPI_File_write_all_end(fh, write_buf_ptr, &status);
   TOGGLE_PTR(write_buf_ptr);
   MPI_File_write_all_begin(fh, write_buf_ptr, bufcount, buftype);
}

/* DOUBLE-BUFFER epilog:
 *   wait for final write to complete.
 */
MPI_File_write_all_end(fh, write_buf_ptr, &status);


/* buffer cleanup */
free(buffer1);
free(buffer2);
}
```

8 Language Bindings

MPI-1 specifies bindings for C and Fortran 77. MPI-2 adds bindings for C++ and specifies two levels of Fortran support that allow MPI programs to be written in Fortran-90, the current definition of Fortran.

8.1 C++

Here we discuss the design of the C++ bindings for MPI. The bindings themselves are given throughout the book below each function definition.

8.1.1 Overview

This section presents a complete C++ language interface for MPI. There are some issues specific to C++ that must be considered in the design of this interface that go beyond the simple description of language bindings. In particular, in C++, we must be concerned with the design of objects and their interfaces, rather than just the design of a language-specific functional interface to MPI. Fortunately, the original design of MPI was based on the notion of objects, so a natural set of classes is already part of MPI.

In some cases, MPI-2 provides new names for the C bindings of deprecated MPI-1 functions. In this case, the C++ binding matches the new C name — there is no binding for the deprecated name.

8.1.2 Design

The C++ language interface for MPI is designed according to the following criteria:

1. The C++ language interface consists of a small set of classes with a lightweight functional interface to MPI. The classes are based up the fundamental MPI object types (e.g., communicator, group, etc.).

2. The MPI C++ language bindings provide a semantically correct interface to MPI.

3. To the greatest extent possible, the C++ bindings for MPI functions are member functions of MPI classes.

Rationale. Providing a lightweight set of MPI objects that correspond to the basic MPI types is the best fit to MPI's implicit object-based design; methods can be supplied for these objects to realize MPI functionality. The existing C bindings can be used in C++ programs, but much of the expressive power of the C++

language is forfeited. On the other hand, while a comprehensive class library would make user programming more elegant, such a library is not suitable as a language binding for MPI since a binding must provide a direct and unambiguous mapping to the specified functionality of MPI. ▯

8.1.3 C++ Classes for MPI

All MPI classes, constants, and functions are declared within the scope of an MPI namespace. Thus, instead of the MPI_ prefix that is used in C and Fortran, MPI functions essentially have an MPI:: prefix.

Advice to implementors.   Although namespace is officially part of the draft ANSI C++ standard, as of this writing it not yet widely implemented in C++ compilers. Implementations using compilers without namespace may obtain the same scoping through the use of a noninstantiable MPI class. (To make the MPI class noninstantiable, all constructors must be private.) ▯

The members of the MPI namespace are those classes corresponding to objects implicitly used by MPI. An abbreviated definition of the MPI namespace for MPI-1 and its member classes is as follows:

```
namespace MPI {
    class Comm                              {...};
    class Intracomm : public Comm           {...};
    class Graphcomm : public Intracomm      {...};
    class Cartcomm  : public Intracomm      {...};
    class Intercomm : public Comm           {...};
    class Datatype                          {...};
    class Errhandler                        {...};
    class Exception                         {...};
    class Group                             {...};
    class Op                                {...};
    class Request                           {...};
    class Prequest  : public Request        {...};
    class Status                            {...};
};
```

Additionally, the following classes are defined for MPI-2:

```
namespace MPI {
  class File                            {...};
  class Grequest  : public Request      {...};
  class Info                            {...};
  class Win                             {...};
};
```

Note that there are a small number of derived classes and that virtual inheritance is *not* used.

8.1.4   Class Member Functions for MPI

Besides the member functions that constitute the C++ language bindings for MPI, the C++ language interface has additional functions (as required by the C++ language). In particular, the C++ language interface must provide a constructor and destructor, an assignment operator, and comparison operators.

The bindings take advantage of some important C++ features, such as reference and **const** semantics. Declarations (which apply to all MPI member classes) for construction, destruction, copying, assignment, comparison, and mixed-language operability are also provided.

Except where indicated, all nonstatic member functions (except for constructors and the assignment operator) of MPI member classes are virtual functions.

Rationale.   Providing virtual member functions is an important part of design for inheritance. Virtual functions can be bound at runtime, which allows users of libraries to redefine the behavior of objects already contained in a library. There is a small performance penalty that must be paid (the virtual function must be looked up before it can be called). However, users concerned about this performance penalty may be able to force compile-time function binding. ☐

Example 8.1   This example shows a derived MPI class.

```
class foo_comm : public MPI::Intracomm {
public:
  void Send(const void* buf, int count, const MPI::Datatype& type,
            int dest, int tag) const
  {
    // Class library functionality
```

```
    MPI::Intracomm::Send(buf, count, type, dest, tag);
    // More class library functionality
  }
};
```

Advice to implementors.   Implementors must be careful to avoid unintended side effects from class libraries that use inheritance, especially in layered implementations. For example, if MPI_BCAST is implemented by repeated calls to MPI_SEND or MPI_RECV, the behavior of MPI_BCAST cannot be changed by derived communicator classes that might redefine MPI_SEND or MPI_RECV. The implementation of MPI_BCAST must explicitly use the MPI_SEND (or MPI_RECV) of the base `MPI::Comm` class. ▯

8.1.5 Semantics

The semantics of the member functions constituting the C++ language binding for MPI are specified by the MPI function description itself. Here, we specify the semantics for those portions of the C++ language interface that are not part of the language binding. In this subsection, functions are prototyped using the type `MPI::⟨CLASS⟩` rather than listing each function for every MPI class; the word ⟨CLASS⟩ can be replaced with any valid MPI class name (e.g., `Group`), except as noted.

Construction and Destruction. The default constructor and destructor are prototyped as follows:

```
MPI::<CLASS>()
```

```
~MPI::<CLASS>()
```

   In terms of construction and destruction, opaque MPI user-level objects behave like handles. Default constructors for all MPI objects except MPI::Status create corresponding MPI::*_NULL handles. That is, when an MPI object is instantiated, comparing it with its corresponding MPI::*_NULL object will return **true**. The default constructors do not create new MPI opaque objects. Some classes have a member function `Create()` for this purpose.

Example 8.2   In the following code fragment, the test will return **true** and the message will be sent to cout.

```
void foo()
{
```

```
  MPI::Intracomm bar;

if (bar == MPI::COMM_NULL)
    cout << "bar is MPI::COMM_NULL" << endl;
}
```

The destructor for each MPI user-level object does *not* invoke the corresponding MPI_*_FREE function (if it exists).

Rationale.   MPI_*_FREE functions are not automatically invoked for the following reasons:

1.   Automatic destruction contradicts the shallow-copy semantics of the MPI classes.

2.   The model put forth in MPI makes memory allocation and deallocation the responsibility of the user, not the implementation.

3.   Calling MPI_*_FREE upon destruction could have unintended side effects, including triggering collective operations (this also affects the copy, assignment, and construction semantics). In the following example, we would want neither foo_comm nor bar_comm to automatically invoke MPI_*_FREE upon exit from the function. (The copy constructor and assignment operator used in the example are described in the next section.)

```
void example_function()
{
  MPI::Intracomm foo_comm(MPI::COMM_WORLD), bar_comm;
  bar_comm = MPI::COMM_WORLD.Dup();
  // rest of function
}
```

                                                                                        ☐

Copy and Assignment.   The copy constructor and assignment operator are prototyped as follows:

```
MPI::<CLASS>(const MPI::<CLASS>& data)
```

```
MPI::<CLASS>& MPI::<CLASS>::operator=(const MPI::<CLASS>& data)
```

In terms of copying and assignment, opaque MPI user-level objects behave like handles. Copy constructors perform handle-based (shallow) copies. MPI::Status objects are exceptions to this rule. These objects perform deep copies for assignment and copy construction.

Advice to implementors.   Each MPI user-level object is likely to contain, by value or by reference, implementation-dependent state information. The assignment and copying of MPI object handles may simply copy such information. □

Example 8.3 Example using assignment operator. In this example, `MPI::Intracomm::Dup()` is *not* called for `foo_comm`. The object `foo_comm` is simply an alias for `MPI::COMM_WORLD`. But `bar_comm` is created with a call to `MPI::Intracomm::Dup()` and is therefore different from `foo_comm` (and thus different from `MPI::COMM_WORLD`). `baz_comm` becomes an alias for `bar_comm`. If one of `bar_comm` or `baz_comm` is freed with MPI_COMM_FREE it will be set to MPI::COMM_NULL. The state of the other handle will be undefined—it will be invalid, but not necessarily set to MPI::COMM_NULL.

```
MPI::Intracomm foo_comm, bar_comm, baz_comm;

foo_comm = MPI::COMM_WORLD;
bar_comm = MPI::COMM_WORLD.Dup();
baz_comm = bar_comm;
```

Comparison.   The comparison operators are prototyped as follows:

```
bool MPI::<CLASS>::operator==(const MPI::<CLASS>& data) const
```

```
bool MPI::<CLASS>::operator!=(const MPI::<CLASS>& data) const
```

The member function `operator==()` returns `true` only when the handles reference the same internal MPI object, `false` otherwise. `operator!=()` returns the boolean complement of `operator==()`. However, since the `Status` class is not a handle to an underlying MPI object, it does not make sense to compare `Status` instances. Therefore, the `operator==()` and `operator!=()` functions are not defined on the `Status` class.

Constants.   Constants are singleton objects and are declared `const`. Note that not all globally defined MPI objects are constant. For example, `MPI::COMM_WORLD` and `MPI::COMM_SELF` are not `const`.

8.1.6   C++ Datatypes

Table 8.1.6 lists all of the C++ predefined MPI datatypes and their corresponding C and C++ datatypes, Table 8.1.6 lists all of the Fortran predefined MPI datatypes and their corresponding Fortran 77 datatypes. Table 8.1.6 lists the C++ names for all other MPI datatypes.

Table 8.1
C++ names for the MPI C and C++ predefined datatypes, and their corresponding C/C++ datatypes.

MPI datatype	C datatype	C++ datatype
MPI::CHAR	char	char
MPI::WCHAR	wchar_t	wchar_t
MPI::SHORT	signed short	signed short
MPI::INT	signed int	signed int
MPI::LONG	signed long	signed long
MPI::SIGNED_CHAR	signed char	signed char
MPI::UNSIGNED_CHAR	unsigned char	unsigned char
MPI::UNSIGNED_SHORT	unsigned short	unsigned short
MPI::UNSIGNED	unsigned int	unsigned int
MPI::UNSIGNED_LONG	unsigned long	unsigned long int
MPI::FLOAT	float	float
MPI::DOUBLE	double	double
MPI::LONG_DOUBLE	long double	long double
MPI::BOOL		bool
MPI::COMPLEX		Complex<float>
MPI::DOUBLE_COMPLEX		Complex<double>
MPI::LONG_DOUBLE_COMPLEX		Complex<long double>
MPI::BYTE		
MPI::PACKED		

MPI::BYTE and MPI::PACKED conform to the same restrictions as MPI_BYTE and MPI_PACKED (see I-2.2.2 and I-3.12). Table 8.4 defines groups of MPI predefined datatypes. Valid datatypes for each reduction operation are specified in Table 8.5 in terms of the groups defined in Table 8.4.

MPI::MINLOC and MPI::MAXLOC perform just as their C and Fortran counterparts; see Section I-4.11.3.

8.1.7 Communicators

The `MPI::Comm` class hierarchy makes explicit the different kinds of communicators implicitly defined by MPI and allows them to be strongly typed. Since the original design of MPI defined only one type of handle for all types of communicators, the following clarifications are provided for the C++ design.

Table 8.2
C++ names for the MPI Fortran predefined datatypes, and their corresponding Fortran 77
datatypes.

MPI datatype	Fortran datatype
MPI::CHARACTER	CHARACTER(1)
MPI::INTEGER	INTEGER
MPI::REAL	REAL
MPI::DOUBLE_PRECISION	DOUBLE PRECISION
MPI::LOGICAL	LOGICAL
MPI::F_COMPLEX	COMPLEX
MPI::BYTE	
MPI::PACKED	

Types of communicators. There are five different types of communicators:
`MPI::Comm`, `MPI::Intercomm`, `MPI::Intracomm`, `MPI::Cartcomm`, and `MPI::`-
`Graphcomm`. `MPI::Comm` is the abstract base communicator class, encapsulating
the functionality common to all MPI communicators. `MPI::Intercomm`
and `MPI::Intracomm` are derived from `MPI::Comm`. `MPI::Cartcomm` and
`MPI::Graphcomm` are derived from `MPI::Intracomm`.

Note that functions for collective communication are members of the MPI::Comm
class. However, since the collective operations do not make sense on the base class
(since an MPI::Comm is neither an intercommunicator nor an intracommunicator),
these functions are pure virtual.

Advice to users. Initializing a derived class with an instance of a base class is
not legal in C++. For instance, it is not legal to initialize a MPI::Cartcomm from
an MPI::Intracomm. Moreover, because MPI::Comm is an abstract base class, it is
noninstantiable, so that it is not possible to have an object of class MPI::Comm.
However, it is possible to have a reference or a pointer to an MPI::Comm.

Example 8.4 The following code is erroneous.

```
MPI::Intracomm intra = MPI::COMM_WORLD.Dup();
MPI::Cartcomm cart(intra);          // This is erroneous
```

Table 8.3
C++ names for other MPI datatypes. Implementations may also define other optional types
(e.g., MPI::INTEGER16).

MPI datatype	Description
MPI::FLOAT_INT	C/C++ reduction type
MPI::DOUBLE_INT	C/C++ reduction type
MPI::LONG_INT	C/C++ reduction type
MPI::TWOINT	C/C++ reduction type
MPI::SHORT_INT	C/C++ reduction type
MPI::LONG_DOUBLE_INT	C/C++ reduction type
MPI::LONG_LONG	Optional C/C++ type
MPI::UNSIGNED_LONG_LONG	Optional C/C++ type
MPI::TWOREAL	Fortran reduction type
MPI::TWODOUBLE_PRECISION	Fortran reduction type
MPI::TWOINTEGER	Fortran reduction type
MPI::F_DOUBLE_COMPLEX	Optional Fortran type
MPI::INTEGER1	Explicit size type
MPI::INTEGER2	Explicit size type
MPI::INTEGER4	Explicit size type
MPI::INTEGER8	Explicit size type
MPI::REAL4	Explicit size type
MPI::REAL8	Explicit size type
MPI::REAL16	Explicit size type

MPI::COMM_NULL. The specific type of MPI::COMM_NULL is implementation dependent. MPI::COMM_NULL must be able to be used in comparisons and initializations with all types of communicators. MPI::COMM_NULL must also be able to be passed to a function that expects a communicator argument in the parameter list (provided that MPI::COMM_NULL is an allowed value for the communicator argument).

Rationale.   There are several possibilities for implementation of MPI::COMM_NULL. Specifying its required behavior, rather than its realization, provides maximum flexibility to implementors. □

Example 8.5   The following example demonstrates the behavior of assignment and comparison using MPI::COMM_NULL.

Table 8.4
Groups of predefined datatypes

C integer:	MPI::INT, MPI::LONG, MPI::SHORT, MPI::UNSIGNED_SHORT, MPI::UNSIGNED, MPI::UNSIGNED_LONG, MPI::SIGNED_CHAR, MPI::UNSIGNED_CHAR
Fortran integer:	MPI::INTEGER
Floating point:	MPI::FLOAT, MPI::DOUBLE, MPI::REAL, MPI::DOUBLE_PRECISION, MPI::LONG_DOUBLE
Logical:	MPI::LOGICAL, MPI::BOOL
Complex:	MPI::F_COMPLEX, MPI::COMPLEX, MPI::F_DOUBLE_COMPLEX, MPI::DOUBLE_COMPLEX, MPI::LONG_DOUBLE_COMPLEX
Byte:	MPI::BYTE

Table 8.5
Valid datatypes for reduction operations

Op	Allowed Types
MPI::MAX, MPI::MIN	C integer, Fortran integer, Floating point
MPI::SUM, MPI::PROD	C integer, Fortran integer, Floating point, Complex
MPI::LAND, MPI::LOR, MPI::LXOR	C integer, Logical
MPI::BAND, MPI::BOR, MPI::BXOR	C integer, Fortran integer, Byte

```
MPI::Intercomm comm;
comm = MPI::COMM_NULL;                  // assign with COMM_NULL
if (comm == MPI::COMM_NULL)             // true
   cout << "comm is NULL" << endl;
if (MPI::COMM_NULL == comm)             // note -- a different function!
   cout << "comm is still NULL" << endl;
```

Dup() is not defined as a member function of MPI::Comm, but it is defined for the derived classes of MPI::Comm. Dup() is not virtual and it returns its OUT parameter by value.

MPI::Comm::Clone(). The C++ language interface for MPI includes a new function Clone(). MPI::Comm::Clone() is a pure virtual function. For the derived communicator classes, Clone() behaves like Dup() except that it returns a new object by reference. The Clone() functions are prototyped as follows:

```
namespace MPI {
   Comm&           Comm::Clone() const = 0;
   IntraComm& IntraComm::Clone() const;
   InterComm& InterComm::Clone() const;
   CartComm&   CartComm::Clone() const;
   GraphComm& GraphComm::Clone() const;
};
```

Rationale. To be consistent with the language-neutral specification of MPI, Dup() must return its OUT parameter by value, rather than by reference. Since the Dup() method for each derived class must return a different class by value, C++ does not allow Dup() to be a virtual function. Clone() instead provides the "virtual Dup()" functionality that is expected by C++ programmers and library writers. Since Clone() returns a new object by reference, users are responsible for eventually deleting the object (this is in contrast with the typical MPI model for memory management). A new method is introduced to provide this functionality rather than changing the semantics of Dup(). □

Advice to implementors. Within their class declarations, prototypes for Clone() and Dup() might look like the following:

```
namespace MPI {
   class Comm {
      virtual Comm& Clone() const = 0;
   };

   class Intracomm : public Comm {
      Intracomm Dup() const { ... };
      virtual Intracomm& Clone() const { ... };
   };

   class Intercomm : public Comm {
      Intercomm Dup() const { ... };
      virtual Intercomm& Clone() const { ... };
```

```
  };
  // Cartcomm and Graphcomm are similarly defined
};
```

Compilers that do not support the variable return type feature of virtual functions may return a reference to `Comm`. Users can cast to the appropriate type as necessary. ▯

8.1.8 Exceptions

The C++ language interface for MPI includes the predefined error handler `MPI::ERRORS_THROW_EXCEPTIONS` for use with the `Set_errhandler()` member functions. `MPI::ERRORS_THROW_EXCEPTIONS` can only be set or retrieved by C++ functions. If a non-C++ program causes an error that invokes the `MPI::ERRORS_THROW_EXCEPTIONS` error handler, the exception will pass up the calling stack until C++ code can catch it. If there is no C++ code to catch it, the behavior is undefined. In a multithreaded environment or if a nonblocking MPI call throws an exception while making progress in the background, the behavior is implementation dependent.

The error handler `MPI::ERRORS_THROW_EXCEPTIONS` causes an `MPI::Exception` to be thrown for any MPI result code other than `MPI::SUCCESS`. The public interface to `MPI::Exception` class is defined as follows:

```
namespace MPI {
  class Exception {
  public:

    Exception(int error_code);

    int Get_error_code() const;
    int Get_error_class() const;
    const char *Get_error_string() const;
  };
};
```

Advice to implementors.   The exception will be thrown within the body of `MPI::ERRORS_THROW_EXCEPTIONS`. It is expected that control will be returned to the user when the exception is thrown. Some MPI functions specify certain return information in their parameters if an error occurs and `MPI_ERRORS_RETURN` has been

specified. The same type of return information must be provided when exceptions
are thrown. For example, MPI_WAITALL puts an error code for each request in
the corresponding entry in the status array and returns MPI_ERR_IN_STATUS. When
using MPI::ERRORS_THROW_EXCEPTIONS, it is expected that the error codes in the
status array will be set appropriately before the exception is thrown. □

8.1.9 Mixed-Language Operability

The C++ language interface provides functions listed below for mixed-language
operability. These functions provide for a seamless transition between C and C++.
For the case where the C++ class corresponding to <CLASS> has derived classes,
functions are also provided for converting between the derived classes and the C
MPI_<CLASS>.

MPI::<CLASS>& MPI::<CLASS>::operator=(const MPI_<CLASS>& data)

MPI::<CLASS>(const MPI_<CLASS>& data)

MPI::<CLASS>::operator MPI_<CLASS>() const

These functions are discussed in Section 2.2.4.

8.1.10 Profiling

This section specifies the requirements of a C++ profiling interface to MPI.

Advice to implementors. Since the main goal of profiling is to intercept function
calls from user code, it is the implementor's decision how to layer the underlying
implementation to allow function calls to be intercepted and profiled. If an implementation of the MPI C++ bindings is layered on top of MPI bindings in another
language (such as C), or if the C++ bindings are layered on top of a profiling
interface in another language, no extra profiling interface is necessary because the
underlying MPI implementation already meets the MPI profiling interface requirements.

Native C++ MPI implementations that do not have access to other profiling interfaces must implement an interface that meets the requirements outlined in this
section.

High-quality implementations can implement the interface outlined in this section
in order to promote portable C++ profiling libraries. Implementors may wish
to provide an option whether to build the C++ profiling interface or not; C++
implementations that are already layered on top of bindings in another language or

another profiling interface will have to insert a third layer to implement the C++ profiling interface. ☐

To meet the requirements of the C++ MPI profiling interface, an implementation of the MPI functions *must*:

1.   Provide a mechanism through which all of the MPI defined functions may be accessed with a name shift. Thus all of the MPI classes and static member functions (which normally start with the prefix "MPI::") should also be accessible with the prefix "PMPI::."

2.   Ensure that those MPI functions that are not replaced may still be linked into an executable image without causing name clashes.

3.   Document the implementation of different language bindings of the MPI interface if they are layered on top of each other, so that profiler developers know whether they must implement the profile interface for each binding, or can economize by implementing it only for the lowest level routines.

4.   Where the implementation of different language bindings is is done through a layered approach (e.g., the C++ binding is a set of "wrapper" functions which call the C implementation), ensure that these wrapper functions are separable from the rest of the library.

This is necessary to allow a separate profiling library to be correctly implemented, since (at least with Unix linker semantics) the profiling library must contain these wrapper functions if it is to perform as expected. This requirement allows the author of the profiling library to extract these functions from the original MPI library and add them into the profiling library without bringing along any other unnecessary code.

5.   Provide a no-op routine MPI::Pcontrol in the MPI library.

Advice to implementors.   There are (at least) two apparent options for implementing the C++ profiling interface: inheritance or containment. An inheritance-based approach may not be attractive because it may require a virtual inheritance implementation of the communicator classes. Thus, it is most likely that implementors will contain PMPI objects within the corresponding MPI objects. The containment scheme is outlined below.

The "real" entry points to each routine can be provided within a namespace PMPI. The nonprofiling version can then be provided within a namespace MPI.

Containing instances of `PMPI` objects in the `MPI` handles provides the "has a" relationship that is necessary to implement the profiling scheme.

Each instance of an `MPI` object simply "wraps up" an instance of a `PMPI` object. `MPI` objects can then perform profiling actions before invoking the corresponding function on their internal `PMPI` object. This is true for base classes and derived classes; there is a `PMPI` class hierarchy directly corresponding to the `MPI` hierarchy.

The key to making the profiling work by simply re-linking programs is to have a header file that *declares* all the `MPI` functions. The functions must be *defined* elsewhere, and compiled into a library. MPI constants should be declared **extern** in the `MPI` namespace. For example, the following is an excerpt from a sample `mpi.h` file:

Example 8.6   Sample `mpi.h` file.

```
namespace PMPI {
  class Comm {
  public:
    int Get_size() const;
  };
  // etc.
};

namespace MPI {
public:
  class Comm {
  public:
    int Get_size() const;

  private:
    PMPI::Comm pmpi_comm;
  };
};
```

Note that all constructors, the assignment operator, and the destructor in the `MPI` class will need to initialize/destroy the internal `PMPI` object as appropriate.

The definitions of the functions must be in separate object files; the `PMPI` class member functions and the nonprofiling versions of the `MPI` class member functions can be compiled into libmpi.a, while the profiling versions can be compiled into libpmpi.a. Note that the PMPI class member functions and the MPI constants must be in different object files from the nonprofiling MPI class member functions in the libmpi.a library to prevent multiple definitions of MPI class member function names when linking both libmpi.a and libpmpi.a. For example:

Example 8.7   pmpi.cc, to be compiled into libmpi.a.

```
int PMPI::Comm::Get_size() const
{
  // Implementation of MPI_COMM_SIZE
}
```

Example 8.8   constants.cc, to be compiled into libmpi.a.

```
const MPI::Intracomm MPI::COMM_WORLD;
```

Example 8.9   mpi_no_profile.cc, to be compiled into libmpi.a.

```
int MPI::Comm::Get_size() const
{
  return pmpi_comm.Get_size();
}
```

Example 8.10   mpi_profile.cc, to be compiled into libpmpi.a.

```
int MPI::Comm::Get_size() const
{
  // Do profiling stuff
  int ret = pmpi_comm.Get_size();
  // More profiling stuff
  return ret;
}
```

8.1.11 Cross-Reference

The C++ bindings use *this and return values in place of IN and OUT function arguments. To clarify the relationship between the language independent specification of function arguments and the C++ bindings, the following tables provide a cross-reference of all MPI functions and their corresponding C++ bindings. Also given in the tables is a listing of the MPI arguments that correspond to *this and to returned values.

MPI Function	C++ Function	Arguments	
		*this	Return
MPI_ABORT	Comm::Abort()	comm	void
MPI_ACCUMULATE	Win::Accumulate()	win	void
MPI_ADDRESS	<none>		
MPI_ADD_ERROR_CLASS	Add_error_class()	<none>	errorclass
MPI_ADD_ERROR_CODE	Add_error_code()	<none>	errorcode
MPI_ADD_ERROR_STRING	Add_error_string()	<none>	void
MPI_ALLGATHERV	Comm::Allgatherv()	comm	void
MPI_ALLGATHER	Comm::Allgather()	comm	void
MPI_ALLOC_MEM	Alloc_mem()	<none>	baseptr
MPI_ALLREDUCE	Comm::Allreduce()	comm	void
MPI_ALLTOALLV	Comm::Alltoallv()	comm	void
MPI_ALLTOALLW	Comm::Alltoallw()	comm	void
MPI_ALLTOALL	Comm::Alltoall()	comm	void
MPI_ATTR_DELETE	<none>		
MPI_ATTR_GET	<none>		
MPI_ATTR_PUT	<none>		
MPI_BARRIER	Comm::Barrier()	comm	void
MPI_BCAST	Comm::Bcast()	comm	void
MPI_BSEND_INIT	Comm::Bsend_init()	comm	request
MPI_BSEND	Comm::Bsend()	comm	void
MPI_BUFFER_ATTACH	Attach_buffer()	<none>	void
MPI_BUFFER_DETACH	Detach_buffer()	<none>	size
MPI_CANCEL	Request::Cancel()	request	void
MPI_CARTDIM_GET	Cartcomm::Get_dim()	comm	ndims
MPI_CART_COORDS	Cartcomm::Get_coords()	comm	void
MPI_CART_CREATE	Intracomm::Create_cart()	comm_old	comm_cart
MPI_CART_GET	Cartcomm::Get_topo()	comm	void
MPI_CART_MAP	Cartcomm::Map()	comm	newrank
MPI_CART_RANK	Cartcomm::Get_cart_rank()	comm	rank
MPI_CART_SHIFT	Cartcomm::Shift()	comm	void
MPI_CART_SUB	Cartcomm::Sub()	comm	newcomm
MPI_CLOSE_PORT	Close_port()	<none>	void
MPI_COMM_ACCEPT	Intracomm::Accept()	comm	newcomm
MPI_COMM_CALL_ERRHANDLER	Comm::Call_errhandler()	comm	void
MPI_COMM_COMPARE	static Comm::Compare()	<none>	result
MPI_COMM_CONNECT	Intracomm::Connect()	comm	newcomm
MPI_COMM_CREATE_ERRHANDLER	static Comm::Create_errhandler()	<none>	errhandler

MPI Function	C++ Function	Arguments	
		*this	Return
MPI_COMM_CREATE_-KEYVAL	static Comm::Create_keyval()	<none>	comm_-keyval
MPI_COMM_CREATE	Intercomm::Create()	comm	newcomm
	Intracomm::Create()	comm	newcomm
MPI_COMM_DELETE_-ATTR	Comm::Delete_attr()	comm	void
MPI_COMM_-DISCONNECT	Comm::Disconnect()	comm	void
MPI_COMM_DUP	Intracomm::Dup()	comm	newcomm
	Intercomm::Dup()	comm	newcomm
	Comm::Clone()	comm	&newcomm
MPI_COMM_FREE_-KEYVAL	static Comm::Free_keyval()	<none>	void
MPI_COMM_FREE	Comm::Free()	comm	void
MPI_COMM_GET_ATTR	Comm::Get_attr()	comm	flag
MPI_COMM_GET_-ERRHANDLER	Comm::Get_errhandler()	comm	errhandler
MPI_COMM_GET_NAME	Comm::Get_name()	comm	void
MPI_COMM_GET_-PARENT	static Comm::Get_parent()	<none>	parent
MPI_COMM_GROUP	Comm::Get_group()	comm	group
MPI_COMM_JOIN	static Comm::Join()	<none>	intercomm
MPI_COMM_RANK	Comm::Get_rank()	comm	rank
MPI_COMM_REMOTE_-GROUP	Intercomm::Get_remote_-group()	comm	group
MPI_COMM_REMOTE_-SIZE	Intercomm::Get_remote_-size()	comm	size
MPI_COMM_SET_ATTR	Comm::Set_attr()	comm	void
MPI_COMM_SET_-ERRHANDLER	Comm::Set_errhandler()	comm	void
MPI_COMM_SET_NAME	Comm::Set_name()	comm	void
MPI_COMM_SIZE	Comm::Get_size()	comm	size
MPI_COMM_SPAWN_-MULTIPLE	Intracomm::Spawn_-multiple()	comm	intercomm
MPI_COMM_SPAWN	Intracomm::Spawn()	comm	intercomm
MPI_COMM_SPLIT	Intercomm::Split()	comm	newcomm
	Intracomm::Split()	comm	newcomm
MPI_COMM_TEST_INTER	Comm::Is_inter()	comm	flag
MPI_DIMS_CREATE	Compute_dims()	<none>	void
MPI_ERRHANDLER_-CREATE	<none>		
MPI_ERRHANDLER_-CREATE	<none>		

MPI Function	C++ Function	Arguments *this	Return
MPI_ERRHANDLER_FREE	Errhandler::Free()	errhandler	void
MPI_ERRHANDLER_GET	\<none\>		
MPI_ERRHANDLER_SET	\<none\>		
MPI_ERROR_CLASS	Get_error_class()	\<none\>	errorclass
MPI_ERROR_STRING	Get_error_string()	\<none\>	void
MPI_EXSCAN	Intracomm::Exscan()	comm	void
MPI_FILE_CALL_-ERRHANDLER	File::Call_errhandler()	fh	void
MPI_FILE_CLOSE	File::Close()	fh	void
MPI_FILE_CREATE_-ERRHANDLER	static File::Create_-errhandler()	\<none\>	errhandler
MPI_FILE_DELETE	static File::Delete()	\<none\>	void
MPI_FILE_GET_AMODE	File::Get_amode()	fh	amode
MPI_FILE_GET_-ATOMICITY	File::Get_atomicity()	fh	flag
MPI_FILE_GET_BYTE_-OFFSET	File::Get_byte_offset()	fh	offset
MPI_FILE_GET_-ERRHANDLER	File::Get_errhandler()	file	errhandler
MPI_FILE_GET_GROUP	File::Get_group()	fh	group
MPI_FILE_GET_INFO	File::Get_info()	fh	info_used
MPI_FILE_GET_-POSITION_SHARED	File::Get_position_-shared()	fh	offset
MPI_FILE_GET_POSITION	File::Get_position()	fh	offset
MPI_FILE_GET_SIZE	File::Get_size()	fh	size
MPI_FILE_GET_TYPE_-EXTENT	File::Get_type_extent()	fh	extent
MPI_FILE_GET_VIEW	File::Get_view()	fh	void
MPI_FILE_IREAD_AT	File::Iread_at()	fh	request
MPI_FILE_IREAD_-SHARED	File::Iread_shared()	fh	request
MPI_FILE_IREAD	File::Iread()	fh	request
MPI_FILE_IWRITE_AT	File::Iwrite_at()	fh	request
MPI_FILE_IWRITE_-SHARED	File::Iwrite_shared()	fh	request
MPI_FILE_IWRITE	File::Iwrite()	fh	request
MPI_FILE_OPEN	static File::Open()	\<none\>	fh
MPI_FILE_PREALLOCATE	File::Preallocate()	fh	void
MPI_FILE_READ_ALL_-BEGIN	File::Read_all_begin()	fh	void
MPI_FILE_READ_ALL_END	File::Read_all_end()	fh	void
MPI_FILE_READ_ALL	File::Read_all()	fh	void

		Arguments	
MPI Function	C++ Function	*this	Return
MPI_FILE_READ_AT_ALL_-BEGIN	File::Read_at_all_-begin()	fh	void
MPI_FILE_READ_AT_ALL_-END	File::Read_at_all_end()	fh	void
MPI_FILE_READ_AT_ALL	File::Read_at_all()	fh	void
MPI_FILE_READ_AT	File::Read_at()	fh	void
MPI_FILE_READ_-ORDERED_BEGIN	File::Read_ordered_-begin()	fh	void
MPI_FILE_READ_-ORDERED_END	File::Read_ordered_-end()	fh	void
MPI_FILE_READ_-ORDERED	File::Read_ordered()	fh	void
MPI_FILE_READ_SHARED	File::Read_shared()	fh	void
MPI_FILE_READ	File::Read()	fh	void
MPI_FILE_SEEK_SHARED	File::Seek_shared()	fh	void
MPI_FILE_SEEK	File::Seek()	fh	void
MPI_FILE_SET_-ATOMICITY	File::Set_atomicity()	fh	void
MPI_FILE_SET_-ERRHANDLER	File::Set_errhandler()	file	void
MPI_FILE_SET_INFO	File::Set_info()	fh	void
MPI_FILE_SET_SIZE	File::Set_size()	fh	void
MPI_FILE_SET_VIEW	File::Set_view()	fh	void
MPI_FILE_SYNC	File::Sync()	fh	void
MPI_FILE_WRITE_ALL_-BEGIN	File::Write_all_begin()	fh	void
MPI_FILE_WRITE_ALL_-END	File::Write_all_end()	fh	void
MPI_FILE_WRITE_ALL	File::Write_all()	fh	void
MPI_FILE_WRITE_AT_-ALL_BEGIN	File::Write_at_all_-begin()	fh	void
MPI_FILE_WRITE_AT_ALL	File::Write_at_all()	fh	void
MPI_FILE_WRITE_AT_END	File::Write_at_all_-end()	fh	void
MPI_FILE_WRITE_AT	File::Write_at()	fh	void
MPI_FILE_WRITE_-ORDERED_BEGIN	File::Write_ordered_-begin()	fh	void
MPI_FILE_WRITE_-ORDERED_END	File::Write_ordered_-end()	fh	void
MPI_FILE_WRITE_-ORDERED	File::Write_ordered()	fh	void
MPI_FILE_WRITE_-SHARED	File::Write_shared()	fh	void

| | | Arguments | |
MPI Function	C++ Function	*this	Return
MPI_FILE_WRITE	File::Write()	fh	void
MPI_FINALIZE	Finalize()	<none>	void
MPI_FINALIZED	Is_finalized()	<none>	flag
MPI_FREE_MEM	Free_mem()	<none>	void
MPI_GATHERV	Comm::Gatherv()	comm	void
MPI_GATHER	Comm::Gather()	comm	void
MPI_GET_ADDRESS	Get_address()	<none>	address
MPI_GET_COUNT	Status::Get_count()	status	count
MPI_GET_ELEMENTS	Status::Get_elements()	status	count
MPI_GET_PROCESSOR_- NAME	Get_processor_name()	<none>	void
MPI_GET	Win::Get()	win	void
MPI_GRAPHDIMS_GET	Graphcomm::Get_dims()	comm	void
MPI_GRAPH_CREATE	Intracomm::Create_- graph()	comm_old	comm_graph
MPI_GRAPH_GET	Graphcomm::Get_topo()	comm	void
MPI_GRAPH_MAP	Graphcomm::Map()	comm	newrank
MPI_GRAPH_- NEIGHBORS_COUNT	Graphcomm::Get_- neighbors_count()	comm	nneighbors
MPI_GRAPH_NEIGHBORS	Graphcomm::Get_- neighbors()	comm	void
MPI_GREQUEST_- COMPLETE	Grequest::Complete()	request	void
MPI_GREQUEST_START	static Grequest::Start()	<none>	request
MPI_GROUP_COMPARE	static Group::Compare()	<none>	result
MPI_GROUP_- DIFFERENCE	static Group::Difference()	<none>	newgroup
MPI_GROUP_EXCL	Group::Excl()	group	newgroup
MPI_GROUP_FREE	Group::Free()	group	void
MPI_GROUP_INCL	Group::Incl()	group	newgroup
MPI_GROUP_- INTERSECTION	static Group::Intersect()	<none>	newgroup
MPI_GROUP_RANGE_- EXCL	Group::Range_excl()	group	newgroup
MPI_GROUP_RANGE_- INCL	Group::Range_incl()	group	newgroup
MPI_GROUP_RANK	Group::Get_rank()	group	rank
MPI_GROUP_SIZE	Group::Get_size()	group	size
MPI_GROUP_- TRANSLATE_RANKS	static Group::Translate_- ranks()	<none>	void

MPI Function	C++ Function	*this	Return
			Arguments
MPI_GROUP_UNION	static Group::Union()	<none>	newgroup
MPI_IBSEND	Comm::Ibsend()	comm	request
MPI_INFO_CREATE	static Info::Create()	<none>	info
MPI_INFO_DELETE	Info::Delete()	info	void
MPI_INFO_DUP	Info::Dup()	info	newinfo
MPI_INFO_FREE	Info::Free()	info	void
MPI_INFO_GET_NKEYS	Info::Get_nkeys()	info	nkeys
MPI_INFO_GET_NTHKEY	Info::Get_nthkey()	info	void
MPI_INFO_GET_VALUELEN	Info::Get_valuelen()	info	flag
MPI_INFO_GET	Info::Get()	info	flag
MPI_INFO_SET	Info::Set()	info	void
MPI_INITIALIZED	Is_initialized()	<none>	flag
MPI_INIT_THREAD	Init_thread()	<none>	provided
MPI_INIT	Init()	<none>	void
MPI_INTERCOMM_CREATE	Intracomm::Create_intercomm()	local_comm	newintercomm
MPI_INTERCOMM_MERGE	Intercomm::Merge()	intercomm	newintracomm
MPI_IPROBE	Comm::Iprobe()	comm	flag
MPI_IRECV	Comm::Irecv()	comm	request
MPI_IRSEND	Comm::Irsend()	comm	request
MPI_ISEND	Comm::Isend()	comm	request
MPI_ISSEND	Comm::Issend()	comm	request
MPI_IS_THREAD_MAIN	Is_thread_main()	<none>	flag
MPI_KEYVAL_CREATE	<none>		
MPI_KEYVAL_FREE	<none>		
MPI_LOOKUP_NAME	Lookup_name()	<none>	void
MPI_OPEN_PORT	Open_port()	<none>	void
MPI_OP_CREATE	Op::Init()	op	void
MPI_OP_FREE	Op::Free()	op	void
MPI_PACK_EXTERNAL_SIZE	Datatype::Pack_external_size()	datatype	size
MPI_PACK_EXTERNAL	Datatype::Pack_external()	datatype	void
MPI_PACK_SIZE	Datatype::Pack_size()	datatype	size
MPI_PACK	Datatype::Pack()	datatype	void
MPI_PCONTROL	Pcontrol()	<none>	void
MPI_PROBE	Comm::Probe()	comm	void
MPI_PUBLISH_NAME	Publish_name()	<none>	void
MPI_PUT	Win::Put()	win	void
MPI_QUERY_THREAD	Query_thread()	<none>	provided
MPI_RECV_INIT	Comm::Recv_init()	comm	request

MPI Function	C++ Function	Arguments	
		*this	Return
MPI_RECV	Comm::Recv()	comm	void
MPI_REDUCE_SCATTER	Comm::Reduce_scatter()	comm	void
MPI_REDUCE	Comm::Reduce()	comm	void
MPI_REGISTER_DATAREP	Register_datarep()	<none>	void
MPI_REQUEST_FREE	Request::Free()	request	void
MPI_REQUEST_GET_STATUS	Request::Get_status()	request	flag
MPI_RSEND_INIT	Comm::Rsend_init()	comm	request
MPI_RSEND	Comm::Rsend()	comm	void
MPI_SCAN	Intracomm::Scan()	comm	void
MPI_SCATTERV	Comm::Scatterv()	comm	void
MPI_SCATTER	Comm::Scatter()	comm	void
MPI_SENDRECV_REPLACE	Comm::Sendrecv_replace()	comm	void
MPI_SENDRECV	Comm::Sendrecv()	comm	void
MPI_SEND_INIT	Comm::Send_init()	comm	request
MPI_SEND	Comm::Send()	comm	void
MPI_SSEND_INIT	Comm::Ssend_init()	comm	request
MPI_SSEND	Comm::Ssend()	comm	void
MPI_STARTALL	static Prequest::Startall()	<none>	void
MPI_START	Prequest::Start()	request	void
MPI_STATUS_SET_CANCELLED	Status::Set_cancelled()	status	void
MPI_STATUS_SET_ELEMENTS	Status::Set_elements()	staus	void
MPI_TESTALL	static Request::Testall()	<none>	flag
MPI_TESTANY	static Request::Testany()	<none>	flag
MPI_TESTSOME	static Request::Testsome()	<none>	outcount
MPI_TEST_CANCELLED	Status::Is_cancelled()	status	flag
MPI_TEST	Request::Test()	request	flag
MPI_TOPO_TEST	Comm::Get_topology()	comm	status
MPI_TYPE_COMMIT	Datatype::Commit()	datatype	void
MPI_TYPE_CONTIGUOUS	Datatype::Create_contiguous()	oldtype	newtype
MPI_TYPE_CREATE_DARRAY	Datatype::Create_darray()	oldtype	newtype

MPI Function	C++ Function	Arguments	
		*this	Return
MPI_TYPE_CREATE_F90_-COMPLEX	static Datatype::Create_f90_-complex()	<none>	newtype
MPI_TYPE_CREATE_F90_-INTEGER	static Datatype::Create_f90_-integer()	<none>	newtype
MPI_TYPE_CREATE_F90_-REAL	static Datatype::Create_f90_-real()	<none>	newtype
MPI_TYPE_CREATE_-HINDEXED	Datatype::Create_-hindexed()	oldtype	newtype
MPI_TYPE_CREATE_-HVECTOR	Datatype::Create_-hvector()	oldtype	newtype
MPI_TYPE_CREATE_-INDEXED_BLOCK	Datatype::Create_-indexed_block()	oldtype	newtype
MPI_TYPE_CREATE_-KEYVAL	static Datatype::Create_-keyval()	<none>	type_-keyval
MPI_TYPE_CREATE_-RESIZED	Datatype::Resized()	oldtype	newtype
MPI_TYPE_CREATE_-STRUCT	static Datatype::Create_-struct()	<none>	newtype
MPI_TYPE_CREATE_-SUBARRAY	Datatype::Create_-subarray()	oldtype	newtype
MPI_TYPE_DELETE_-ATTR	Datatype::Delete_attr()	type	void
MPI_TYPE_DUP	Datatype::Dup()	type	newtype
MPI_TYPE_EXTENT	<none>		
MPI_TYPE_FREE_KEYVAL	static Datatype::Free_keyval()	<none>	void
MPI_TYPE_FREE	Datatype::Free()	datatype	void
MPI_TYPE_GET_ATTR	Datatype::Get_attr()	type	flag
MPI_TYPE_GET_-CONTENTS	Datatype::Get_-contents()	datatype	void
MPI_TYPE_GET_-ENVELOPE	Datatype::Get_-envelope()	datatype	void
MPI_TYPE_GET_EXTENT	Datatype::Get_extent()	datatype	void
MPI_TYPE_GET_NAME	Datatype::Get_name()	type	void
MPI_TYPE_GET_TRUE_-EXTENT	Datatype::Get_true_-extent()	datatype	void
MPI_TYPE_HINDEXED	<none>		

		Arguments	
MPI Function	C++ Function	*this	Return
MPI_TYPE_HVECTOR	\<none\>		
MPI_TYPE_INDEXED	Datatype::Create_-indexed()	oldtype	newtype
MPI_TYPE_LB	\<none\>		
MPI_TYPE_MATCH_SIZE	static Datatype::Match_size()	\<none\>	type
MPI_TYPE_SET_ATTR	Datatype::Set_attr()	type	void
MPI_TYPE_SET_NAME	Datatype::Set_name()	type	void
MPI_TYPE_SIZE	Datatype::Get_size()	datatype	size
MPI_TYPE_STRUCT	\<none\>		
MPI_TYPE_UB	\<none\>		
MPI_TYPE_VECTOR	Datatype::Create_-vector()	oldtype	newtype
MPI_UNPACK_EXTERNAL	Datatype::Unpack_-external()	datatype	void
MPI_UNPACK	Datatype::Unpack()	datatype	void
MPI_UNPUBLISH_NAME	Unpublish_name()	\<none\>	void
MPI_WAITALL	static Request::Waitall()	\<none\>	void
MPI_WAITANY	static Request::Waitany()	\<none\>	index
MPI_WAITSOME	static Request::Waitsome()	\<none\>	outcount
MPI_WAIT	Request::Wait()	request	void
MPI_WIN_CALL_-ERRHANDLER	Win::Call_errhandler()	win	void
MPI_WIN_COMPLETE	Win::Complete()	win	void
MPI_WIN_CREATE_-ERRHANDLER	static Win::Create_-errhandler()	\<none\>	errhandler
MPI_WIN_CREATE_-KEYVAL	static Win::Create_keyval()	\<none\>	win_keyval
MPI_WIN_CREATE	static Win::Create()	\<none\>	win
MPI_WIN_DELETE_ATTR	Win::Delete_attr()	win	void
MPI_WIN_FENCE	Win::Fence()	win	void
MPI_WIN_FREE_KEYVAL	static Win::Free_keyval()	\<none\>	void
MPI_WIN_FREE	Win::Free()	win	void
MPI_WIN_GET_ATTR	Win::Get_attr()	win	flag
MPI_WIN_GET_-ERRHANDLER	Win::Get_errhandler()	win	errhandler
MPI_WIN_GET_GROUP	Win::Get_group()	win	group
MPI_WIN_GET_NAME	Win::Get_name()	win	void
MPI_WIN_LOCK	Win::Lock()	win	void

| MPI Function | C++ Function | Arguments | |
		*this	Return
MPI_WIN_POST	Win::Post()	win	void
MPI_WIN_SET_ATTR	Win::Set_attr()	win	void
MPI_WIN_SET_-ERRHANDLER	Win::Set_errhandler()	win	void
MPI_WIN_SET_NAME	Win::Set_name()	win	void
MPI_WIN_START	Win::Start()	win	void
MPI_WIN_TEST	Win::Test()	win	flag
MPI_WIN_UNLOCK	Win::Unlock()	win	void
MPI_WIN_WAIT	Win::Wait()	win	void
MPI_WTICK	Wtick()	<none>	wtick
MPI_WTIME	Wtime()	<none>	wtime

8.2 Fortran Support

8.2.1 Overview

Fortran 90 is the current international Fortran standard. MPI-2 Fortran bindings are Fortran 90 bindings that in most cases are "Fortran 77 friendly." That is, with few exceptions (e.g., KIND-parameterized types and the mpi module, both of which can be avoided) Fortran 77 compilers should be able to compile MPI programs.

Rationale.   Fortran 90 contains numerous features designed to make it a more "modern" language than Fortran 77. It seems natural that MPI should be able to take advantage of these new features with a set of bindings tailored to Fortran 90. MPI does not (yet) use many of these features because of a number of technical difficulties. ▯

MPI defines two levels of Fortran support, described in Sections 8.2.3 and 8.2.4. A third level of Fortran support is envisioned, but is not included in MPI-2. In the rest of this section, "Fortran" shall refer to Fortran 90 (or its successor) unless qualified.

Basic Fortran Support: An implementation with this level of Fortran support provides the original Fortran bindings specified in MPI-1, with small additional requirements specified in Section 8.2.3.

Extended Fortran Support: An implementation with this level of Fortran support provides Basic Fortran Support plus additional features that specifically support Fortran 90, as described in Section 8.2.4.

A compliant MPI-2 implementation providing a Fortran interface must provide Extended Fortran Support unless the target compiler does not support modules or KIND-parameterized types.

8.2.2   Problems with Fortran Bindings for MPI

This section discusses a number of problems that may arise when using MPI in a Fortran program. It is intended as advice to users, and clarifies how MPI interacts with Fortran. It does not add to the standard, but is intended to clarify the standard.

As noted in the original MPI specification, the interface violates the Fortran standard in several ways. While these cause few problems for Fortran 77 programs, they become more significant for Fortran 90 programs, so that users must exercise care when using new Fortran 90 features. The violations were originally adopted and have been retained because they are important for the usability of MPI. The rest of this section describes the potential problems in detail. It supersedes and replaces the discussion of Fortran bindings in the original MPI specification (for Fortran 90, not Fortran 77). The following MPI features are inconsistent with Fortran 90.

1.   An MPI subroutine with a choice argument may be called with different argument types.

2.   An MPI subroutine with an assumed-size dummy argument may be passed an actual scalar argument.

3.   Many MPI routines assume that actual arguments are passed by address and that arguments are not copied on entrance to or exit from the subroutine.

4.   An MPI implementation may read or modify user data (e.g., communication buffers used by nonblocking communications) concurrently with a user program that is executing outside of MPI calls.

5.   Several named "constants," such as MPI_BOTTOM, MPI_IN_PLACE, MPI_STATUS_IGNORE, MPI_STATUSES_IGNORE, MPI_ERRCODES_IGNORE, MPI_ARGV_NULL, and MPI_ARGVS_NULL are not ordinary Fortran constants and require a special implementation. See Section 1.5.4 for more information.

6.   The memory allocation routine MPI_ALLOC_MEM can't be usefully used in Fortran without a language extension that allows the allocated memory to be associated with a Fortran variable.

MPI-1 contains several routines that take address-sized information as input or return address-sized information as output. In C such arguments are of type MPI_Aint and in Fortran of type INTEGER. On machines where integers are smaller than addresses, these routines can lose information. In MPI-2 the use of these functions has been deprecated and they have been replaced by routines taking `INTEGER` arguments of `KIND=MPI_ADDRESS_KIND`. A number of new MPI-2 functions also take `INTEGER` arguments of nondefault `KIND`. See Section 1.6 for more information.

Problems Due to Strong Typing.   All MPI functions with choice arguments associate actual arguments of different Fortran datatypes with the same dummy argument. This is not allowed by Fortran 77, and in Fortran 90 is technically only allowed if the function is overloaded with a different function for each type. In C, the use of `void*` formal arguments avoids these problems.

The following code fragment is technically illegal and may generate a compile-time error.

```
integer i(5)
real     x(5)
...
call mpi_send(x, 5, MPI_REAL, ...)
call mpi_send(i, 5, MPI_INTEGER, ...)
```

In practice, it is rare for compilers to do more than issue a warning, though there is concern that Fortran 90 compilers are more likely to return errors.

It is also technically illegal in Fortran to pass a scalar actual argument to an array dummy argument. Thus the following code fragment may generate an error since the buf argument to MPI_SEND is declared as an assumed-size array `<type>` `buf(*)`.

```
integer a
call mpi_send(a, 1, MPI_INTEGER, ...)
```

Advice to users.   In the event that you run into one of the problems related to type checking, you may be able to work around it by using a compiler flag, by compiling separately, or by using an MPI implementation with Extended Fortran Support as described in Section 8.2.4. An alternative that will usually work with variables local to a routine but not with arguments to a function or subroutine is to use the `EQUIVALENCE` statement to create another variable with a type accepted by the compiler. □

Problems Due to Data Copying and Sequence Association.   Implicit in MPI is the idea of a contiguous chunk of memory accessible through a linear address space. MPI copies data to and from this memory. An MPI program specifies the location of data by providing memory addresses and offsets. In the C language, sequence association rules plus pointers provide all the necessary low-level structure.

In Fortran 90, user data is not necessarily stored contiguously. For example, the array section A(1:N:2) involves only the elements of A with indices 1, 3, 5, ... The same is true for a pointer array whose target is such a section. Most compilers ensure that an array that is a dummy argument is held in contiguous memory if it is declared with an explicit shape (e.g., B(N)) or is of assumed size (e.g., B(*)). If necessary, they do this by making a copy of the array into contiguous memory. Both Fortran 77 and Fortran 90 are carefully worded to allow such copying to occur, but few Fortran 77 compilers do it.[1]

Because MPI dummy buffer arguments are assumed-size arrays, this leads to a serious problem for a nonblocking call: the compiler copies the temporary array back on return but MPI continues to copy data to the memory that held it. For example, consider the following code fragment:

```
real a(100)
call MPI_IRECV(a(1:100:2), MPI_REAL, 50, ...)
```

Since the first dummy argument to MPI_IRECV is an assumed-size array (<type> buf(*)), the array section a(1:100:2) is copied to a temporary before being passed to MPI_IRECV, so that it is contiguous in memory. MPI_IRECV returns immediately, and data is copied from the temporary back into the array a. Sometime later, MPI may write to the address of the deallocated temporary. Copying is also a problem for MPI_ISEND since the temporary array may be deallocated before the data has all been sent from it.

Most Fortran 90 compilers do not make a copy if the actual argument is the whole of an explicit-shape or assumed-size array or is a "simple" section such as A(1:N) of such an array. (We define "simple" more fully in the next paragraph.) Also, many compilers treat allocatable arrays the same as they treat explicit-shape arrays in this regard (though we know of one that does not). However, the same is not true for assumed-shape and pointer arrays; since they may be discontiguous, copying is often done. It is this copying that causes problems for MPI as described in the previous paragraph.

Our formal definition of a "simple" array section is

```
name ( [:,]... [<subscript>]:[<subscript>] [,<subscript>]... )
```

---

[1]Technically, the Fortran standards are worded to allow noncontiguous storage of any array data.

That is, there are zero or more dimensions that are selected in full, then one dimension selected without a stride, then zero or more dimensions that are selected with a simple subscript. Examples are

```
A(1:N), A(:,N), A(:,1:N,1), A(1:6,N), A(:,:,1:N)
```

Because of Fortran's column-major ordering, where the first index varies fastest, a simple section of a contiguous array will also be contiguous.[2]

The same problem can occur with a scalar argument. Some compilers, even for Fortran 77, make a copy of some scalar dummy arguments within a called procedure. That this can cause a problem is illustrated by the example

```
call user1(a,rq)
call MPI_WAIT(rq,status,ierr)
write (*,*) a

subroutine user1(buf,request)
call MPI_IRECV(buf,...,request,...)
end
```

If a is copied, MPI_IRECV will alter the copy when it completes the communication and will not alter a itself.

Note that copying will almost certainly occur for an argument that is a nontrivial expression (one with at least one operator or function call), a section that does not select a contiguous part of its parent (e.g., A(1:n:2)), a pointer whose target is such a section, or an assumed-shape array that is (directly or indirectly) associated with such a section.

If there is a compiler option that inhibits copying of arguments, in either the calling or called procedure, this should be employed.

If a compiler makes copies in the calling procedure of arguments that are explicit-shape or assumed-size arrays, simple array sections of such arrays, or scalars, and if there is no compiler option to inhibit this, then this compiler cannot be used for applications that use MPI_GET_ADDRESS, or any nonblocking MPI routine. If a compiler copies scalar arguments in the called procedure and there is no compiler option to inhibit this, then this compiler cannot be used for applications that use memory references across subroutine calls as in the example above.

---

[2]To keep the definition of "simple" simple, we have chosen to require all but one of the section subscripts to be without bounds. A colon without bounds makes it obvious both to the compiler and to the reader that the whole of the dimension is selected. It would have been possible to allow cases where the whole dimension is selected with one or two bounds, but this means for the reader that the array declaration or most recent allocation has to be consulted and for the compiler that a runtime check may be required.

Special Constants.   MPI requires a number of special "constants" that cannot be implemented as normal Fortran constants, including MPI_BOTTOM, MPI_STATUS_-IGNORE, MPI_IN_PLACE, MPI_STATUSES_IGNORE and MPI_ERRCODES_IGNORE. In C, these are implemented as constant pointers, usually as NULL and are used where the function prototype calls for a pointer to a variable, not the variable itself.

In Fortran the implementation of these special constants may require the use of language constructs that are outside the Fortran standard. Using special values for the constants (e.g., by defining them through **parameter** statements) is not possible because an implementation cannot distinguish these values from legal data. Typically these constants are implemented as predefined static variables (e.g., a variable in an MPI-declared **COMMON** block), relying on the fact that the target compiler passes data by address. Inside the subroutine, this address can be extracted by some mechanism outside the Fortran standard (e.g., by Fortran extensions or by implementing the function in C).

Fortran 90 Derived Types.   MPI does not explicitly support passing Fortran 90 derived types to choice dummy arguments. Indeed, for MPI implementations that provide explicit interfaces through the **mpi** module a compiler will reject derived type actual arguments at compile time. Even when no explicit interfaces are given, users should be aware that Fortran 90 provides no guarantee of sequence association for derived types or arrays of derived types. For instance, an array of a derived type consisting of two elements may be implemented as an array of the first elements followed by an array of the second. Use of the **SEQUENCE** attribute may help here.

The following code fragment shows one possible way to send a derived type in Fortran. The example assumes that all data is passed by address.

```
type mytype
   integer i
   real x
   double precision d
end type mytype

type(mytype) foo
integer blocklen(3), type(3)
integer(MPI_ADDRESS_KIND) disp(3), base

call MPI_GET_ADDRESS(foo%i, disp(1), ierr)
call MPI_GET_ADDRESS(foo%x, disp(2), ierr)
```

```
call MPI_GET_ADDRESS(foo%d, disp(3), ierr)

base = disp(1)
disp(1) = disp(1) - base
disp(2) = disp(2) - base
disp(3) = disp(3) - base

blocklen(1) = 1
blocklen(2) = 1
blocklen(3) = 1

type(1) = MPI_INTEGER
type(2) = MPI_REAL
type(3) = MPI_DOUBLE_PRECISION

call MPI_TYPE_CREATE_STRUCT(3, blocklen, disp, type, newtype, &
                            ierr)
call MPI_TYPE_COMMIT(newtype, ierr)

! unpleasant to send foo%i instead of foo, but it works for scalar
! entities of type mytype
call MPI_SEND(foo%i, 1, newtype, ...)
```

A Problem with Register Optimization.   MPI provides operations that may be hidden from the user code and run concurrently with it, accessing the same memory as user code. Examples include the data transfer for an MPI_IRECV. The optimizer of a compiler will assume that it can recognize periods when a copy of a variable can be kept in a register without reloading from or storing to memory. When the user code is working with a register copy of some variable while the hidden operation reads or writes the memory copy, problems occur. This section discusses register optimization pitfalls.

When a variable is local to a Fortran subroutine (i.e., not in a module or COMMON block), the compiler will assume that it cannot be modified by a called subroutine unless it is an actual argument of the call. In the most common linkage convention, the subroutine is expected to save and restore certain registers. Thus, the optimizer will assume that a register which held a valid copy of such a variable before the call will still hold a valid copy on return.

Normally users are not afflicted with this. But the user should pay attention to this section if in his/her program a buffer argument to an MPI_SEND, MPI_RECV, etc., uses a name which hides the actual variables involved. MPI_BOTTOM with an MPI_Datatype containing absolute addresses is one example. Another way is to create a datatype that uses one variable as an anchor and brings along others by using MPI_GET_ADDRESS to determine their offsets from the anchor. The anchor variable would be the only one mentioned in the call. Also attention must be paid if MPI operations are used that run in parallel with the user's application.

The following example shows what Fortran compilers are allowed to do.
This source ...   can be compiled as:

```
call MPI_GET_ADDRESS(buf,bufaddr,        call MPI_GET_ADDRESS(buf,...)
          ierror)
call MPI_TYPE_CREATE_STRUCT(1,1,         call MPI_TYPE_CREATE_STRUCT(...)
          bufaddr,
          MPI_REAL,type,ierror)
call MPI_TYPE_COMMIT(type,ierror)        call MPI_TYPE_COMMIT(...)
val_old = buf                            register = buf
                                          val_old = register
call MPI_RECV(MPI_BOTTOM,1,              call MPI_RECV(MPI_BOTTOM,...)
          type,...)

val_new = buf                            val_new = register
```

The compiler does not invalidate the register because it cannot see that MPI_RECV changes the value of buf. The access of buf is hidden by the use of MPI_GET_ADDRESS and MPI_BOTTOM.

The next example shows extreme, but allowed, possibilities.
Source   compiled as   or compiled as

```
call MPI_IRECV(buf,..req) call MPI_IRECV(buf,..req) call MPI_IRECV(buf,..req)
                          register = buf            b1 = buf
call MPI_WAIT(req,..)     call MPI_WAIT(req,..)     call MPI_WAIT(req,..)
b1 = buf                  b1 := register
```

MPI_WAIT on a concurrent thread modifies buf between the invocation of MPI_IRECV and the finish of MPI_WAIT. But the compiler cannot see any possibility that buf can be changed after MPI_IRECV has returned, and may schedule the load of buf earlier than typed in the source. It has no reason to avoid using a register to hold buf across the call to MPI_WAIT. It also may reorder the instructions as in the case on the right.

To prevent instruction reordering or the allocation of a buffer in a register there are two possibilities in portable Fortran code:

• The compiler may be prevented from moving a reference to a buffer across a call to an MPI subroutine by surrounding the call by calls to an external subroutine with the buffer as an actual argument. Note that if the intent is declared in the external subroutine, it must be OUT or INOUT. The subroutine itself may have an empty body, but the compiler does not know this and has to assume that the buffer may be altered. For example, the above call of MPI_RECV might be replaced by

```
call DD(buf)
call MPI_RECV(MPI_BOTTOM,...)
call DD(buf)
```

with the separately compiled

```
subroutine DD(buf)
  integer buf
end
```

(assuming that buf has type INTEGER). The compiler may be similarly prevented from moving a reference to a variable across a call to an MPI subroutine.

In the case of a nonblocking call, as in the above call of MPI_WAIT, no reference to the buffer is permitted until it has been verified that the transfer has been completed. Therefore, in this case, the extra call ahead of the MPI call is not necessary, that is, the call of MPI_WAIT in the example might be replaced by

```
call MPI_WAIT(req,..)
call DD(buf)
```

• An alternative is to put the buffer or variable into a module or a common block and access it through a USE or COMMON statement in each scope where it is referenced, defined or appears as an actual argument in a call to an MPI routine. The compiler will then have to assume that the MPI procedure (MPI_RECV in the above example) may alter the buffer or variable, provided that the compiler cannot analyze that the MPI procedure does not reference the module or common block.

In the longer term, the attribute VOLATILE is under consideration for Fortran 2000 and would give the buffer or variable the properties needed, but it would inhibit optimization of any code containing the buffer or variable.

In C, subroutines that modify variables that are not in the argument list will not cause register optimization problems. This is because taking pointers to storage objects by using the & operator and later referencing the objects by way of the pointer is an integral part of the language. A C compiler understands the implications, so that the problem should not occur, in general. However, some compilers do offer optional aggressive optimization levels which may not be safe.

8.2.3 Basic Fortran Support

Because Fortran 90 is (for all practical purposes) a superset of Fortran 77, Fortran 90 (and future) programs can use the original Fortran interface. The following additional requirements are added:

1. Implementations are required to provide the file mpif.h, as described in the original MPI-1 specification.

2. mpif.h must be valid and equivalent for both fixed- and free- source form.

Advice to implementors. To make mpif.h compatible with both fixed- and free-source forms, to allow automatic inclusion by preprocessors, and to allow extended fixed-form line length, it is recommended that requirement two be met by constructing mpif.h without any continuation lines. This should be possible because mpif.h contains only declarations and because common block declarations can be split among several lines. To support Fortran 77 as well as Fortran 90, it may be necessary to eliminate all comments from mpif.h. ▯

8.2.4 Extended Fortran Support

Implementations with Extended Fortran Support must provide:

1. An mpi module.

2. A new set of functions to provide additional support for Fortran intrinsic numeric types, including parameterized types: MPI_SIZEOF, MPI_TYPE_-MATCH_SIZE, MPI_TYPE_CREATE_F90_INTEGER, MPI_TYPE_CREATE_F90_REAL and MPI_TYPE_CREATE_F90_COMPLEX. Parameterized types are Fortran intrinsic types that are specified using KIND type parameters. These routines are described in detail in Section 8.2.5.

Additionally, high-quality implementations should provide a mechanism to prevent fatal type mismatch errors for MPI routines with choice arguments.

The mpi Module. An MPI implementation must provide a module named mpi that can be USEd in a Fortran 90 program. This module must:

- Define all named MPI constants.
- Declare MPI functions that return a value.

An MPI implementation may provide in the mpi module other features that enhance the usability of MPI while maintaining adherence to the standard. For example, it may:

- Provide interfaces for all or for a subset of MPI routines.
- Provide INTENT information in these interface blocks.

Advice to implementors. The appropriate INTENT may be different from what is given in the MPI generic interface. Implementations must choose INTENT so that the function adheres to the MPI standard. □

Rationale. The intent given by the MPI generic interface does not in all cases correspond to the correct Fortran INTENT. For instance, receiving into a buffer specified by a datatype with absolute addresses may require associating MPI_BOTTOM with a dummy OUT argument. Moreover, "constants" such as MPI_BOTTOM and MPI_STATUS_IGNORE are not constants as defined by Fortran, but "special addresses" used in a nonstandard way. Finally, the MPI-1 generic intent is changed in several places by MPI-2. For instance, MPI_IN_PLACE changes the sense of an OUT argument to be INOUT. □

Applications may use either the mpi module or the mpif.h include file. An implementation may require use of the module to prevent type mismatch errors (see below).

Advice to users. It is recommended that the mpi module be used even if it is not necessary to use it to avoid type mismatch errors on a particular system. Using a module provides several potential advantages over using an include file. □

It must be possible to link together routines some of which USE mpi and others of which INCLUDE mpif.h.

No Type Mismatch Problems for Subroutines with Choice Arguments. A high-quality MPI implementation should provide a mechanism to ensure that MPI choice arguments do not cause fatal compile-time or runtime errors due to type mismatch. An MPI implementation may require applications to use the mpi module, or require that it be compiled with a particular compiler flag, in order to avoid type mismatch problems.

Advice to implementors. In the case where the compiler does not generate errors, nothing needs to be done to the existing interface. In the case where the compiler may generate errors, a set of overloaded functions may be used (see the paper of M. Hennecke [11]). Even if the compiler does not generate errors, explicit interfaces for all routines would be useful for detecting errors in the argument list. Also, explicit interfaces which give INTENT information can reduce the amount of copying for BUF(*) arguments. ☐

8.2.5 Additional Support for Fortran Numeric Intrinsic Types

The routines in this section are part of Extended Fortran Support described in Section 8.2.4.

MPI-1 provides a small number of named datatypes that correspond to named intrinsic types supported by C and Fortran. These include MPI_INTEGER, MPI_REAL, MPI_INT, MPI_DOUBLE, etc., as well as the optional types MPI_REAL4, MPI_REAL8, etc. There is a one-to-one correspondence between language declarations and MPI types.

Fortran (starting with Fortran 90) provides so-called KIND-parameterized types. These types are declared using an intrinsic type (one of INTEGER, REAL, COMPLEX, LOGICAL and CHARACTER) with an optional integer KIND parameter that selects from among one or more variants. The specific meaning of different KIND values themselves are implementation dependent and not specified by the language. Fortran provides the KIND selection functions selected_real_kind for REAL and COMPLEX types, and selected_int_kind for INTEGER types that allow users to declare variables with a minimum precision or number of digits. These functions provide a portable way to declare KIND-parameterized REAL, COMPLEX and INTEGER variables in Fortran. This scheme is backward compatible with Fortran 77. REAL and INTEGER Fortran variables have a default KIND if none is specified. Fortran DOUBLE PRECISION variables are of intrinsic type REAL with a nondefault KIND. The following two declarations are equivalent:

```
double precision x
real(KIND(0.0d0)) x
```

MPI provides two orthogonal methods to communicate using numeric intrinsic types. The first method can be used when variables have been declared in a portable way—using default KIND or using KIND parameters obtained with the selected_-int_kind or selected_real_kind functions. With this method, MPI automatically selects the correct data size (e.g., 4 or 8 bytes) and provides representation conversion in heterogeneous environments. The second method gives the user complete control over communication by exposing machine representations.

Parameterized Datatypes with Specified Precision and Exponent Range. MPI-1 provides named datatypes corresponding to standard Fortran 77 numeric types—MPI_INTEGER, MPI_COMPLEX, MPI_REAL, MPI_DOUBLE_PRECISION and MPI_DOUBLE_COMPLEX. MPI automatically selects the correct data size and provides representation conversion in heterogeneous environments. The mechanism described in this section extends this MPI-1 model to support portable parameterized numeric types.

The model for supporting portable parameterized types is as follows. Real variables are declared (perhaps indirectly) using selected_real_kind(p, r) to determine the KIND parameter, where p is decimal digits of precision and r is an exponent range. Implicitly MPI maintains a two-dimensional array of predefined MPI datatypes D(p, r). D(p, r) is defined for each value of (p, r) supported by the compiler, including pairs for which one value is unspecified. Attempting to access an element of the array with an index (p, r) not supported by the compiler is erroneous. MPI implicitly maintains a similar array of COMPLEX datatypes. For integers, there is a similar implicit array related to selected_int_kind and indexed by the requested number of digits r. Note that the predefined datatypes contained in these implicit arrays are not the same as the named MPI datatypes MPI_REAL, etc., but a new set.

Advice to implementors. The above description is for explanatory purposes only. It is not expected that implementations will have such internal arrays. ⬜

Advice to users. selected_real_kind() maps a large number of (p,r) pairs to a much smaller number of KIND parameters supported by the compiler. KIND parameters are not specified by the language and are not portable. From the language point of view intrinsic types of the same base type and KIND parameter are of the same type. In order to allow interoperability in a heterogeneous environment, MPI is more stringent. The corresponding MPI datatypes match if and only if they have the same (p,r) value (REAL and COMPLEX) or r value (INTEGER). Thus MPI has many more datatypes than there are fundamental language types. ⬜

MPI_TYPE_CREATE_F90_REAL(p, r, newtype)

IN	p	precision, in decimal digits (integer)
IN	r	decimal exponent range (integer)
OUT	newtype	the requested MPI datatype (handle)

```
int MPI_Type_create_f90_real(int p, int r, MPI_Datatype *newtype)
```

```
MPI_TYPE_CREATE_F90_REAL(P, R, NEWTYPE, IERROR)
    INTEGER P, R, NEWTYPE, IERROR
```

```
static MPI::Datatype MPI::Datatype::Create_f90_real(int p, int r)
```

This function returns a predefined MPI datatype that matches a REAL variable of KIND selected_real_kind(p, r). In the model described above it returns a handle for the element D(p, r). Either p or r may be omitted from calls to selected_real_kind(p, r), but not both. Analogously, either p or r may be set to MPI_UNDEFINED. In communication, an MPI datatype A returned by MPI_TYPE_CREATE_F90_REAL matches a datatype B if and only if B was returned by MPI_TYPE_CREATE_F90_REAL called with the same values for p and r or B is a duplicate of such a datatype. Restrictions on using the returned datatype with the "external32" data representation are given on page 316.

It is erroneous to supply values for p and r not supported by the compiler.

MPI_TYPE_CREATE_F90_COMPLEX(p, r, newtype)

IN	p	precision, in decimal digits (integer)
IN	r	decimal exponent range (integer)
OUT	newtype	the requested MPI datatype (handle)

```
int MPI_Type_create_f90_complex(int p, int r, MPI_Datatype *newtype)
```

```
MPI_TYPE_CREATE_F90_COMPLEX(P, R, NEWTYPE, IERROR)
    INTEGER P, R, NEWTYPE, IERROR
```

```
static MPI::Datatype MPI::Datatype::Create_f90_complex(int p, int r)
```

This function returns a predefined MPI datatype that matches a COMPLEX variable of KIND selected_real_kind(p, r). Either p or r may be omitted from calls to selected_real_kind(p, r), but not both. Analogously, either p or r may be set to MPI_UNDEFINED. Matching rules for datatypes created by this function are

analogous to the matching rules for datatypes created by MPI_TYPE_CREATE_-
F90_REAL. Restrictions on using the returned datatype with the "external32" data
representation are given on page 316.

It is erroneous to supply values for p and r not supported by the compiler.

MPI_TYPE_CREATE_F90_INTEGER(r, newtype)

| IN | r | decimal exponent range, i.e., number of decimal digits (integer) |
| OUT | newtype | the requested MPI datatype (handle) |

```
int MPI_Type_create_f90_integer(int r, MPI_Datatype *newtype)
```

```
MPI_TYPE_CREATE_F90_INTEGER(R, NEWTYPE, IERROR)
    INTEGER R, NEWTYPE, IERROR
```

```
static MPI::Datatype MPI::Datatype::Create_f90_integer(int r)
```

This function returns a predefined MPI datatype that matches an INTEGER variable of KIND selected_int_kind(r). Matching rules for datatypes created by this
function are analogous to the matching rules for datatypes created by MPI_TYPE_-
CREATE_F90_REAL. Restrictions on using the returned datatype with the "exter-
nal32" data representation are given on page 316.

It is erroneous to supply a value for r that is not supported by the compiler.

Example 8.11 This shows how to create the MPI datatypes corresponding to
two Fortran types specified with selected_int_kind and selected_real_kind.

```
integer        longtype, quadtype
integer, parameter :: long = selected_int_kind(15)
integer(long) ii(10)
real(selected_real_kind(30)) x(10)
call MPI_TYPE_CREATE_F90_INTEGER(15, longtype, ierror)
call MPI_TYPE_CREATE_F90_REAL(30, MPI_UNDEFINED, quadtype, ierror)
...

call MPI_SEND(ii, 10, longtype, ...)
call MPI_SEND(x,  10, quadtype, ...)
```

Advice to users. The datatypes returned by the above functions are predefined
datatypes. They cannot be freed; they do not need to be committed; they can

be used with predefined reduction operations. There are two situations in which they behave differently syntactically, but not semantically, from the MPI named predefined datatypes.

    1.   MPI_TYPE_GET_ENVELOPE returns special combiners that allow a program to retrieve the values of p and r.

    2.   Because the datatypes are not named, they cannot be used as compile-time initializers or otherwise accessed before a call to one of the MPI_TYPE_CREATE_F90_ routines.

If a variable was declared specifying a nondefault KIND value that was not obtained with selected_real_kind() or selected_int_kind(), the only way to obtain a matching MPI datatype is to use the size-based mechanism described in the next section. ▯

Rationale.   The MPI_TYPE_CREATE_F90_REAL/COMPLEX/INTEGER interface needs as input the original range and precision values to be able to define useful and compiler-independent external (Section 7.5.2) or user-defined (Section 7.5.3) data representations, and in order to be able to perform automatic and efficient data conversions in a heterogeneous environment. ▯

Datatypes and external32 representation.   We now specify how the datatypes described in this section behave when used with the "external32" external data representation described in Section 7.5.2.

The external32 representation specifies data formats for integer and floating point values. Integer values are represented in two's complement big-endian format. Floating point values are represented by one of three IEEE formats. These are the IEEE "Single," "Double" and "Double Extended" formats, requiring 4, 8 and 16 bytes of storage, respectively. For the IEEE "Double Extended" formats, MPI specifies a Format Width of 16 bytes, with 15 exponent bits, bias = +10383, 112 fraction bits, and an encoding analogous to the "Double" format.

The external32 representations of the datatypes returned by MPI_TYPE_CREATE_F90_REAL/COMPLEX/INTEGER are given by the following rules. For MPI_TYPE_CREATE_F90_REAL:

if	$(p > 33)$ or $(r > 4931)$ then	external32 representation is undefined
else if	$(p > 15)$ or $(r > 307)$ then	external32_size = 16
else if	$(p > 6)$ or $(r > 37)$ then	external32_size = 8
else		external32_size = 4

For MPI_TYPE_CREATE_F90_COMPLEX: twice the size as for MPI_TYPE_CREATE_-
F90_REAL. For MPI_TYPE_CREATE_F90_INTEGER:

$$
\begin{array}{lll}
\text{if} & (r > 38) \text{ then} & \text{external32 representation is undefined} \\
\text{else if} & (r > 18) \text{ then} & \text{external32\_size} = 16 \\
\text{else if} & (r > 9) \text{ then} & \text{external32\_size} = 8 \\
\text{else if} & (r > 4) \text{ then} & \text{external32\_size} = 4 \\
\text{else if} & (r > 2) \text{ then} & \text{external32\_size} = 2 \\
\text{else} & & \text{external32\_size} = 1 \\
\end{array}
$$

If the external32 representation of a datatype is undefined, the result of using the
datatype directly or indirectly (i.e., as part of another datatype or through a duplicated datatype) in operations that require the external32 representation is undefined. These operations include MPI_PACK_EXTERNAL, MPI_UNPACK_EXTERNAL
and many MPI_FILE functions, when the "external32" data representation is used.
The ranges for which the external32 representation is undefined are reserved for
future standardization.

Support for Size-specific MPI Datatypes. MPI-1 provides named datatypes
corresponding to optional Fortran 77 numeric types that contain explicit byte
lengths—MPI_REAL4, MPI_INTEGER8, etc. This section describes a mechanism that
generalizes this model to support all Fortran numeric intrinsic types.

We assume that for each **typeclass** (integer, real, complex) and each word size
there is a unique machine representation. For every pair (**typeclass**, **n**) supported
by a compiler, MPI must provide a named size-specific datatype. The name of
this datatype is of the form MPI_<TYPE>n in C and Fortran and of the form
MPI::<TYPE>n in C++ where <TYPE> is one of REAL, INTEGER and COMPLEX,
and **n** is the length in bytes of the machine representation. This datatype locally
matches all variables of type (**typeclass**, **n**). The list of names for such types
includes:

```
MPI_REAL4       MPI_INTEGER1
MPI_REAL8       MPI_INTEGER2
MPI_REAL16      MPI_INTEGER4
MPI_COMPLEX8    MPI_INTEGER8
MPI_COMPLEX16   MPI_INTEGER16
MPI_COMPLEX32
```

In MPI-1 these datatypes are all optional and correspond to the optional, nonstandard declarations supported by many Fortran compilers. In MPI-2, one datatype

is required for each representation supported by the compiler. To be backward compatible with the interpretation of these types in MPI-1, we assume that the nonstandard declarations REAL*n, INTEGER*n, always create a variable whose representation is of size **n**. All these datatypes are predefined.

Additional size-specific types, such as MPI_LOGICAL1 (corresponding to LOGICAL*1) may be defined by implementations, but are not required by the MPI standard.

The following functions allow a user to obtain a size-specific MPI datatype for any intrinsic Fortran type.

MPI_SIZEOF(x, size)

IN	x	a Fortran variable of numeric intrinsic type (choice)
OUT	size	size of machine representation of that type (integer)

```
MPI_SIZEOF(X, SIZE, IERROR)
    <type> X
    INTEGER SIZE, IERROR
```

This function returns the size in bytes of the machine representation of the given variable. It is a generic Fortran routine and has a Fortran binding only.

Advice to users. This function is similar to the C and C++ sizeof operator but behaves slightly differently. If given an array argument, it returns the size of the base element, not the size of the whole array. □

Rationale. This function is not available in other languages because it is not necessary.

□

MPI_TYPE_MATCH_SIZE(typeclass, size, type)

IN	typeclass	generic type specifier (integer)
IN	size	size, in bytes, of representation (integer)
OUT	type	datatype with correct type, size (handle)

```
int MPI_Type_match_size(int typeclass, int size, MPI_Datatype *type)
```

```
MPI_TYPE_MATCH_SIZE(TYPECLASS, SIZE, TYPE, IERROR)
```

```
     INTEGER TYPECLASS, SIZE, TYPE, IERROR

static MPI::Datatype MPI::Datatype::Match_size(int typeclass,
    int size)
```

typeclass is one of MPI_TYPECLASS_REAL, MPI_TYPECLASS_INTEGER and MPI_-
TYPECLASS_COMPLEX, corresponding to the desired **typeclass** (MPI::TYPECLASS_-
REAL, MPI::TYPECLASS_INTEGER and MPI::TYPECLASS_COMPLEX in C++). The
function returns an MPI datatype matching a local variable of type (**typeclass**,
size).

This function returns a reference (handle) to one of the predefined named datatypes, not a duplicate. This type cannot be freed. MPI_TYPE_MATCH_SIZE can
be used to obtain a size-specific type that matches a Fortran numeric intrinsic type
by first calling MPI_SIZEOF in order to compute the variable size, and then calling
MPI_TYPE_MATCH_SIZE to find a suitable datatype. In C and C++, one can use
the C function sizeof(), instead of MPI_SIZEOF. In addition, for variables of default
kind the variable's size can be computed by a call to MPI_TYPE_GET_EXTENT,
if the **typeclass** is known. It is erroneous to specify a size not supported by the
compiler.

Rationale.   This is a convenience function. Without it, it can be tedious to find
the correct named type. See advice to implementors below. ☐

Advice to implementors.   This function can be implemented as a series of tests.

```
int MPI_Type_match_size(int typeclass, int size,
                        MPI_Datatype *rtype)
{
  switch(typeclass) {
      case MPI_TYPECLASS_REAL: switch(size) {
        case 4: *rtype = MPI_REAL4; return MPI_SUCCESS;
        case 8: *rtype = MPI_REAL8; return MPI_SUCCESS;
        default: error(...);
      }
      case MPI_TYPECLASS_INTEGER: switch(size) {
        case 4: *rtype = MPI_INTEGER4; return MPI_SUCCESS;
        case 8: *rtype = MPI_INTEGER8; return MPI_SUCCESS;
        default: error(...);
      }
```

```
    ... etc ...
  }
}
```

☐

Communication With Size-specific Types. The usual type matching rules apply to size-specific datatypes: a value sent with datatype MPI_<TYPE>n can be received with this same datatype on another process. Most modern computers use 2's complement for integers and IEEE format for floating point. Thus, communication using these size-specific datatypes will not entail loss of precision or truncation errors.

Advice to users. Care is required when communicating in a heterogeneous environment. Consider the following code:

```
real(selected_real_kind(5)) x(100)
call MPI_SIZEOF(x, size, ierror)
call MPI_TYPE_MATCH_SIZE(MPI_TYPECLASS_REAL, size, xtype, ierror)
if (myrank .eq. 0) then
    ... initialize x ...
    call MPI_SEND(x, xtype, 100, 1, ...)
else if (myrank .eq. 1) then
    call MPI_RECV(x, xtype, 100, 0, ...)
endif
```

This may not work in a heterogeneous environment if the value of size is not the same on process 1 and process 0. There should be no problem in a homogeneous environment. To communicate in a heterogeneous environment, there are at least four options, if one does not use size-specific (nonstandard) declarations, such as REAL*8. The first is to declare variables of default type and use the MPI datatypes for these types, e.g., declare a variable of type REAL and use MPI_REAL. The second is to use selected_real_kind or selected_int_kind and with the functions of the previous section. The third is to declare a variable that is known to be the same size on all architectures (e.g., selected_real_kind(12) on almost all compilers will result in an 8-byte representation). The fourth is to carefully check representation size before communication. This may require explicit conversion to a variable of size that can be communicated and handshaking between sender and receiver to agree on a size.

Note finally that using the "external32" representation for I/O requires explicit attention to the representation sizes. Consider the following code:

```
real(selected_real_kind(5)) x(100)
call MPI_SIZEOF(x, size, ierror)
call MPI_TYPE_MATCH_SIZE(MPI_TYPECLASS_REAL, size, xtype, ierror)

if (myrank .eq. 0) then
   call MPI_FILE_OPEN(MPI_COMM_SELF, 'foo',              &
                 MPI_MODE_CREATE+MPI_MODE_WRONLY,        &
                 MPI_INFO_NULL, fh, ierror)
   call MPI_FILE_SET_VIEW(fh, 0, xtype, xtype, 'external32', &
                     MPI_INFO_NULL, ierror)
   call MPI_FILE_WRITE(fh, x, 100, xtype, status, ierror)
   call MPI_FILE_CLOSE(fh, ierror)
endif

call MPI_BARRIER(MPI_COMM_WORLD, ierror)

if (myrank .eq. 1) then
   call MPI_FILE_OPEN(MPI_COMM_SELF, 'foo', MPI_MODE_RDONLY, &
                 MPI_INFO_NULL, fh, ierror)
   call MPI_FILE_SET_VIEW(fh, 0, xtype, xtype, 'external32', &
                     MPI_INFO_NULL, ierror)
   call MPI_FILE_WRITE(fh, x, 100, xtype, status, ierror)
   call MPI_FILE_CLOSE(fh, ierror)
endif
```

If processes 0 and 1 are on different machines, this code may not work as expected if the size is different on the two machines. []

9 Conclusions

"We are probably the first generation of message-passing programmers."

"We are also probably the last generation of message-passing programmers."

This exchange (paraphrased from one that actually occurred during a meeting of the MPI Forum) illustrates the position in which MPI (or, more generally, message-passing programming) currently finds itself.

On the one hand, message passing is a (relatively) mature paradigm for parallel programming. The development of MPI has provided a message-passing library standard which, coupled with implementations from high-performance computer vendors, will have a lasting impact on the field of high-performance computing. With a platform-independent standard, applications and libraries can exist well beyond the lifetime of their original hardware (and in fact do not have to be written with a particular hardware platform in mind).

On the other hand, computer technology continues to evolve at a breakneck pace, and development efforts in hardware, system software, and language and compiler design all seek to make parallel programming more portable, more scalable, and more transparent. It remains to be seen when (or if) these technologies will combine to obviate message passing.

What is clear, however, is that for the foreseeable future, message passing will continue be an important technology for scalable parallel computing and that it will be a stepping stone to whatever technology or technologies ultimately replace it.

9.1 Extensions to MPI

Given that MPI was extended once, it is natural to ask if it is likely (or even planned) that there will be further extensions to MPI. The answer is yes, there will probably be extensions to MPI, but there are no plans to reconvene the MPI Forum in the near future. Thus, any extensions made to MPI must remain unofficial in the near term.

During the course of the two years that the MPI Forum convened for MPI-2, many ideas were explored that are not included in the final MPI-2 Standard. We discuss those briefly here since these ideas are likely starting points for further development of MPI. These ideas are discussed more fully in the *MPI Journal of Development*[6], or JOD, where a chapter is devoted to each issue.

Spawning Independent Processes. A number of issues were not covered in MPI-2 regarding dynamic process management, particularly with regard to management of processes with which the spawning processes do not intend to communicate. These issues were discussed at length by the Forum in the context of dynamic process management but ultimately were not included in the standard. Facilities for process signalling and monitoring are examples of functionality proposed in this chapter.

Threads and MPI. Shared-memory and distributed-memory parallel computing are not necessarily competing programming models. Since clusters of SMPs are a viable (and important) parallel computing resource, one particularly interesting (and most likely inevitable) discussion is how to effectively combine thread programming and MPI. Functions normally associated with threads and shared variables are extended to distributed memory situations.

Communicator ID. The MPI-1 Forum carefully defined communicators so that communicator creation need not always be a synchronizing operation. This makes the notion of a global identifier for each communicator problematic. An approach to the problem is discussed in this chapter.

Miscellany. This chapter discusses Miscellaneous topics in the MPI JOD, in particular single-copy routines for use in shared-memory environments and new datatype constructors.

Toward a Full Fortran 90 Interface. As seen in Chapter 8, a complete Fortran 90 interface for MPI is problematic. This chapter describes an approach to providing a more elaborate Fortran 90 interface.

Two-phase Collective Communication. Non-blocking collective operations present difficult implementation issues, particularly in the absence of threads. The Forum spent considerable time discussing non-blocking collective operations. Non-blocking variants of the routines in I-4 were first replaced by the related "two-phase" collective operations, which offer many of the same advantages as non-blocking operations, but eventually it was decided not to include them in the Standard. The specifications are presented in this chapter. The two-phase operations for collective I/O are the only remnants of these operations.

Real Time MPI. Real-time requirements suggest both additions to, and subtractions from, the MPI-1 and MPI-2 specifications. The real-time subcommittee of the MPI Forum invested considerable work in this chapter, but eventually decided not to propose it for inclusion in the MPI-2 Standard. The work to produce a specification for a real-time message-passing library that will be strongly related to the MPI specification is ongoing (See http://www.mpirt.org/).

9.2   Implementation and Adoption of MPI-2

Unlike MPI-1, which had the `mpich` implementation [10] being developed in conjunction (and evolving) with the standard itself, MPI-2 has not had a reference implementation accompanying it through its development process.

Nevertheless, as of this writing, there is one known complete MPI-2 implementation, by Fujitsu.

Hewlett-Packard has announced (May, 1998) that their MPI now contains an implementation of the most important one-sided operations.

As with MPI-1, MPI-2 was designed with layerability in mind (indeed, several parts of MPI-2 were developed precisely to extend the layerability of MPI) and this has allowed several major portions of MPI-2 to be developed. Several research efforts have exploited the layerability of MPI using the facilities in Chapter 6 to provide public implementations of MPI-2 I/O [25]. Users can expect to see MPI-2 I/O features from several vendors and other developers as well before the end of 1998. For example, Sun Microsystems has already announced support for many of the MPI-2 I/O routines. In addition, C++ binding layers for MPI are available publicly from `http://www.cse.nd.edu/~lsc/research/mpi2c++/` and `http://www.erc.msstate.edu/labs/icdcrl/mpi++`. Similarly layered C++ bindings for MPI should be available soon from several vendors.

References

[1] David Bailey, Tim Harris, William Saphir, Rob van der Wijngaart, Alex Woo, and Maurice Yarrow. The NAS parallel benchmarks 2.0. Technical Report NAS-95-020, NASA Ames Research Center, Moffett Field, CA 94035-1000, December 1995.

[2] Rajesh Bordawekar, Juan Miguel del Rosario, and Alok Choudhary. Design and evaluation of primitives for parallel I/O. In *Proceedings of Supercomputing '93*, pages 452–461, 1993.

[3] Juan Miguel del Rosario, Rajesh Bordawekar, and Alok Choudhary. Improved parallel I/O via a two-phase run-time access strategy. In *IPPS '93 Workshop on Input/Output in Parallel Computer Systems*, pages 56–70, 1993. Also published in Computer Architecture News 21(5), December 1993, pages 31–38.

[4] Message Passing Interface Forum. MPI: A Message-Passing Interface Standard (version 1.1). Technical report, 1995. http://www.mpi-forum.org.

[5] Message Passing Interface Forum. MPI-2: Extensions to the Message-Passing Interface. Technical report, 1997. http://www.mpi-forum.org.

[6] Message Passing Interface Forum. MPI-2 Journal of Development. Technical report, 1997. http://www.mpi-forum.org.

[7] Message Passing Interface Forum. MPI2: A Message-Passing Interface Standard. *The International Journal of High Performance Computing Applications*, 12:1–299, 1998. Special issue on MPI.

[8] A. Geist, A. Beguelin, J. Dongarra, W. Jiang, R. Manchek, and V. Sunderam. *PVM: A Users' Guide and Tutorial for Networked Parallel Computing*. MIT Press, 1994. The book is available electronically, the url is ftp://www.netlib.org/pvm3/book/pvm-book.ps.

[9] W. Gropp and E. Lusk. Dynamic process management in an MPI setting. In *Proceedings of the Seventh IEEE Symposium on Parallel and Distributed Processing, October 25–28, 1995, San Antonio, Texas*, pages 530–534. IEEE Computer Society Press, 1995.

[10] William Gropp, Ewing Lusk, Nathan Doss, and Anthony Skjellum. A high-performace, portable implementation of the MPI message passing interface standard. *Parallel Computing*, (22):789–828, 1996.

[11] Michael Hennecke. A Fortran 90 interface to MPI version 1.1. Technical Report 63/96, Rechenzentrum, Universität Karlsruhe, D-76128 Karlsruhe, Germany, June 1996. Available via world wide web from http://www.uni-karlsruhe.de/~Michael.Hennecke/Publications/#MPI_F90.

[12] IEEE, New York. *IEEE Standard for Information Technology— POSIX Fortran 77 Language Interfaces —Part 1: System Application Program Interface (API)*, 1992.

[13] Institute of Electrical and Electronics Engineers, New York. *IEEE Standard for Binary Floating-Point Arithmetic, ANSI/IEEE Standard 754-1985*, 1985.

[14] International Organization for Standardization, Geneva. *Information processing—8-bit single-byte coded graphic character sets—Part 1: Latin alphabet No. 1*, 1987.

[15] International Organization for Standardization, Geneva. *Information technology—Portable Operating System Interface (POSIX)—Part 1: System Application Program Interface (API) [C Language]*, December 1996.

[16] P. J. Komisky. Performance analysis of an implementation of the beam and warming implicit factored scheme on the ncube hypercube. In *Proceedings of the 3rd Symposium on the Frontiers of Massively Parallel Computation*. College Park, MD, October 8-10, 1990.

[17] David Kotz. Disk-directed I/O for MIMD multiprocessors. In *Proceedings of the 1994 Symposium on Operating Systems Design and Implementation*, pages 61–74, November 1994. Updated as Dartmouth TR PCS-TR94-226 on November 8, 1994.

[18] S. J. Lefflet, R. S. Fabry, W. N. Joy, P. Lapsley, S. Miller, and C. Torek. An advanced 4.4BSD interprocess communication tutorial, Unix programmer's supplementary documents (PSD) 21. Technical report, Computer Systems Research Group, Depertment of Electrical Engineering and Computer Science, University of California, Berkeley, 1993. Also available at http://www.netbsd.org/Documentation/lite2/psd/.

[19] Bill Nitzberg. Performance of the iPSC/860 Concurrent File System. Technical Report RND-92-020, NAS Systems Division, NASA Ames, December 1992.

[20] William J. Nitzberg. *Collective Parallel I/O*. PhD thesis, Department of Computer and Information Science, University of Oregon, December 1995.

[21] *4.4BSD Programmer's Supplementary Documents (PSD)*. O'Reilly and Associates, 1994.

[22] K. E. Seamons, Y. Chen, P. Jones, J. Jozwiak, and M. Winslett. Server-directed collective I/O in Panda. In *Proceedings of Supercomputing '95*, December 1995.

[23] Mark Snir, Steve Otto, Steven Huss-Lederman, David Walker, and Jack Dongarra. *MPI: The Complete Reference (Second Edition)*. MIT Press, 1998.

[24] Rajeev Thakur and Alok Choudhary. An Extended Two-Phase Method for Accessing Sections of Out-of-Core Arrays. *Scientific Programming*, 5(4):301–317, Winter 1996.

[25] Rajeev Thakur, William Gropp, and Ewing Lusk. An abstract-device interface for implementing portable parallel-I/O interfaces. In *Proceedings of the Sixth Symposium on the Frontiers of Massively Parallel Computation*, pages 180–187, October 1996.

[26] *The Unicode Standard, Version 2.0*. Addison-Wesley, 1996. ISBN 0-201-48345-9.

Constants Index

Function Index

Index